Universal Abandon?

THE POLITICS
OF POSTMODERNISM

CULTURAL ⚱ POLITICS

A series from the Social Text collective

Universal "Abandon?

THE POLITICS
OF POSTMODERNISM

Andrew Ross, editor
(for the Social Text collective)

University of Minnesota Press/Minneapolis

Published by the University of Minnesota Press
2037 University Avenue Southeast, Minneapolis MN 55414.
Published simultaneously in Canada
by Fitzhenry & Whiteside Limited, Markham.
Printed in the United States of America.

This book corresponds to a special issue of *Social Text*
(Volume 7, no. 3, Winter 1989).

Library of Congress Cataloging-in-Publication Data

Universal abandon? : the politics of postmodernism / edited by Andrew
Ross for Social Text.
    p. cm. —(Cultural politics)
    Includes index.
    ISBN 0-8166-1679-5. ISBN 0-8166-1680-9 (pbk.)
    1. Criticism. 2. Politics and literature. 3. Postmodernism.
4. Marxist criticism. I. Ross, Andrew, 1956-   II. Social Text
(Organization). III. Series: Cultural politics (Minneapolis, Minn.)
PN98.P64U55 1988
801'.95'0904—dc19   88-10134
                                              CIP

4 – 5 –90

CONTENTS

ACKNOWLEDGMENT

Research assistance was provided by Marjorie Howes, Allan Hepburn, and the Princeton University Research Council for the Humanities.

A. R.

INTRODUCTION
Andrew Ross

In his introduction to a collection of essays published in 1986, *Post-modernism and Politics*, Jonathan Arac pointed out that postmodern criticism had chosen, from the first, to be "worldly."[1] As the debate about postmodernism itself broadens daily it has emerged as a full-blown discussion about the nature and future of social modernity. Consequently, the question of *worldliness* has taken on ever more grandiose implications. What world? Whose world? and What possible world? Suddenly, postmodernism has become an epic production almost in spite of itself, or at least in spite of what many saw initially as one of its possibly vital impulses—a dissenting response to the epic, or universal, claims of modernism. Suddenly, we are faced again with the big questions that the last two decades of cultural and sexual politics had taught us to regard with suspicion. For some, these are questions for which the lessons of this two-decade period of micropolitics have prepared many of the necessary responses: in other words, a politics of the local and the particular and a politics of racial, sexual, and ethnic difference are not only symptoms of, but also essential strategies for coping with a postmodernist culture that advertises itself as decentered, transnational, and pluralistic and even as boasting its own unconscious. For others, however, these big questions are simply questions that appeal to abstract propositions about the global and therefore betray a new spirit of *contemptus mundi* for everyday life struggles and domestic problems at large.

Clearly, many other responses in this debate are possible, for post-modernism means many things to many people. It is a debate from which no one, this time, ought to be excluded. It is important to recognize that postmodernist culture is a real medium in which we all live to some extent, no matter how unevenly its effects are lived and felt across the jagged spectrum of color, sex, class, region, and nationality. It hardly seems useful anymore to dismiss postmodernism as a mere "fashion that is already dead," as Dario Fo does in a recent interview: "Fashion . . . is what results when there is not a fundamental, real reason, ideology, or morality behind a discourse. In other words, when discourse doesn't make an argument."[2] Nor does it clarify very much to point, as Fo might have done, to the use of the term *postmodernist* (not to mention the flourishing evidence of its practices) in the pages of fashion magazines as evidence of the rapid assimilation and popular corruption of a once pristine, intellectual phenomenon; postmodernism, after all, holds the promise of a cultural politics that would have no institutional boundaries, high or low, and that would fight over, if not infiltrate, every last inch of new historical terrain.

But Fo's comments about postmodernism's lack of substance go much further than simply begging the question of institutional terrain. Ultimately, of course, Fo's appeal is to the *materialist* bedrock of the marxist tradition. One need only quote one of the first footnotes in *Capital*, on exchange-value, to summon up the efficient, mordant wit of Marx himself on this same topic:

> In the seventeenth century, many English authors continued to write "worth" for "use-value" and "value" for "exchange-value," this being accordant with the genius of a language which prefers an Anglo-Saxon word for an actual thing, and a Romance word for its reflexion.[3]

While we might savor Marx's *bon mot*, we can also take retrospective pleasure in the prescience of his observation, for today's reader cannot help but interpret these lines in the light of the "critique of the political economy of the sign," to use Baudrillard's phrase, which *poststructuralism* ushered in, and which has so transformed the face of marxist thinking in recent years. While Marx himself was uncomfortable with the most vulgar appeals to materialism, few would now disagree that the specter that has come to haunt marxist analysis has been the fear of losing sight of "the actual [Anglo-Saxon] thing," a fear that is invoked, for example, in what Fo derisively refers to as the moment "when discourse doesn't have an argument."

Of course, the question of the exact determinate role of material conditions in cultural analysis is the site of a long and involved debate within marxism itself. This question cannot be wholly reduced to the set of propositions about language, epistemology, and psychosexuality upon which poststructuralism rests its powerful and troubling claims. But this is not to say that the claims of poststructuralism have not had a radical effect on the way in which we talk about the relationship between material and cultural conditions. No one is able to read or interpret the *text*—social, historical, or cultural—in quite the same unmediated way, and with quite the same confidence, after the poststructuralist revolution. So, too, the radical emphasis of poststructuralism on circuits of pleasure that override and disrupt the controlled hedonism of consumer capitalism is a lesson that will not be forgotten, even as an "age of permissions" flinches under the tragic pressure of the AIDS crisis, and the prolonged conservative backlash to the sixties. Most profound of all, though this consequence is perhaps the least developed in practice, poststructuralism allowed us to engage and contest the ideological surface of popular discourses without automatically reaching out for the comfortable political "truths" that lie behind the often reactionary face of the popular.

More and more, however, we have come to see poststructuralism as a belated response to the vanguardist innovations of high modernism. Poststructuralism is the critical revolution that was delayed: it is the continuation of modernism by other means. In *theory*, its genealogical origins (in fact, all of its important "breaks") have been traced to Marx, Freud, Nietzsche, and, in a more instrumental way, to Saussure. In *practice*, its tribute to uncertainty was fulfilled in the historical tradition of the European avant-garde. As an *institution* of critical and theoretical practice, it earned its radical credentials in the wake of the more broad-based challenge to academic process and discipline that was mounted in the late sixties. For privileged students, however, weaned on the monuments of modernist culture, poststructuralism seemed to make perfect sense: it made nothing strange. And for those less privileged, with less or little access to academically certified knowledge and information, its critical advocacy of negative capability—of withdrawing from traditionally empowered positions—could often only be read as a patronizing parody of their own lack of an empowered voice. Whether it liked it or not, poststructuralism, as a *late modernist* phenomenon, bore with it many of the elitist strains so characteristic of the modernist heyday. Increasingly, then, the claims of poststructuralism have been placed in a larger context, or "condition," of which they have been seen equally as a symptom and as a determining cause. This larger condition—postmodernism—addresses a whole range of material conditions that are no longer consonant with the dominant rationality of modernism and its technological commitment to finding *solutions* in every sphere of social and cultural life. What we think of as the "postmodern condition" speaks to a complex conjuncture of conditions. For example, it encompasses the vestigial personal revolutions in self-liberation and communal participation initiated by the countercultural movements of the sixties *just as* it entails the dramatic, postwar restructuring of capitalism in the West and in the multinational global economy; it involves the everyday effects of the new media and communication technology *as well as* the great redistribution of power, population, and wealth that has accompanied the new structures of commodity production.

The history of the term *postmodernism* has been adequately charted.[4] In its migration from a specific set of cultural distinctions proposed by literary critics in the fifties to its current significance as the subject of a debate about global questions, postmodernism has accumulated an abundance of sedimented meanings. To cite Dick Hebdige's by no means exhaustive inventory of contexts, tendencies, and objects, postmodern can be used today to refer to:

> the decor of a room, the design of a building, the diegesis of a film, the construction of a record, or a "scratch" video, a TV commercial, or an arts documentary, or the "intertextual" relations between them, the layout of a page in a fashion magazine or critical journal, an anti-teleological tendency within epistemology, the attack on the "metaphysics of presence," a general attenuation of feeling, the collective chagrin and morbid projections of a post-War generation of Baby Boomers confronting disillusioned middle age, the "predicament" of reflexivity, a group of rhetorical tropes, a proliferation of surfaces, a new phase in commodity fetishism, a fascination for "images," codes and styles, a process of cultural, political or existential fragmentation and/or crisis, the "de-centering" of the subject, an "incredulity towards metanarratives," the replacement of unitary power axes by a pluralism of power/discourse formations, the "implosion of meaning," the collapse of cultural

hierarchies, the dread engendered by the threat of nuclear self-destruction, the decline of the University, the functioning and effects of the new miniaturized technologies, broad societal and economic shifts into a "media," "consumer" or "multinational" phase, a sense (depending on whom you read) of placelessness or the abandonment of placelessness ("critical regionalism") or (even) a generalized substitution of spatial for temporal co-ordinates.[5]

This profusion of meanings may offend the purist, who would want to restrict the understanding and use of the term to a more limited context, in order, for example, to preserve the incorruptibility of some pet postmodernist practice. But the category of postmodernism—the collection of practices that call themselves postmodern—has, for better or worse, refused any such process of distillation. That it has achieved such diverse cultural currency as a term thereby demonstrates what has been seen as one of postmodernism's most provocative lessons; that terms are by no means guaranteed their meanings, and that these meanings can be appropriated and redefined for different purposes, different contexts, and, more important, different causes. In fact, this politics of appropriation, for so long exclusively the discursive preserve of the colonizer, has more recently been crucial to groups on the social margin, who have preferred, under certain circumstances, to struggle for recognition and legitimacy on established "metropolitan" political ground rather than run the risk of ghettoization by insisting on the "authenticity" of their respective group identities, ethnic, sexual, or otherwise. Again, however, it is important to point out that this strategy (the politics of appropriation, mimicry, plagiarism, the simulacrum) is unevenly recognized and practiced across the spectrum of these "marginal" social groups and movements. For those closest to the center—white, Western, middle-class feminists, for example—it has had the greatest appeal; for those farther away, it often looks simply like a new kind of assimilation or collaboration. Consequently, the politics of color, gender, class, and sexual orientation remains, in large part, tied to an essentialist notion of political identity. A postmodern politics cannot afford to be blind to the powerful force and affectivity of these essentialist claims, even though it is often seen as opposed to, or at least committed to the deconstruction of, such claims. At the very least, such a politics must accept essentialism itself as *one* of the many subject positions that inform its radical pluralism. At best, it ought to recognize that moments of "identity" are historically effective (they are the result of a shared material and discursive history) and therefore have a concrete existence even when and where the political consistency of such moments may be theoretically untenable.

Despite what looks like the declaration of an open season on the meaning of the term *postmodernist*, much of the recent discussion (and the contributors to this present volume are no exception) has followed upon a particular "debate," fueled by contributions in the early eighties from three figures, all white, male, marxists or ex-marxists: Jürgen Habermas, Jean-François Lyotard, and Fredric Jameson.[6] Daniel Bell's earlier contribution, *The Cultural Contradictions of Capitalism*, is more often ignored (again, the contributors to this volume of essays are no exception) or, in the case of Habermas, simply reviled. This is not just because of Bell's crablike neoconservatism in cultural matters (Bell would refuse this label in political and economic spheres), nor is it because his arguments speak to a more exclusively American context and history and are not addressed to the larger claims that arise out of the arguments of the other three. In fact, Bell is not especially insular in his views. It is just that his polemical cast of mind cannot include any consideration of the way in which postmodernism, as Stuart Hall puts it, is "about how the world dreams itself to be 'American.' "[7]

As long as the world goes on dreaming itself to be "American," what will undoubtedly be charted and debated in coming years will be the pervasive effects of postmodernism in its "management" of the various cultural economies of non-Western countries, still struggling to negotiate the effects of underdevelopment induced by Western modes of "modernization." Until very recently, however, discussion of the Habermas-Lyotard-Jameson debates has focused on the political and philosophical traditions that underlie or "ground" Western liberal capitalism and its various socialist alternatives. If these traditions, liberal and marxist alike, are rooted in the Enlightenment project of social, cultural, and political rationality, they are also tied to propositions about the *universality* of that project—as a social logic through which the world ought to transform itself in the image of Western men. Western Enlightenment philosophy thereby creates a world of universals in order to imagine itself as universal for the rest of the world. For the left, the liberal humanist interpretation of this project—extending all the way from its benign tolerance of the imperialist "mission" in the name of the rationality of "progress" to its Panglossian vision of a wired-up "global village" of free and equal communication, creatively managed by the transnational giants of the telecommunications industry—has long been considered bankrupt. So, too, the moment of social democracy—the heyday of welfare capitalism—has been eroded by the new right, its historic compromise between capital and labor broken up, if not dismantled, and thereby revealed as a social vision with only limited, and not universal, applications.

But the orthodox marxist tradition, as established by the Second International, is equally a discourse of universals: founded on and maintained by an analysis of the universality of the social functions of particular social classes, especially that of the revolutionary proletariat; committed to the rationality of progress, planning, and freedom through emancipation, revolutionary or otherwise; and sustained by its belief in necessity, in the shape of a teleological "idea" of History. These foundational elements of marxism have long been challenged, in the realm of both theory and practice. In the debates about postmodernism, these challenges have, as it were, come home to roost. For postmodernism has become a convenient rallying point around which Western intellectuals have gathered to debate the continuing worth or the wholesale abandonment of the universal propositions that provide the ground for the Enlightenment idea of politics and social transformation. (In this respect, its significance extends beyond the limits of the equally contentious debates about realism and formalism that involved Lukács, Benjamin, Brecht, and Adorno in the thirties). It should be noted, however, that the alacrity with which its participants have sprung to debate these large questions signals in itself the resurrection of the position of the "universal intellectual" (as opposed to Foucault's "specific intellectual"), who speaks as, and on behalf of, the consciousness of society as a whole. This is a position concomitant with the universalist marxist tradition itself, and it brings back with it the moral high ground that has been shunned by new types of organic intellectuals—most notably feminist, ethnic, gay, and nonmetropolitan—who have had little to gain and much to lose from concerning themselves with the often metaphysical questions of macropolitics. It is an intellectual position, then, whose very privileges are under scrutiny in this context, because it begs one of the political questions of postmodernism itself—the role of the intellectual in an age that rejects intellectual vanguardism and vanguardist intellectuals alike.

If we accept nonetheless, at the largest philosophical level of the debate, that the political status of claims to universality is at stake, then the following question ought to be addressed. *In whose interests is it, exactly, to declare the abandonment of universals?* For it is here that we may face the ethical question of postmodernism, a question about its political "horizon" (or lack thereof).

No matter how the ethical stakes are divided today, it is clear that we can no longer envisage a grand tug-of-war between Capital and Labor (the old "war of manoeuvre" in which a gain on one side is necessarily a loss on the other). In addition, the emergence of the new social movements and new political subjects has so radically pluralized the agenda of the left that gains for some cannot be universalized as gains for all. In *Hegemony and Socialist Strategy*, a book widely discussed as a prospectus for a postmodernist politics, Ernesto Laclau and Chantal Mouffe argue that there are no necessary links, for example, between the interests of women and the interests of workers. These links have to be *articulated*, or bound together, from contest to contest, and from moment to moment. The result is an agenda appropriate to a modern Gramscian war of position; a field of heterogeneous positions and sometimes contradictory discourses, often with no common content and no overall guarantee of a progressive outcome.

While the cogency and force of these new movements have transformed the agenda of opposition to racism, sexism, homophobia, and other institutions of oppression, the left's view of Capital itself as a supremely rational and monolithic, domination-producing system has tended to remain in place, if not always in favor. Whether it is personified as the great Satan whose multinational mark is everywhere, and whose arguments are cunningly persuasive (that is, unless our will to resist its service is strong enough—remember Eisenhower in 1960: "Capital is a curious thing with perhaps no nationality. It flows where it is served best"), or whether, in a more Thomist way, its logic is held to be perfect, finite, and accountable, Capital, or rather, our imaginary of Capital, still belongs for the most part to a demonology of the Other. This is a demonology that inhibits understanding and action as much as it artificially keeps alive older forms of *ressentiment* that have little or no purchase on a postmodern consumer society. In such a society, for example, it is unrealistic to heroicize declarations of immunity to the contagious forms of the commodity world when so much of our social lives is lived as consumers. We simply cannot afford to take the high ground if our popular culture and everyday life, saturated as they are with the effects of commodification, are to be important sites of contestation, and if new and popular images of modern, material life are to be constructed.

Because of this new demand for realism on everyday life issues, the classical explanatory system of marxism, dependent on the stable category of Capital as its universal model of explanation, has been further challenged. The comforts provided by the totalizing, explanatory power of marxist categories are no longer enough to help us make sense of the fragmented and various ways in which people live and negotiate the everyday life of consumer capitalism. This is *not* to say that the structure of multinational capitalism, with its new global grid of information and its new international divisions of labor, is beyond explanation, or without significance. On the contrary, it is to say that such an explanation cannot in itself account for the complex ideological processes through which our various, local insertions into that global economy are represented and reproduced. The debate about the culture of postmodernism is very much a debate about the *instability* of these ideological processes. And it is precisely because this instability is most palpably felt at the level of everyday life that a postmodernist politics must complete the Gramscian move to extend the political into all spheres, domains and practices of our culture. Everything is contestable; nothing is off-limits; and no outcomes are guaranteed. These are the conditions of a "philosophy of praxis," which demands of its disciples that they put aside, for the time being, the rank-and-file state of mind—in other words, their willing suspension of disbelief in a fixed ethical horizon.

(Is there a contradiction here? Yes, although it is often reduced to a crude formulation—how does one recognize the cogency of particular political struggles and allegiances if one has no clearly defined goals? This formulation may, in fact, beg the question, if what is at stake here is a redefinition of politics itself; redefined, for example, to account for those arrangements of power that devolve upon the body, sexuality, the unconscious, and so on. In effect, the contradiction of postmodernist politics is one that a more traditional ethics

on the left cannot easily accommodate if it still insists on a concept of
"politics"—*real* actions and events in the political sphere—that is
always above and beyond what continues to be disparaged as the
[merely] potentially political effects of cultural transformations.)

Today's postmodernist critique of totalism and universalism arises
from social and political conditions different from those that produced earlier debates within Western marxism about the role of
totality within the Hegelian tradition. Although a postmodernist politics might share some of the formal aspects of, say, Adorno's "negative dialectics," it has not been obliged, as Adorno and others were,
to declare and affirm its distance from the politics of authoritarian
centralism, otherwise known as totalitarianism. Somewhat remote
from the experience of fascism and Stalinism, its relation to a
"center" has been historically different, and articulated, primarily,
within the domestic context of Western liberal capitalism. As a result,
postmodernist politics has been posed as a politics of difference,
wherein many of the voices of color, gender, and sexual orientation,
newly liberated from the margins, have found representation under
conditions that are not exclusively tailored to the hitherto heroicized
needs and interests of white, male intellectuals and/or white, male
workers. In this respect we can only see social gains. On the other
hand, this new field of difference brings with it a new arrangement of
power and therefore new structures of inequality; it has to be seen in
the context of the transformed conditions of capitalist production
and the new patterns of unequal development in the West and elsewhere. On the one hand, then, gains on the level of representation;
on the other, new structures of exploitation and oppression. Both of
these need to be viewed side by side as dual effects of the conditions
under which a politics of difference has emerged.

A similar caveat could be offered in all the instances in which the
effects of "universal abandon" are discussed. In the everyday dictums
of popular discourse, for example, "universals," even if they almost
always advocate passivity, are the very *real* vehicles of common
sense—"you can't fight city hall"; "a bad workman always blames his
tools"; "a woman's work is never done"; and so forth. These sedimented perceptions cannot simply be demystified. To understand
their power requires analysis of how people use such expressions,
not always in the same way, to make sense of their world. On the
other hand, to actively reconstruct this "common sense" in an oppo-

sitional way requires more than a commitment to negative capability—*not* to be always in the position of unveiling a truth beyond the ideological facade of popular "sense." It also requires a willingness to engage with the concrete effects of that sense in the everyday culture at large. To merely dismiss the fixity of these popular frames of reference is also to dismiss the given histories (even if they are histories of oppression) that explain them, and thus to play into the hands of political practices that profit from a maximum of mobility and a minimum of history.

Finally, to ask whose interests are served by "universal abandon" is not to hark back to a more straightforward kind of oppositional politics—our interests or their interests?—in which the left clearly "owned" or appropriated what the right had lost. On the contrary, it is to problematize the very question of interests in an age when interests can no longer be universalized, and for a politics in which identities are not already *there*, to be reflected as unitary in already constituted forms of struggle. To ask such a question is necessarily to survey the uneven effects of "universal abandon" on our social and cultural landscapes. In asking that question, finally, we are obliged to fall back upon, not the faith, hope, and charity of History, but those resources at hand that can help shape a reconstructed agenda for our times, and a popular imagery of the future.

The essays and interviews collected here (with the exception of Jacqueline Rose's and that of Nancy Fraser and Linda Nicholson) were written and prepared for this volume. Contributors were asked to respond to what they saw as the most significant political issues to have emerged out of their work within and around the postmodernism debates. The selections appear here in no especially significant order, except that they are framed by two wide-ranging interviews (with Fredric Jameson and Cornel West, two members of the *Social Text* collective with whom this volume was produced).

Readers could no doubt find certain categories under which to group the primary topics addressed by the authors included in the volume: questions of race, ethnicity, and neocolonialism (Cornel West, George Yúdice, Paul Smith); questions of feminism and sexual difference (Nancy Fraser and Linda Nicholson, Laura Kipnis, Jacqueline Rose); questions of popular culture (Lawrence Grossberg, Meaghan Morris); the vanguardist debates within the art world (Abigail

Solomon-Godeau, Hal Foster); and, in addition, those questions about politics, philosophy, and culture that have, historically, been more central to the Western tradition (Fredric Jameson, Chantal Mouffe, Stanley Aronowitz, Ernesto Laclau). These categories, however, are by no means exhaustive, nor were they conceived, primarily, as categories of selection. So, too, whereas some of the essays are exclusively concerned with the problematic of a particular field of inquiry, others range more generally across the entire field of the debate: from the local to the global, from low to high culture, from the personal, or domestic, to public affairs of state. Taken together, they do not intend to represent any directed attempt at forging a consensus about the politics of postmodernism, nor do they propose an agenda for a postmodernist politics. As a collection of interventions, however, they demand, in no uncertain terms, that the question of postmodernism—Universal Abandon?—remains a question and not an answer.

NOTES

1. Jonathan Arac, ed., *Postmodernism and Politics* (Minneapolis: University of Minnesota Press, 1986), IX.

2. Anders Stephanson and Daniela Salvioni, "A Short Interview with Dario Fo," *Social Text* 16 (Winter 1986/87); 167.

3. Karl Marx, *Capital*, trans. Eden Paul and Cedar Paul (New York: E. P. Dutton, 1930), 4.

4. Andreas Huyssen, *After the Great Divide: Modernism, Mass Culture, Postmodernism* (Bloomington: Indiana University Press, 1986), 179-221.

5. Dick Hebdige, "Postmodernism and 'The Other Side,' " *Journal of Communication Inquiry* 10 (Summer 1986), 78.

6. Jürgen Habermas, "Modernity—An Incomplete Project," in *The Anti-Aesthetic: Essays on Postmodern Culture*, ed. Hal Foster (Port Townsend, Wash.: Bay Press, 1983), 3-15; Jean-François Lyotard, *The Postmodern Condition* (Minneapolis: University of Minnesota Press, 1984); Fredric Jameson, "Postmodernism, or the Cultural Logic of Late Capitalism," *New Left Review* 146 (1984), 53-92.

7. S. Elizabeth Bird et al., "On Postmodernism and Articulation: An Interview with Stuart Hall," ed. Lawrence Grossberg, *Journal of Communication Inquiry* 10 (Summer 1986), 46.

What handicaps Bell in this, of course, is his intellectual formation in the United States as a Cold War anti-Stalinist. While he does not share the often extreme accommodationist stance of many of his generation of anti-Stalinist intellectuals, his worldview, quite literally, is still dependent upon a partiality for American exceptionalism, and even nationalism: one of his favorite maxims is that "One can be a critic of one's country without being an enemy of its promises." See "Our Country—1984," in *Partisan Review: The Fiftieth Anniversary Edition*, ed. William Phillips (New York: Stein & Day, 1984), 155.

Universal Abandon?

THE POLITICS
OF POSTMODERNISM

Regarding Postmodernism—A Conversation with Fredric Jameson

Anders Stephanson

Anders Stephanson: Your argument about postmodernism has two levels: on the one hand, an inventory of constitutive features, and on the other, an account of a vaster reality which these features are said to express.

Fredric Jameson: The idea is to create a mediatory concept, to construct a model that can be articulated in, and descriptive of, a whole series of different cultural phenomena. This unity, or system, is then placed in a relation to the infrastructural reality of late capitalism. The aim, in other words, is to provide something that can face in two directions: a principle for the analysis of cultural texts, which is at the same time a working system that can show the general ideological function of all these features taken together. I'm not sure that my analysis has covered all the essentials, but I tried to range across a set of qualitatively different things, starting with the visual, passing through the temporal, and then returning to a new conception of space itself.

Since our first concepts of postmodernism have tended to be negative (i.e., it isn't this, it isn't that, it isn't a whole series of things that modernism was), I begin by comparing modernism and postmodernism. However, the object is ultimately a positive description, not in any sense of value (so that postmodernism would then be "better" than modernism) but to grasp postmodernism as a new cultural logic in its own right, as something more than a mere reaction. Historically, of course, it *did* begin as a reaction against the institutionalization of modernism in universities, museums, and concert halls, and against the canonization of a certain kind of architecture. This entrenchment is felt to be oppressive by the generation that comes of age, roughly speaking, in the 1960s; and, not surprisingly, it then systematically tries to make a breathing space for itself by repudiating modernist values. In the literary context, values thus repudiated include complexity and ambiguity of language, irony, the concrete universal, and the construction of elaborate symbolic system. The specific features would of course have been different in other arts.

AS: You begin the exploration with an analysis of depth and surface in painting.

FJ: I wanted to focus on a certain flatness, not to be confused with the way in which modernist painting famously reconquered the surface of the painting. I describe this in terms of the disappearance of a certain *depth*, a word I wanted to function in a deliberately ambiguous way. I meant not only visual depth—which was already happening in modern painting—but also interpretative depth, the idea that the object is fascinating because of the density of its secrets, which are then to be uncovered by interpretation. All this vanishes. Similarly, because the idea of interpretive depth is a subtheme of the relation between postmodernism in the arts and contemporary theory, I tried to show how this goes along with a new kind of conceptualization which no longer involves *philosophical* notions of depth, that is, various hermeneutics in which one interprets an appearance in terms of some underlying reality, which these philosophies then uncode. Finally, historicity and historical depth, which used to be called historical consciousness or the sense of the past, are abolished. In short, objects fall into the world and become decoration again; visual depth and systems of interpretation fade away, and something peculiar happens to historical time.

This is then accompanied by a transformation of the depth of psychological *affect*, in that a particular kind of phenomenological or emotional reaction to the world disappears. Symptomatic here is the changeover from anxiety—the dominant feeling or affect in modernism—to a different system in which schizophrenic or drug language gives the key notion. I am referring to what the French have started to call *intensities* of highs and lows. These have nothing to do with "feelings" that offer clues to meaning in the way anxiety did. Anxiety is a hermeneutic emotion, expressing an underlying nightmare state of the world; whereas highs and lows really don't imply anything about the world, because you can feel them on whatever occasion. They are no longer *cognitive*.

AS: **You speak here of "the hysterical sublime" and "the exhilaration of the gleaming surface."** In the "dialectical intensification of the autoreferentiality of all modern culture," we face a complete lack of affect punctured by moments of extreme intensity.

FJ: Dialectically, in the conscious sublime, it is the self that touches the limit; here it is the body that is touching its limits, "volatilized," in this experience of images, to the point of being outside itself, or losing itself. What you get is a reduction of time to an instant in a most intense final punctual experience of all these things, but it is no longer *subjective* in the older sense in which a personality is standing in front of the Alps, knowing the limits of the individual subject and the human ego. On the contrary, it is a kind of nonhumanist experience of limits beyond which you get dissolved.

AS: **Whereupon we reach the temporal aspect.**

FJ: Yes. The visual metaphoric depth gives way to a description of temporal disconnection and fragmentation, the kind of thing embodied, for example, in John Cage's music. Discontinuity in sound and time is then seen as emblematic of the disappearance of certain relationships to history and the past. Analogously, it is related to the way we describe a text today as the production of discontinuous sentences without any larger unifying forms. A rhetoric of texts replaces older notions of a work organized according to this or that form. Indeed, the very language of form disappears.

AS: **During the sixties, I was once told that the average camera movement—a change of view, a zoom, a pan—did not go below something like one per 7.5 seconds in an ordinary thirty-second commercial, the reason being that this was considered the optimum of what human perception could handle. Now, it is down to something like 3.5 or less. I have actually timed commercials in which there is about one change every two seconds, fifteen changes in a matter of thirty seconds.**

FJ: We are approaching a logic of subliminality there and your example effectively illustrates this new logic of difference to which we are being programmed—these increasingly rapid and empty breaks in our time. Each training in an increased tempo is a training in feeling that it is natural to shift from one thing to another.

AS: Paik's video art is, as you say, a valuable postmodernist place to explore this problem.

FJ: As a kind of training in a new logic of difference. An empty formal training or programming in a new way of perceiving difference.

AS: What exactly is that new way of perceiving difference?

FJ: I tried to put this in the slogan "difference relates." The very perception of breaks and difference becomes a meaning in itself; yet not a meaning that has content but one that seems to be a meaningful, yet new, form of unity. This kind of view does not pose the problem "How do we relate those things, how do we turn those things back into continuities or similarities?" It simply says "When you register difference, something positive is happening in your mind." It's a way of getting rid of content.

AS: From this diagnosis of the temporal you proceed to the spatial.

FJ: I then link these two sets of features (surface and fragmentation) in terms of the spatialization of time. Time has become a perpetual present and thus spatial. Our relationship to the past is now a spatial one.

AS: Why does it necessarily become spatial?

FJ: One privileged language in modernism—take that of Marcel Proust or Thomas Mann for example—always used temporal description. That notion of "deep time," Bergsonian time, seems radically irrelevant to our contemporary experience, which is one of a perpetual spatial present. Our *theoretical* categories also tend to become spatial: structural analyses with graphs of synchronic multiplicities of spatially related things (as opposed to, say, the dialectic and its temporal moments), and languages like Foucault's, with its empty rhetoric of cutting, sorting, and modifying, a kind of spatial language in which you organize data like a great block to be chopped up in various ways. This happens to be how I, in particular, "use" Foucault, with limitations that will probably infuriate his disciples. Much of Foucault, on the other hand, was already familiar: the binary opposition between center and margin was largely developed in Sartre/Saint Genet; the concepts of power had emerged in many places, but fundamentally in the anarchist tradition; and the totalizing strategies of his various schemes also have many analogies from Weber on. I propose, rather, to consider Foucault in terms of the *cognitive mapping* of power, the construction of spatial picture-models, and the transfer of conceptions of social power and its forms onto powerful spatial figures. But then, of course, once put that way, Foucault's own figures—the grid, for example—become starkly relativized and cease to be theories as such.

AS: **Where does "hyperspace" come into the spatial argument?**

FJ: Normal space is made up of things, or organized by things. Here we are talking about the dissolution of things. In this final moment, one cannot talk about components anymore. We used to talk about this in terms of subject-object dialectics; but in a situation in which subjects and objects have been dissolved, hyperspace is the ultimate of the object-pole, and intensity the ultimate of the subject-pole, though we no longer have subjects and objects.

At any rate, the notion of spatialization replacing temporalization leads back to architecture and new experiences of space which I think are very different from any previous moments of the space of the city, to name one example. What is striking about the new urban ensembles around Paris, for example, is that there is *absolutely no perspective at all*. Not only has the street disappeared (that was already the task of modernism), but all profiles have disappeared as well. This is bewildering, and I use existential bewilderment in this new postmodern space to make a final diagnosis of the loss of our ability to *position ourselves within this space and cognitively map it*. This is then projected back on the emergence of a global, multinational culture that is decentered and cannot be visualized, a culture in which one cannot position oneself. That is the conclusion.

AS: **To be more specific, you use, very elegantly, Portman's Bona-venture Hotel in Los Angeles as an example: a mirror facade, a self-enclosed structure in which it is impossible to orientate oneself. Yet the new commercial spaces around Rodeo Drive are the very opposite of what you describe: quaint squares, readily visible spaces where things can be purchased in quite obvious and conventional ways.**

FJ: But that is the Disney version of postmodern architecture, the Disneyland pastiche of the older square or piazza or whatever. I picked emblematic things and not, by any means, everything that can be analyzed in that vein. These other examples do not exemplify the hyperspace, but they are certainly exemplary of the production of simulacra. Disney's EPCOT is another excellent example.

AS: In other words, you are referring to his compressed version of the world: little toy countries where you can orientate yourself in no time at all.

FJ: I suppose you can orient yourself because walking paths are available. But where you actually are is a real problem, for you may in fact be in the Florida Everglades and in this case you are not only in a swamp but also in a simulacra of somewhere else. Disneyland is, on the whole, supremely prophetic and paradigmatic of a lot of this stuff.

AS: The emergence of postmodernism is materially tied in your analysis to the rise of American capital on a global scale, dated to the late fifties and early sixties. However, the United States was then actually beginning to experience a relative decline in its postwar dominance: other nations were coming back economically, and there was an upsurge in third-world liberation movements and the return in the first world of oppositional ideologies fashioned very much on the depth model (marxism for one).

FJ: Notions of the discontinuity of culture and economics can account for some of that. The setting in place of American power is one thing; the development of a culture which both reflects and perpetuates that power is a somewhat different matter. The old cultural slate had to be wiped clean, and this could happen in the United States instead of Europe because of the persistence of *l'ancien régime* in European culture. Once modernism broke down, the absence of traditional forms of culture in the United States opened up a field for a whole new cultural production across the board. Individual things could be pioneered in Europe, but a *system* of culture could only emerge from this American possibility. The moment American power begins to be questioned, a new cultural apparatus becomes necessary to reinforce it. The system of postmodernism comes in as the vehicle for a new kind of ideological hegemony that might not have been required before.

AS: Isn't this view close to straightforward functionalism or instrumentalism?

FJ: Yes and no. There is certainly a way in which this system—from the export of American television shows to so-called high cultural values, above all the very logic and practice of "American" consumption itself—is as effective a vehicle for depoliticization as religion may once have been. There had to be channels of transmission, which are laid in place with communications systems, televisions, computers, and so forth. Worldwide, that was really only available in the sixties. Suffice it simply for a power elite to say: "Well, in this situation we need a cultural system which has to correspond to changes that are taking place in people's lives and offer a kind of content." The new life experience embodied in postmodernism is very powerful precisely because it has a great deal of *content* that seems to come as a solution to existential problems.

A lot of other discontinuous systems are going on here too. Some of the *social* effects of American hegemony are not felt until the sixties — the agricultural revolution, for example — so it's wrong to see this merely in terms of political power. Much of the social resistance of the sixties comes when people — peasants, for instance — begin to realize what the neocolonial systems are doing to ways of life that had been exploited before but left relatively intact. The emergence of resistance does not necessarily mean merely rolling back American influence; it can be a symptom of the disintegrating forces of that influence on deeper levels of social life than the political one.

AS: When you depict the capitalist destruction of van Gogh's world of peasant shoes and Heidegger's country pathway, you do so in terms of Tafuri's account of the modernist project in architecture: the aim of ensuring that the future holds no surprises, the idea of "planification" and elimination of future risk. This seems a valid point. However, you skate over rather easily the modernizing features of marxism itself, the results of which are clear and obvious in the unthinking destruction of the environment in Soviet-style societies. Planification with a vengeance, which actually prepares the grounds for future disaster. The obliteration of Heidegger's pathway can thus be seen as an integral feature of any modernizing ethic.

FJ: Plainly, in an advanced society, our immediate oppositional tendency is to talk about restraining technological progress. I am not sure poor societies always have that option. Some of these features, what is happening to cities like Moscow, are part of what could be called the cultural debt crisis. Think of the sixties and seventies, when the Soviets were sucked into the world system and began to believe they had to have tourists and build big hotels. One has to distinguish between the Promethean scenario — the struggle with nature — and other kinds of commodification that they really get from us in a lot of ways.

AS: Yet Stalin was a great admirer of American technology and Taylorist efficiency. The fact that the Soviets engage in this sort of destruction is not only rooted in their wanting to catch up with the West or having to compete with the West, but also embedded in a certain kind of marxist theory. By delineating the problematic in an exclusively capitalist domain, you render yourself open to the objection that a strong element of conquering nature and older "logics" exists in marxist as well as capitalist thought. Marcuse's analysis of Soviet theory is surely unequivocal on this point. If your argument, in short, is built on the idea of the relentless ordering of the world in terms of the commodifying logic of capital, it must also be clear that certain marxisms are far from innocent.

FJ: I agree. But the emphasis on production and productivity and on catching up with capitalism is at least part of the rivalry that capitalism has laid on these underdeveloped countries: they have to catch up. Therefore, we have a very elaborate dialectical process where these societies have found it necessary to go beyond self-sufficiency or autarchy to generate modernization for many reasons, like armament.

AS: Yes, but the conception of modernity is there from the outset.

FJ: That is indeed an ideological conception, and it no doubt needs to be rethought.

AS: Your model goes from the microlevel, assorted things here and there, to the macrolevel, represented by Mandel's concept of Late Capitalism. These "homologies" between the three moments of capital and the three moments in cultural development (realism, modernism, and postmodernism) lend credence to descriptions of your position as unreconstructed Lukácsianism. It does seem to be a case of expressive causality, correspondences and all. However, it is difficult to see how one can preserve a consistent political commitment if one adopts poststructuralist fantasies of pure contingency and nonrelation. In a nutshell, a certain amount of reductionism is necessary. Hence, objections to the actual concept of the three stages of capitalism aside, I think the idea of this kind of model is perfectly proper. Problems arise, however, with the mediating instances, the way in which you jump from the minute to the staggeringly global.

FJ: But Lukács takes a moralizing position on modernism that is neither historical nor dialectical. He thinks it is something essentially morally wrong that can be eliminated by an effort of the will. That position is very different from my presentation of something that seems *more* morally horrendous, namely postmodernism. As for expressive causality, I find it paradoxical that a discontinuous and dialectical model of something can be criticized for being an idealistic continuity that includes a telos. Each of these moments is dialectically different from each other and has different laws and modes of operation. I also make a place for overdetermination; that is, some things are enabled by developments in the cultural realm that tie into others at certain conjunctures. I don't think that's what one would do in a model of "the Spirit of the Age." For example, the notion of hegemony is not normally thought to be Hegelian. In talking about a certain kind of cultural hegemony, I have left a space for oppositional, or enclaves of, resistance, all kinds of things not integrated into the global model but necessarily defined against it. I can see how in some very loose and general sense one can make the sort of characterization you made, and in the same loose and general sense it wouldn't bother me. If we talk about the specifics, however, I would want to see what reprehensible things it ended up doing before I accepted it. On the other hand, as you say, any attempt to be systematic potentially attracts those criticisms because one is trying to make a reduction.

AS: **What distinguishes your concept of postmodernism is in fact that it does not designate as a stylistic mode but as a *cultural dominant*. In that way it bears little relation to the ideas of everyone from Tafuri to Lyotard.**

FJ: Two points here. First, it's important to understand that this notion of a dominant does not exclude forms of resistance. In fact, the whole point for me in undertaking this analysis was the idea that one wouldn't be able to measure the effectiveness of resistance unless one knew what the dominant forces were. My conception of postmodernism is thus not meant to be monolithic, but to allow evaluations of other currents within this system — which cannot be measured unless one knows what the system is.

Second, I want to propose a dialectical view in which we see postmodernism neither as immoral, frivolous or reprehensible because of its lack of high seriousness, nor as good in the McLuhanist, celebratory sense of the emergence of some wonderful new utopia. Features of both are going on at once. Certain aspects of postmodernism can be seen as relatively positive, such as the return of storytelling after the sort of poetic novels that modernism used to produce. Other features are obviously negative (the loss of a sense of history for example). All in all, these developments have to be confronted as a historical situation rather than as something to be morally deplored or simply celebrated.

AS: **Moralizing aside, is postmodernism not predominantly negative from a marxist perspective?**

FJ: Think of its popular character and the relative democratization involved in various postmodernist forms. This is an experience of culture accessible to far more people than the older modernist languages were. Certainly, that cannot be altogether bad. Culturalization on a very wide front might be deplored by people for whom modernism was a very sophisticated language to be conquered by dint of self-formation, of which postmodernism is then a bastardization and vulgarization. Why this should be condemned from a leftist standpoint is however not clear to me.

AS: **In that sense, no, but as you yourself have emphasized, simple opposition to totality in the name of some celebrated fragmentation and heterogeneity renders the very idea of critique difficult.**

FJ: Yet even heterogeneity is a positive thing: the social rhetoric of differences is reflected in this, which in itself is surely not a bad thing. The point is that many of these seemingly negative features can be looked at positively if they are seen historically. If one views them as items in a defense of postmodern art, they don't look the same. Postmodern architecture is demonstrably a symptom of democratization, of a new relationship of culture to people, but this does not mean that one can defend or glamorize the buildings of the postmodernists because they are populist buildings.

AS: **It is obvious, nevertheless, that postmodernist discourse makes it difficult to say things about the whole.**

FJ: One of the ways of to describe this is as a modification in the very nature of the cultural sphere: a loss of the autonomy of culture, or a case of culture falling into the world. As you say, this makes it much more difficult to speak of cultural systems and to evaluate them in isolation. A whole new theoretical problem is posed. Thinking at once negatively and positively about it is a beginning, but what we need is a new vocabulary. The languages that have been useful in talking about culture and politics in the past don't really seem adequate to this historical moment.

AS: Yet you retain the classical marxist paradigm: the master narrative underneath this search for a new vocabulary is very traditional.

FJ: Traditional in a sense, but it implies a third stage of capitalism which is not present in Marx.

AS: Nor indeed is the second one, "monopoly capitalism," which was invented by the Second International and bought wholesale, with very bad results, by the Third.

FJ: The marxist framework is still indispensable for understanding the new historical content, which demands, not a modification of the marxist framework, but an expansion of it.

AS: Why is that clear?

FJ: Contemporary marxist economics and social science is not a rewriting of nineteenth-century marxism. This can be dramatized, as Mandel does, by saying that it is not that reality has evolved away from the model or that this is no longer the capitalism analyzed by Marx, but that it is a much closer, purer version of capitalism. A feature of this third stage is that the precapitalist enclaves have systematically been penetrated, commodified, and assimilated to the dynamics of the system. If the original instruments of marxism are unserviceable, it is not that marxism is wrong now but that it is *truer* now than in Marx's time. Hence we need an expansion, rather than a replacement, of these instruments.

AS: The old Lukácsian model of truth and false consciousness is, I suppose, one casualty in this regard.

FJ: In the more interesting parts of Lukács, that is not in fact the model. Let me put that in a more personal way. Obviously, there is false consciousness, and there are moments when one wants to denounce certain things as sheer false consciousness, which is essentially a political decision and part of a struggle that has to be. In ideological analysis, on the other hand, the denunciation of works of art for embodying false consciousness was possible only in a more heterogeneous class situation, in which the working classes were a nation within the nation and did not consume bourgeois culture. When one takes a stand in such circumstances, one can see that certain kinds of objects — Proust's writings, for example — are decadent in the sense that it is not the mode in which either experience or artistic form makes any sense to people who work. From that view-point one can denounce the decadence and false consciousness which Proust undoubtedly embodied. But now, when these class differences are no longer secured by social isolation and the process of massive democratic culturalization continues, there is no space outside for the left to occupy. My position on ideological analysis of works of art today is, therefore, that you don't denounce them from the outside. If you want to denounce their false consciousness, you have to do it from the inside and it has to be a *self-critique*. It is not that false consciousness doesn't exist anymore—perhaps because it is everywhere—but we have to talk about it in a different way.

AS: You propose, then, to preserve "the moment of truth" in post-modernism. What exactly is it?

FJ: I am using contemporary German post-Hegelian language here. Ideological analysis from that vantage point means talking about the moment of truth and the moment of untruth, and in this case I am trying to say that insofar as postmodernism *really expresses* multinational capitalism, there is some cognitive content to it. It is articulating something that is going on. If the subject is lost in it, and if in social life the psychic subject has been decentered by late capitalism, this art faithfully and authentically registers that. That is its moment of truth.

AS: Modernism, as you have argued, emerges at the same time as mass culture, to which it is thus inextricably linked. Postmodernism can then be seen as the collapse of these two into one again. Terry Eagleton has reformulated this as a kind of sick joke on the historical avant-garde, in which the attempt by the avant-garde to break down the boundaries between art and social life suddenly becomes a reactionary implosion.

FJ: It's not a matter of becoming that, but being *revealed* as that. The other version of that account, which I find very persuasive, is that of Tafuri in connection with architecture. He tries to show that the protopolitical aesthetic revolution first laid out in Schiller—i.e., "We must change our existential experience and that will in itself be a revolution"—is virtually taken over word for word by Le Corbusier: "We change the space we live in and then we don't need political revolution." The protopolitical impulse of modernism, according to Tafuri, is necessarily always predicated on exclusion, for the radical new space of the modern thing must begin by a gesture of excluding the old fallen space that is to be revolutionized. Implicit here is the belief that this new space will fan out and transform the old space. Instead, it simply remains an enclave space; and when the existential and cultural spatial revolution fails to take hold in this fallen, outlying world, the building or work of art becomes an isolated monument, testifying to its own sterility or impotence. It ceases to be a revolutionary gesture. So what Eagleton is ironizing is, in Tafuri's account, already implicit in the first modernisms.

AS: There is a misreading of your reading of Tafuri which seems to say that by calling for a "properly Gramscian architecture" you are simply calling for some cleared enclave of resistance; but that is not quite what you are arguing.

FJ: In my appeal to a Gramscian architecture, I also mentioned Lefebvre. I was thinking not of an architectural practice as such but of an awareness that the locus of our new reality, and the cultural politics by which it must be confronted, is that of space. We must therefore begin to think of cultural politics in terms of space and the struggle for space. Then we are no longer thinking in old categories of critical distance but in some new way in which the disinherited and essentially modernist language of subversion and negation is conceived differently. Tafuri's argument is couched in cultural terms, but what matters in any defeat or success of a plan to transform the city is political power, control over speculation and land values, and so on. That's a very healthy awareness of the infrastructure.

AS: How does this differ from traditional politics?

FJ: The difference is that the political is projected onto at least two levels: the practical matter of this place, this terrain, and these resistances; and then above and beyond that, the cultural vision of Utopian space of which this particular enclave is but a specific figure. All of which can be said in a more banal way in terms of the decay of the very concept of socialism, which we can observe everywhere (in all three worlds). It is a matter of reinventing that concept as a powerful cultural and social vision, something one does not do simply by repeating a worn-out name or term. But it is a two-level strategy: the specific space or place *and* the global vision of which the first is only one particular manifestation or local fulfillment. Add to this the fact and problem of the new global systemic space and we have a demand made on the political imagination that is historically unparalleled. Let me put it this way: There exists today a global capitalist, or late capitalist culture, which we call, as is now apparent, postmodernism. It is a tremendously powerful force which, in sheer gravitational attraction and capability of diffusion, is known, or used to be known, as cultural imperialism. Nothing like a global socialist culture exists as a distinct oppositional force and style to this. On the other hand, when one proposes such a political project to some of the interested parties, they rightly begin at once to worry about the dissolution of that national situation and culture which has generally played such a powerful role in socialist revolutions. What is wanted, therefore, is a new relationship between a global cultural style and the specificity and demands of a concrete local or national situation.

AS: Is the spatial aspect not really what Social Democrats in Europe have been concerned with, sometimes successfully, for a longtime?

FJ: The problem with the social democratic governments is that they've gained power in a nation-state whose economic realities are really controlled by the international market. They are therefore not in control of their own national space. Ultimately, I am talking about a global space which is not abstract or speculative. I am talking about the fact that the proletariat of the first world is now in the third world and that production is taking place around the Pacific basin or wherever. These are practical realities, and the control of national space may itself be an outmoded idea in a situation of multinationals.

AS: Indeed, one may take your macroanalysis to mean that the task of radical first-world intellectuals is a kind of "third-worldism." This, to my mind, recalls various "bribery theories" of the 1960s— using the absence of movement among the Western working class as a justification for fixation on other, and less quiescent, continents. Eventually these positions were discarded and rightly so.

FJ: The attractiveness of "third-worldism" as an ideology rises and falls with the condition of the third world itself, but the political movement going on today—such as there is—is in places like Nicaragua and South Africa. Surely, then, the third world is still very much alive as a possibility. It is not a matter of cheering for third-world countries to make their revolution; it is a dialectical matter of seeing that we here are involved in these areas and are busy trying to put them down, that they are part of our power relations.

AS: But that tends to end up in moralism: "We shouldn't do this and we shouldn't do that in the third world." Once one has realized that, what is there to do? No particular politics follows as far as the first world itself is concerned. One tends to end up with Paul Sweezy's position that the only thing to do is prevent interventions in the third world. This strikes me as a bit barren.

FJ: Well, what are the alternatives? We are talking about culture, and culture is a matter of awareness; and it would not be bad to generate the awareness that we in the superstate are at all times a presence in third-world realities, that our affluence and power are in the process of doing something to them. The form this awareness takes in American culture has to do not only with foreign policy but also with the notion that the United States itself is a third-world country. In a way, we have become the biggest third-world country, because of unemployment, nonproduction, the flight of factories, and so on.

AS: Why does that make us a third-world country? It seems like the definition of a first-world country.

FJ: If the third world is defined, as it sometimes has been, as the development of underdevelopment, it does seem clear that we have begun to do this to ourselves as well. In any case, the apparent return to some finance capitalism with dizzying edifices of credit and paper no longer reposing on the infrastructure or "ground" of real production offers some peculiar analogies to current (poststructuralist) theory itself. Let's say that here the first world—if it does not revert back into third-world realities—unexpectedly, and in a peculiar dialectical reversal, begins to touch some features of third-world experience, perhaps another reason third-world culture has lately become one of our passionate interests.

AS: In arguing against condemnation and celebration, you wish to encourage a critique that goes through postmodernism in a sort of "homeopathic" way.

FJ: To undo postmodernism homeopathically by the methods of postmodernism: to work at dissolving the pastiche by using all the instruments of pastiche itself, to reconquer some genuine historical sense by using the instruments of what I have called substitutes for history.

AS: How is this "homeopathic" operation to be understood more specifically?

FJ: The figure of homeopathic medicine here does not imply that the culture functions in only that way, but it is often the case. Modernism, for example, was an experience of nascent commodification that fought reification by means of reification, in terms of reification. It was itself a gigantic process of reification internalized as a homeopathic way of seizing on this force, mastering it, and opposing the result to reifications passively submitted to in external reality. I am wondering whether some positive features of postmodernism couldn't do that as well: attempt somehow to master these things by choosing them and pushing them to their limits. There is a whole range of so-called oppositional arts, whether it's punk writing or ethnic writing, that really try to use postmodern techniques—though for obvious reasons I dislike the term *technique*—to go through and beyond. It's certainly wrong to go down the list of contemporary trends and, once again, in typical left-wing fashion, try to find out which is progressive. The only way through a crisis of space is to invent a new space.

AS: **Despite the disappearance of a *sense* of history, there is no lack of historical elements in postmodern culture.**

FJ: When I talked about the loss of history, I didn't mean the disappearance of images of history, for instance, in the case of nostalgia film. The increasing number of films about the past are no longer historical; they are images, simulacra, and pastiches of the past. They are effectively a way of satisfying a chemical craving for historicity, using a product that substitutes for and blocks it.

AS: **But historical images are, in a way, always substitutes.**

FJ: That is not the way Lukács analyzed the historical novel in its emergent form. I would also argue that something like science fiction can occasionally be looked at as a way of breaking through to history in a new way; achieving a distinctive historical consciousness by way of the future rather than the past; and becoming conscious of our present as the past of some unexpected future, rather than as the future of a heroic national past (the traditional historical novel of Lukács). But nostalgia art gives us the image of various generations of the past as fashion-plate images that entertain no determinable ideological relationship to other moments of time: they are not the outcome of anything, nor are they the antecedents of our present; they are simply images. This is the sense in which I describe them as substitutes for any genuine historical consciousness rather than specific new forms of the latter.

AS: **The cannibalizing of styles is part and parcel of this type of "historicity."**

FJ: This is what architects call historicism, the eclectic use of dead languages.

AS: I first became aware of this a couple of years ago with regard to fashion, when the fifties was being mined, along with its ideological orientation: the schlock of the Eisenhower epoch, fascination with television series of that period, and so forth. Now, when that seems exhausted, there is excavation of the sixties, not the politicized sixties but the sixties of the go-go girls. One can imagine that even the militant sixties can be used for stylistic innovation, rather in the manner in which Macy's department store instantly transforms East Village vogues into commercial values.

FJ: Perhaps one could write a history of these nostalgias. It would be plausible to say that in a moment of exhaustion with politics, the images that are cannibalized and offered by nostalgia film are those of a great depoliticized era. Then, when unconsciously political drives begin to reawaken, they are contained by offering images of a politicized era. We are all happy to have a movie like *Reds*, but is that not also a nostalgia film?

AS: Perhaps, but nostalgia is difficult to avoid in popular depictions of the past.

FJ: A historical situation is at stake, and one can't wish this postmodern blockage of historicity out of existence by mere self-critical self-consciousness. If it's true that we have real difficulty imagining the radical difference with the past, this difficulty cannot be overcome by an act of the will or by deciding that this is the wrong kind of history to have and that we ought to do it in some other way. This, for me, is the fascination with Doctorow's novels. Here is a radical left-wing novelist who has seized the whole apparatus of nostalgia art, pastiche, and postmodernism to work himself through them instead of attempting to resuscitate some older form of social realism, an alternative that would in itself become another pastiche. Doctorow's is not necessarily the only possible path, but I find it an intriguing attempt to undo postmodernism "homeopathically" by the methods of postmodernism: to work at dissolving the pastiche by using all the instruments of pastiche itself and to reconquer some genuine historical sense by using the instruments of what I have called substitutes for history.

In your terms this might be another version of "third-worldism" in the cultural sense. We come back to looking for some alternative place which is neither the past of the first world, the great moment of modernism, nor its present, which is that of schizophrenic textuality.

AS: But how is it possible, in a mode of cultural expression that by definition is superficial, to say anything about deep structures? After all, the essence of marxism is to reveal something about what "really is."

FJ: Doctorow is still my best example, for by turning the past into something which is obviously a black simulacrum, he suddenly makes us realize that this is the only image of the past we have; in truth, a projection on the walls of Plato's cave. This, if you like, is negative dialectics, or negative theology, an insistence on the very flatness and depthlessness of the thing which makes what isn't there very vivid. That is not negligible. It is not the reinvention of some sense of the past wherein one would fantasize about a healthier age of deeper historical sense: the use of these very limited instruments shows their limits. And it is not *ironic*.

AS: But how does one use that perception of difference to get somewhere else? If you resort to homology, you've basically done the same thing that you criticize in *Reds* but not in Doctorow's work.

FJ: The problem of homologies (and the unsatisfactory nature of these parallels or analogies between levels) has been a constant theoretical concern for me. Something like the homology does seem difficult to avoid when one attempts to correlate distinct semiautonomous fields. I've played with alternative concepts: Sartre's notion of the *analagon* and Peirce's concept of the *interpretant*. Both of these stress the operation of reading analogies off the allegorical object, rather than discovering them ontologically, as "realities" in the world. And each seems, in addition, to contribute a little toward clarifying the process I've called cognitive mapping, the invention of ways of using one object and one reality to get a mental grasp of something else which one cannot represent or imagine. As an emblem of this process, I might offer the picture of those hypersterilized laboratory chambers into which enormous gloves and instruments protrude, manipulated by the scientist from the outside. The normal body is doing one thing, but the results are taking place in another space altogether and according to other dimensions, other parameters. It must be a bewildering set of tasks to exercise, as far from our normal bodily operations as the deductive or abductive appropriation of the banana is for the laboratory monkey. But, if it were possible, this would give you an idea of the new kinds of representational processes demanded here.

AS: **The personal "style" so typical of modernism has, according to you become a mere code in postmodernism.**

FJ: This is another feature developed primarily by poststructuralism, namely, the eclipse of the old personal subject and ego. Modernism was predicated on the achievement of some unique personal style that could be parlayed out to the subject of genius, the charismatic subject, or the supersubject, if you like. If that subject has disappeared, the styles linked to it are no longer possible. A certain form of depersonalization thus seems implicit in all of this: even when modernism itself is pastiched, it is only an imitation of style, not a style.

Still, I always insist on a third possibility beyond the old bourgeois ego and the schizophrenic subject of our organization society today: a *collective subject*, decentered but not schizophrenic. It emerges in certain forms of storytelling that can be found in third-world literature, in testimonial literature, in gossip and rumors, and in things of this kind. It is a storytelling which is neither personal in the modernist sense, nor depersonalized in the pathological sense of the schizophrenic text. It is decentered, since the stories you tell there as an individual subject don't belong to you; you don't control them the way the master subject of modernism would. But you don't just suffer them in the schizophrenic isolation of the first-world subject of today. None of this reinvents style in the older sense.

AS: **Some years ago, in a wholly different context, you called the brushstroke the very sign of the modern genius, pointing specifically to de Kooning's metabrushstroke as the last gasp of some individualizing art. Yet, the next morning, neoexpressionism brought back this megabrushstroke with a vengeance. Would you then say that this was pastiche, not the surviving element of some older modernism?**

FJ: Some of it is merely a pastiche of modernist subjectivity.

AS: **On the other hand, certain of these painters, Immendorf for instance, were quite explicitly political, with interesting stories to tell.**

FJ: A lot of it is European or comes from the semiperiphery of the American core (e.g., Canada). It would seem, for instance, that neoexpressionism flourished particularly in Italy and Germany, the two Western countries that experienced the historical "break" of fascism. Here one could argue with Habermas, who sees the German version of neoexpressionism as reactionary. We, on the other hand, could perhaps use it in other ways, not classifying it as a morbid attempt to reinvent a subjectivity, which in the German tradition is tainted anyway.

AS: And now we see the return of minimalism, blank surfaces, and "neo-geo" forms looking rather like sixties and early seventies to me. The cannibalization of styles has apparently been "revved up," conceivably ending in some furious, vertiginous act of biting its own tail.

You suggest an interesting connection between Tafuri's rigorous anti-utopianism—his almost Adornian negative dialectics of architecture—and Venturi's celebration of Las Vegas: the system, for both, is essentially a massively all-encompassing one which cannot be changed. The difference is that Tafuri stoically refuses it, while Venturi invents ways of "relaxing" within it.

FJ: For Tafuri, Venturi is himself part of an opposition which is rather that of Mies to Venturi. The one solution is that of absolute Mallarméan purity and silence; the other is the abandonment of that final attempt at negative purity and the falling back into the world. The problem with Venturi's architecture or his "solution"—characteristic of many poststructuralisms today—is the appeal to irony, which is a *modernist* solution. He wants to use the language of the vernacular of Las Vegas, but, being engaged in art and aesthetics, he also has to have some kind of minimal distance to it. All of this art, as Tafuri says, is predicated on distance, and distance is always a failure: since it distances itself from what it wants to change, it can't change it.

AS: This reminds me of your criticism of Lyotard's concept of postmodernism: he claims to have eliminated the master narratives but then smuggles them back in again.

FJ: His most famous statement on postmodernism is that it should prepare for the return of the great modernisms. Now does that mean the return of the great master narratives? Is there not some nostalgia at work here? On the other hand, insofar as the refusal of narratives is viewed as the place of the perpetual present, of anarchist science, to use Feyerabend's term (the random breaking of paradigms and so on), we're in full postmodernism.

AS: So the master narratives in that sense are not dead.

FJ: All one has to do is look at the reemergence of religious para-digms, whether it is in Iran or liberation theology or American fundamentalism. There are all kinds of master narratives in this world, which is presumably beyond narrative.

AS: The appropriation of modernism in the United States, when it comes, is quite different from the European predecessors. Though in itself a depoliticized art, postwar modernism here is nevertheless *employed* in very instrumental ways.

FJ: The political elements of "original modernism" in its historical emergence were left out in this process of transplantation so that the various modernisms have been read as subjectivizing and inward-turning. Other features vanished too. The whole utopian and aesthetico-political element in modern architecture, Le Corbusier for example, is no longer visible when we are talking about great monuments and conventions imitated in the schools. At the same time, one must say that this modernism was no longer being produced: there was not a living modernism that could have been encouraged in a different way.

AS: Somewhere you mention Habermas's defense of the idea of a possible high modernism again and point out that this seems to be a defense against a political reaction which in West Germany is still really antimodernist. In this country the situation is in fact the opposite, is it not? The Hilton Kramers here are obviously not defending radicalism. Defense of postmodernism—one thinks of Tom Wolfe—can, on the other hand, also be associated with right-wing politics.

FJ: The modernism Hilton Kramer wants to go back to is the sub-jectivizing modernism of the 1950s, the American reading of mod-ernism that has been sullied, and has lost its purity and so must be recovered. However, Habermas's modernism (I hesitate to call it the genuine article) is seen in the context of 1910 and is therefore something very different. Modernism elsewhere died a natural death and is thus no longer available, but in Germany modernism was of course cut short by nazism; thus, there is an unfulfilled character to that project which I presume someone like Habermas can attempt to take up again. But that option is not viable for us.

AS: The *coupure* in the "dominant" occurs, as you outline it, in the late fifties or early sixties. Art becomes completely enmeshed in the political economy of its own sphere, which in turn becomes part of a greater economic system. Emblematic among the pictorial artists here is Warhol, with whom you contrast van Gogh in the initial delineation of modernism/postmodernism. Warhol is perhaps almost too obvious an example. How does a contemporary of his like Rauschenberg fit in?

FJ: Rauschenberg is transitional, coming in at the tail end of abstract expressionism, but now in his most recent stuff is developing a whole panoply of ways of doing postmodernism. His new works are all collage surfaces with photographic images, including, symptomatically, both modernist and postmodernist ones in the same work. The other thing about Rauschenberg is that he works a lot in third-world countries where many of these photographs are taken.

In dealing with postmodernism, one can isolate people who made some pioneering contributions, but aesthetic questions about how great these contributions are—questions that can legitimately be posed when you're dealing with modernism—make little sense. I don't know how great Rauschenberg is, but I saw a wonderful show of his in China, a glittering set of things that offered all kinds of postmodernist experiences. But when they're over, they're over. The textual object is not, in other words, a work of art, a masterwork like the modernist monument was. The appreciation of the work no longer requires the attachment of some permanent evaluation of it as with the modernist painters or writers, and in that sense it is more of what I sometimes call a disposable text. You go into a Rauschenberg show and experience a process undertaken in very expert and inventive ways, and when you leave it, it's over.

AS: What was the reaction of the Chinese audience?

FJ: Fascination, puzzlement. I tried to explain postmodernism to my Chinese students, but for a general Chinese audience it would simply be "Western art." It must be understood in our historical context: it isn't just modern art in general, but a specific moment of it.

AS: How are the traditional ways of apprehending art changing with all the great social transformations now going on in China? Is there an attempt to rejuvenate modernist notions of creativity, to replace tradition with Western subjectivity?

FJ: It is not being replaced in that way. There is considerable translation of Western bestsellers but also of high culture; translations of

Faulkner's *The Sound and the Fury* and Alice Walker's *The Color Purple*, but also lots of Arthur Hailey. Maybe I can explain it in terms of theory. The Chinese are now interested in two kinds of theory: Western theory and traditional Chinese theory. It is felt that both of these are levers that can get them out of the kind of essentially Soviet cultural theory in which they were trained in the fifties. As Deng Youmei, one of the most interesting Chinese writers, said to me: "We are not much interested in Western modernism as such. We are bored by novels that don't tell stories." In other words, the elaborate symbolism you find in James Joyce or Virginia Woolf doesn't do anything for them. Right after the fall of the Gang of Four, it was important to recoup some of what had been forgotten, but when I got there and thought I was bringing some enlightenment about Kafka, they informed me that they had been interested in this at the end of the 1970s but not anymore. Deng You-mei said: "What you have to realize is that for us realism is also Western. Our realisms come out of the Western traditions; certainly the dominant realism of the 1950s was the Soviet one. We think there is something different from both modernism and realism and that is traditional Chinese storytelling."

This is the third world's input into the whole poststructuralist debate on representation, which is loosely assimilated to realism over here: if it is representation and realism, it's bad, and you want to break it up with the decentered subject and so on. But these Chinese strings of episodic narratives fall outside this framework. They are an example of going back to the sort of storytelling that one finds both in the third world's discovery of its own way of telling stories *and* in a certain form of postmodernism. So one has to rethink this question of realism and representation in the Chinese context. I took a tour through some famous grottoes with stalactites. Imagine the bourgeois public that hates modern art and here in the same way you have a guide with a little light projector who proclaims: "Look at these rocks. There is an old man, three children, there's the goddess, etc." And you think: this is the most rudimentary form of what we denounce as representation in the West, a public that thinks in these terms. But China developed, alongside this popular realistic or representational perception, a very different kind of spatial perception in the evolution of the written characters. It is possible, therefore, that an oppositional culture in China might take the form of a revival of certain kinds of popular ways of seeing things, ways which would not necessarily seem the same to us.

AS: What about allegory here? You have referred to allegory in the third-world novel as well as with regard to postmodernism.

FJ: That was one attempt to theorize that third-world culture is different from our own. In nonhegemonic situations, or in situations of economic or cultural subalternity, there tends to be a reference to the national situation that is always present and always felt in a way that it cannot be in the dominant culture of the superstate. But this type of analysis is not intended as a program for art, to the effect that we should now begin to write allegories.

AS: The Chinese cave mentioned before cannot be described as one of "hyperspace."

FJ: Nor does it really betoken any radical cultural difference. This is exactly what the American tourist would do with the caves in Louisville, Kentucky. Whether a revolutionary peasantry or an American tourist looks at these is not relevant to that conception. If, as Bourdieu has explored, people have no institutional reason to justify to themselves the aesthetic operation, namely by seeing that a little artistic training is somehow good and a sign of social distinction, then they have to have another reason for doing it, which ends up being to see likenesses. Seeing likenesses in this basically mimetic sense is not inherently a sign of the people or the popular either, but it is certainly an interesting index of the relationship of culture to people for whom culture is not a socially signifying property or attribute.

In postmodernism, on the other hand, everyone has learned to consume culture through television and other mass media, so a rationale is no longer necessary. You look at advertising billboards and collages of things because they are there in external reality. The whole matter of how you justify to yourself the time of consuming culture disappears: you are no longer even aware of consuming it. Everything is culture, the culture of the commodity. That's a very significant feature of postmodernism, which accounts for the disappearance from it of the traditional theories, justifications, and rationalizations of what we used to call aesthetics (and of concepts of high culture).

AS: Postmodern art may in some sense be disposable texts, but its monetary value is of course anything but disposable and transient.

Warhol, it should be underlined, does not appear in the model as an *originator*, as traditionally understood. Your object is the *systemic*, not the evaluation of contemporary artists.

FJ: In trying to theorize the systemic, I was using certain of these things as allegories. From this angle it makes no sense to try to look for individual trends, and individual artists are only interesting if one finds some moment in which the system as a whole, or some limit of it, is being touched. Evaluation does come into play, since one can imagine a much less interesting postmodernist exhibition, and one would then have to say that that painter is not as good as Rauschenberg. But this is not the same kind of use of aesthetic axiological evaluation that people felt they were able to do when they were handling modernism, for example, making relative assessments of Proust against Mann.

All the great modernists invented modernism in their own fashion. It is likewise clear that no one postmodernist can give us postmodernism, since the system involves a whole range of things. Warhol is emblematic of one feature of postmodernism and the same goes for Paik. Both artists allow you to analyze and specify something partial, and in that sense their activities are surely original: they have identified a whole range of things to do and have moved in to colonize this new space. However, this is not original in the world-historical sense of the great modernist creator. If one artist actually embodied all of these things, Laurie Anderson, for example, he or she would no doubt be transcending postmodernism. But where Wagner, in the *Gesamtkunstwerk*, may have done something like that in a key moment of modernism, Laurie Anderson's *Gesamtkunstwerk* does not do that for a nonsystematizable system, a nontotalizable system.

AS: This leaves no great space for criticism of individual works. What is the task once one has related the part to the whole?

FJ: If they are no longer *works*, in other words. This is particularly true for video, which one usually sees in batches. You have put your finger on the fundamental methodological problem of the criticism of postmodernism. For to talk about any one of these postmodernist texts is to reify it, to turn it into the work of art it no longer is, to endow it with a permanence and monumentality that it is its vocation to dispel. A critic who is supposed to analyze individual texts is thus faced with almost insuperable problems: the moment one analyzes a single piece of video art one does it violence; one removes some of its provisionality and anonymity and turns it into a masterpiece or at least a privileged text again. It's much easier to deal with it in terms of trends: "Here's a new trend (described as such and such) and here's another." But the whole language of trends is the dialectic of modernism.

AS: We are returning here to the problem of evaluation.

FJ: The Cubans, who have a different system, point out that our sense of value, in a good as well as bad sense, is given to us by the art market. One possible opposite of this would be a situation—I'm expanding on their argument—in which only a few styles would be permitted. But in a country like Cuba, which is devoid of an art market but exceedingly pluralistic culturally, where everything from social realism to pop art to abstract expressionism can be found, there is no mechanism that can say this is more advanced than that. One begins to sense then that the art market has an almost religious-ontological function for us. We don't have to face this radical plurality of styles of "anything goes" because somebody is always around to tell us that "this thing is a little newer than that one." Or more valu-able, since I now think our value system depends on that transmis-sion of the market mechanism.

AS: So how do the Cubans evaluate?

FJ: It is a real problem; they don't know. They confront the death of value (in Nietzsche's version, the death of God) much more intensely than we do. We still have these marvelous theological mechanisms by which we pick things out and sort them. They have a more inter-esting problem of what the value of art would be in a situation of complete freedom, in the Nietzschean sense: freedom, that is, to do anything you want. Value then enters a crisis, also of the Nietzschean type. This is not the case when there is still a market, or when only a few styles are permitted and anyone who pushes against the para-digm can be identified. Then, too, you certainly know where you stand in terms of value.

AS: You say somewhere that the dialectical imagination to which Marcuse refers has atrophied. Yet at the same time you say that a constitutive feature of mass culture is that it satisfies a deep utopian impulse in the consumer. If the imagination has been atrophied, the impulse has not?

FJ: Marcuse, ironically, was the great theorist of the autonomy of culture. The problem is that he reverts in a much simpler manner to

Adorno's modernism, to its autonomy. But Adorno's great aesthetics—the aesthetics one writes when it is impossible to write aesthetics—involves time and death and history: experience is historical and condemned to death in a sense. Marcuse's concept finally simplified that complexity out of Adorno, taking up an older modernist model which is not now helpful. His notion of the utopian impulse is a different matter. The objection there is that he falls back on a position in which the autonomy of art still permits a kind of full expression of the utopian impulse.

AS: Adorno's negative dialectics is criticized in your account for allowing no resistance to the overall system. Nothing, seemingly, is to be done. You point to the similarities here with the poststructuralist tendency to see the system as complete and completely unchangeable in its systematicity; and I suppose one could indeed say that about Foucault, *et al.*, at certain times. The result is pessimism, and it matters less that the first model is dialectical and the latter is one of heterogeneity and contingency. Yet a quick reading of Fredric Jameson leaves one with a distinct residue of pessimism as well.

FJ: The whole point about the loss in postmodernism of the sense of the future is that it also involves a sense that nothing will change and there is no hope. Facile optimism is, on the other hand, not helpful either.

AS: In "going through" poststructuralism and postmodernism and preserving its moment of truth, you are intermittently very hard and negative, quite rightly emphasizing the politically unsavory effects.

FJ: There one can make a distinction. A difference exists between the production of ideologies about this reality and the reality itself. They necessarily demand two different responses. I am not willing to engage this matter of pessimism and optimism about postmodernism, since we are actually referring to capitalism itself: one must know the worst and then see what can be done. I am much more polemical about postmodernist *theories*. Theories which either exalt this or deal with it in moral ways are not productive, and *that* I think one can say something about.

AS: The reconquest of a sense of place here, the attainment of a new cartography, is primarily a call directed to the left itself. We are not referring to any great political practice, but we are arguing with the 1,500 people who happen to be deeply influenced by Deleuze and Guattari, for a large proportion of intellectuals of self-professed radical persuasion would no doubt describe themselves as heavily influenced by poststructuralist ideologies.

FJ: That's why it's worthwhile to get a systemic sense of where all these things come from so that we can see what our influences are and what to do about them. The proliferation of theoretical discourses was healthy because it led to some awareness of their political consequences. In moments of economic crisis or intervention abroad, people can determine more clearly what any given theory does or allows them to do. It is a matter of theoretical and historical self-knowledge, and what I am engaged in is in fact a struggle within theory as much as anything else. If I were making videos, I would talk about this in a different way.

AS: In that respect, yours is a systematic project of building "totalizing" models, something which, to understate the case, has been fairly unpopular among the Western intelligentsia in the last decade. Are people perhaps more receptive now to "model-building"?

FJ: They are more receptive to the historical features of it, to the idea of thinking historically. They are not necessarily more receptive to the marxist version of this historical inquiry, but perhaps they are willing to entertain it on some supermarket-pluralist basis.

AS: The historical dimension counteracts the postmodernist immersion in the present, the dehistoricizing or nonhistorical project. In that sense it goes outside the postmodern paradigm.

FJ: That is essentially the rhetorical trick or solution that I was attempting: to see whether by systematizing something which is resolutely unhistorical, one couldn't force a historical way of thinking *at least about that*. And there are some signs that it is possible to go around it, to *outflank* it.

Radical Democracy: Modern or Postmodern?

Chantal Mouffe

Translated by Paul Holdengräber

What does it mean to be on the left today? In the twilight years of the twentieth century is it in any way meaningful to invoke the Enlightenment ideals that lay behind the project of the transformation of society? We are undoubtedly living through the crisis of the Jacobin imaginary, which has, in diverse ways, characterized the revolutionary politics of the last two hundred years. It is unlikely that marxism will recover from the blows it has suffered; not only the discredit brought upon the Soviet model by the analysis of totalitarianism, but also the challenge to class reductionism posed by the emergence of new social movements. But the fraternal enemy, the social democratic movement, is not in any better shape. It has proved incapable of addressing the new demands of recent decades, and its central achievement, the welfare state, has held up badly under attack from the right, because it has not been able to mobilize those who should have interests in defending its achievements.

As for the ideal of socialism, what seems to be in question is the very idea of progress that is bound up with the project of modernity. In this respect, discussion of the postmodern, which until now had focused on culture, has taken a political turn. Alas, the debate all too quickly petrified around a set of simplistic and sterile positions. Whereas Habermas accuses of conservatism all those who criticize the universalist ideal of the Enlightenment,[1] Lyotard declares with pathos that after Auschwitz the project of modernity has been eliminated.[2] Richard Rorty rightly remarks that one finds on both sides an illegitimate assimilation of the political project of the Enlightenment and its epistemological aspects. This is why Lyotard finds it necessary to abandon political liberalism in order to avoid a universalist philosophy, whereas Habermas, who wants to defend liberalism, holds on, despite all of its problems, to this universalist philosophy.[3] Habermas indeed believes that the emergence of universalist forms of morality and law is the expression of an irreversible collective process of learning, and that to reject this implies a rejection of modernity, undermining the very foundations of democracy's existence. Rorty invites us to consider Blumenberg's distinction, in *The Legitimacy of the Modern Age*, between two aspects of the Enlightenment, that of "self-assertion" (which can be identified with the political project) and that of "self-foundation" (the epistemological project). Once we acknowledge that there is no necessary relation between these two aspects, we are in the position of being able to defend the political project while abandoning the notion that it must be based on a specific form of rationality.

Rorty's position, however, is problematic because of his identification of the political project of modernity with a vague concept of "liberalism," which includes both capitalism and democracy. For, at the heart of the very concept of political modernity, it is important to distinguish two traditions, liberal and democratic, both of which, as MacPherson has shown, are articulated only in the nineteenth century and are thus not necessarily related in any way. Moreover, it would be a mistake to confuse this "political modernity" with "social modernity," the process of modernization carried out under the growing domination of relations of capitalist production. If one fails to draw this distinction between democracy and liberalism, between political liberalism and economic liberalism; if, as Rorty does, one conflates all these notions under the term *liberalism*, then one is driven, under the pretext of defending modernity, to a pure and simple apology for the "institutions and practices of the rich North Atlantic democracies,"[4] which leaves no room for a critique (not even an immanent critique) that would enable us to transform them.

Confronted by this "postmodernist bourgeois liberalism" that Rorty advocates, I would like to show how the project of a "Radical and Plural Democracy," one that Ernesto Laclau and I have already sketched out in our book *Hegemony and Socialist Strategy: Towards a Radical Democratic Politics*,[5] proposes a reformulation of the socialist project that avoids the twin pitfalls of marxist socialism and social democracy, while providing the left with a new imaginary, an imaginary that speaks to the tradition of the great emancipatory struggles but that also takes into account recent theoretical contributions by psychoanalysis and philosophy. In effect, such a project could be defined as being both modern and postmodern. It pursues the "unfulfilled project of modernity," but, unlike Habermas, we believe that there is no longer a role to be played in this project by the epistemological perspective of the Enlightenment. Although this perspective did play an important part in the emergence of democracy, it has become an obstacle in the path of understanding those new forms of politics, characteristic of our societies today, which demand to be approached from a nonessentialist perspective. Hence the necessity of using the theoretical tools elaborated by the different currents of what can be called the postmodern in philosophy and of appropriating their critique of rationalism and subjectivism.[6]

The Democratic Revolution

Different criteria have been suggested for defining modernity. They vary a great deal depending on the particular levels or features one wants to emphasize. I, for one, think that modernity must be defined at the political level, for it is there that social relations take shape and are symbolically ordered. Insofar as it inaugurates a new type of society, modernity can be viewed as a decisive point of reference. In this respect the fundamental characteristic of modernity is undoubtedly the advent of the democratic revolution. As Claude Lefort has shown, this democratic revolution is at the origin of a new kind of institution of the social, in which power becomes an "empty place." For this reason, modern democratic society is constituted as "a society in which power, law and knowledge are exposed to a radical indetermination, a society that has become the theatre of an uncontrollable adventure, so that what is instituted never becomes established, the known remains undetermined by the unknown, the present proves to be undefinable."[7] The absence of power embodied in the person of the prince and tied to a transcendental authority preempts the existence of a final guarantee or source of legitimation; society can no longer be defined as a substance having an organic identity. What remains is a society without clearly defined outlines, a social structure that is impossible to describe from the perspective of a single, or

universal, point of view. It is in this way that democracy is characterized by the "dissolution of the landmarks of certainty."[8] I think that
such an approach is extremely suggestive and useful because it
allows us to put many of the phenomena of modern societies in a
new perspective. Thus, the effects of the democratic revolution can
be analyzed in the arts, theory, and all aspects of culture in general,
enabling one to formulate the question of the relation between
modernity and postmodernity in a new and more productive way.
Indeed, if one sees the democratic revolution as Lefort portrays it, as
the distinctive feature of modernity, it then becomes clear that what
one means when one refers to postmodernity in philosophy is to recognize the impossibility of any ultimate foundation or final legitimation that is constitutive of the very advent of the democratic form of
society and thus of modernity itelf. This recognition comes after the
failure of several attempts to replace the traditional foundation that
lay within God or Nature with an alternative foundation lying in Man
and his Reason. These attempts were doomed to failure from the start
because of the radical indeterminacy that is characteristic of modern
democracy. Nietzsche had already understood this when he proclaimed that the death of God was inseparable from the crisis of
humanism.[9]

Therefore the challenge to rationalism and humanism does not
imply the rejection of modernity but only the crisis of a particular
project within modernity, the Enlightenment project of self-foundation. Nor does it imply that we have to abandon its political project,
which is its achievement of equality and freedom for all. In order to
pursue and deepen this aspect of the democratic revolution, we must
ensure that the democratic project takes account of the full breadth
and specificity of the democratic struggles in our times. It is here that
the contribution of the so-called postmodern critique comes into its
own.

How, in effect, can we hope to understand the nature of these new
antagonisms if we hold on to an image of the unitary subject as the
ultimate source of intelligibility of its actions? How can we grasp the
multiplicity of relations of subordination that can affect an individual
if we envisage social agents as homogeneous and unified entities?
What characterizes the struggles of these new social movements is
precisely the multiplicity of subject-positions, which constitutes a
single agent and the possibility for this multiplicity to become the

site of an antagonism and thereby politicized. Thus the importance of the critique of the rationalist concept of a unitary subject, which one finds not only in poststructuralism but also in psychoanalysis, in the philosophy of language of the late Wittgenstein, and in Gadamer's hermeneutics.

To be capable of thinking politics today, and understanding the nature of these new struggles and the diversity of social relations that the democratic revolution has yet to encompass, it is indispensable to develop a theory of the subject as a decentered, detotalized agent, a subject constructed at the point of intersection of a multiplicity of subject-positions between which there exists no a priori or necessary relation and whose articulation is the result of hegemonic practices. Consequently, no identity is ever definitively established, there always being a certain degree of openness and ambiguity in the way the different subject-positions are articulated. What emerges are entirely new perspectives for political action, which neither liberalism — with its idea of the individual who only pursues his or her own interest — nor marxism — with its reduction of all subject-positions to that of class — can sanction, let alone imagine.

It should be noted, then, that this new phase of the democratic revolution, while it is, in its own way, a result of the democratic universalism of the Enlightenment, also puts into question some of its assumptions. Many of these new struggles do in fact renounce any claim to universality. They show how in every assertion of universality there lies a disavowal of the particular and a refusal of specificity. Feminist criticism unmasks the particularism hiding behind those so-called universal ideals which, in fact, have always been mechanisms of exclusion. Carole Pateman, for example, has shown how classical theories of democracy were based upon the exclusion of women:

> The idea of universal citizenship is specifically modern, and necessarily depends on the emergence of the view that all individuals are born free and equal, or are naturally free and equal to each other. No individual is naturally subordinate to another, and all must thus have public standing as citizens, that upholds their self-governing status. Individual freedom and equality also entails that government can arise only through agreement or consent. We are all taught that the "individual" is a universal category that applies to anyone or everyone, but this is not the case. "The individual" is a man.[10]

The reformulation of the democratic project in terms of radical democracy requires giving up the abstract Enlightenment universalism of an undifferentiated human nature. Even though the emergence of the first theories of modern democracy and of the individual as a bearer of rights was made possible by these very concepts, they have today become a major obstacle to the future extension of the democratic revolution. The new rights that are being claimed today are the expression of differences whose importance is only now being asserted, and they are no longer rights that can be universalized. Radical democracy demands that we acknowledge difference—the particular, the multiple, the heterogeneous—in effect, everything that had been excluded by the concept of Man in the abstract. Universalism is not rejected but particularized; what is needed is a new kind of articulation between the universal and the particular.

Practical Reason: Aristotle Versus Kant

This increasing dissatisfaction with the abstract universalism of the Enlightenment explains the rehabilitation of the Aristotelian concept of *phronesis*. This "ethical knowledge," distinct from knowledge specific to the sciences (*episteme*), is dependent on the ethos, the cultural and historical conditions current in the community, and implies a renunciation of all pretense to universality.[11] This is a kind of rationality proper to the study of human praxis, which excludes all possibility of a "science" of practice but which demands the existence of a "practical reason," a region not characterized by apodictic statements, where the reasonable prevails over the demonstrable. Kant brought forth a very different notion of practical reason, one that required universality. As Ricoeur observes: "By elevating to the rank of supreme principle the rule of universalisation, Kant inaugurated one of the most dangerous ideas which was to prevail from Fichte to Marx; that the practical sphere was to be subject to a scientific kind of knowledge comparable to the scientific knowledge required in the theoretical sphere."[12] So, too, Gadamer criticizes Kant for having opened the way to positivism in the human sciences and considers the Aristotelian notion of *phronesis* to be much more adequate than the Kantian analysis of judgment to grasp the kind of relation existing between the universal and the particular in the sphere of human action.[13]

The development of the postempiricist philosophy of science converges with hermeneutics to challenge the positivistic model of rationality dominant in the sciences. Theorists such as Thomas Kuhn and Mary Hesse have contributed a great deal to this critique by pointing to the importance of rhetorical elements in the evolution of science. It is agreed today that we need to broaden the concept of rationality to make room for the "reasonable" and the "plausible" and to recognize the existence of multiple forms of rationality.

Such ideas are crucial to the concept of a radical democracy in which judgment plays a fundamental role that must be conceptualized appropriately so as to avoid the false dilemmas between, on the one hand, the existence of some universal criterion and, on the other, the rule of arbitrariness. That a question remains unanswerable by science or that it does not attain the status of a truth that can be demonstrated does not mean that a reasonable opinion cannot be formed about it or that it cannot be an opportunity for a rational choice. Hannah Arendt was absolutely right to insist that in the political sphere one finds oneself in the realm of opinion, or "doxa," and not in that of truth, and that each sphere has its own criteria of validity and legitimacy.[14] There are those, of course, who will argue that such a position is haunted by the specter of relativism. But such an accusation makes sense only if one remains in the thrall of a traditional problematic, which offers no alternative between objectivism and relativism.

Affirming that one cannot provide an ultimate rational foundation for any given system of values does not imply that one considers all views to be equal. As Rorty notes, "the real issue is not between people who think one view as good as any other and people who do not. It is between people who think our culture, our purpose or institutions cannot be supported except conversationally and people who still hope for other sorts of support."[15] It is always possible to distinguish between the just and the unjust, the legitimate and the illegitimate, but this can only be done from within a given tradition, with the help of standards that this tradition provides; in fact, there is no point of view external to all tradition from which one can offer a universal judgment. Furthermore, to give up the distinction between logic and rhetoric to which the postmodern critique leads—and where it parts with Aristotle—does not mean that "might makes right" or that one sinks into nihilism. To accept with Foucault that there cannot be an absolute separation between validity and power (since validity is always relative to a specific regime of truth, connected to power) does not mean that we cannot distinguish within a given regime of truth between those who respect the strategy of argumentation and its rules, and those who simply want to impose their power.

Finally, the absence of foundation "leaves everything as it is," as Wittgenstein would say, and obliges us to ask the same questions in a new way. Hence the error of a certain kind of apocalyptical postmodernism which would like us to believe that we are at the threshold of a radically new epoch, characterized by drift, dissemination, and by the uncontrollable play of significations. Such a view remains captive of a rationalistic problematic, which it attempts to criticize. As Searle has pointed out to Derrida: "The real mistake of the classical metaphysician was not the belief that there were metaphysical foundations, but rather the belief that somehow or other such foundations were necessary, the belief that unless there are foundations something is lost or threatened or undermined or just in question."[16]

Tradition and Democratic Politics

Because of the importance it accords to the particular, to the existence of different forms of rationality, and to the role of tradition, the path of radical democracy paradoxically runs across some of the main currents of conservative thinking. One of the chief emphases of conservative thought does indeed lie in its critique of the Enlightenment's rationalism and universalism, a critique it shares with postmodernist thought; this proximity might explain why certain postmodernists have been branded as conservative by Habermas. In fact, the affinities can be found not on the level of the political but in the fact that, unlike liberalism and marxism, both of which are doctrines of reconciliation and mastery, conservative philosophy is predicated upon human finitude, imperfection, and limits. This does not lead unavoidably to a defense of the status-quo and to an antidemocratic vision, for it lends itself to various kinds of articulation.

The notion of tradition, for example, has to be distinguished from that of traditionalism. Tradition allows us to think our own insertion into historicity, the fact that we are constructed as subjects through a series of already existing discourses, and that it is through this tradition which forms us that the world is given to us and all political action made possible. A conception of politics like that of Michael Oakeshott, who attributes a central role to the existing "traditions of behavior" and who sees political action as "the pursuit of an intimation," is very useful and productive for the formulation of radical democracy. Indeed, for Oakeshott,

> Politics is the activity of attending to the general arrangements of a collection of people who, in respect of their common recognition of a manner of attending to its arrangements, compose a single community. . . . This activity, then, springs neither from instant desires, nor from general principles, but from the existing traditions of behavior themselves. And the form it takes, because it can take no other, is the amendment of existing arrangements by exploring and pursuing what is intimated in them.[17]

If one considers the liberal democratic tradition to be the main tradition of behavior in our societies, one can understand the extension of the democratic revolution and development of struggles for equality and liberty in every area of social life as being the pursuit of these "intimations" present in the liberal democratic discourse. Oakeshott provides us with a good example, while unaware of the radical potential of his arguments. Discussing the legal status of women, he declares that

> the arrangements which constitute a society capable of political activity, whether these are customs or institutions or laws or diplomatic decisions, are at once coherent and incoherent; they compose a pattern and at the same time they intimate a sympathy for what does not fully appear. Political activity is the exploration of that sympathy; and consequently, relevant political reasoning will be convincing exposure of a sympathy, present but not yet followed up, and the convincing demonstration that now is the appropriate moment for recognizing it.[18]

He concludes that it is in this way that one is capable of recognizing the legal equality of women. It is immediately apparent how useful reasoning of this kind can be as a justification of the extension of democratic principles.

This importance afforded to tradition is also one of the principal themes of Gadamer's philosophical hermeneutics, which offers us a number of important ways of thinking about the construction of the political subject. Following Heidegger, Gadamer asserts the existence of a fundamental unity between thought, language, and the world. It is through language that the horizon of our present is constituted; this language bears the mark of the past; it is the life of the past in the present and thus constitutes the movement of tradition. The error of the Enlightenment, according to Gadamer, was to discredit "prejudices" and to propose an ideal of understanding which requires that one transcend one's present and free oneself from one's insertion into history. But it is precisely these prejudices that define our hermeneutical situation and constitute our condition of understanding and openness to the world. Gadamer also rejects the opposition drawn up by the Enlightenment between tradition and reason because for him

> tradition is constantly an element of freedom and of history itself. Even the most genuine and solid tradition does not persist by nature because of the inertia of what once existed. It needs to be affirmed, embraced, cultivated. It is, essentially, preservation such as is active in all historical change. But preservation is an act of reason, though an unconspicuous one. For this reason, only what is new, or what is planned, appears as the result of reason. But this is an illusion. Even where life changes violently, as in ages of revolution, far more of the old is preserved in the supposed transformation of everything than anyone knows, and combines with the new to create a new value.[19]

This conception of tradition, as borne through language found in Gadamer, can be made more specific and complex if reformulated in terms of Wittgenstein's "language games." Seen in this light, tradition becomes the set of language games that make up a given community. Since for Wittgenstein language games are an indissoluble union between linguistic rules, objective situations, and forms of life,[20] tradition is the set of discourses and practices that form us as subjects. Thus we are able to think of politics as the pursuit of intimations, which in a Wittgensteinian perspective can be understood as the creation of new usages for the key terms of a given tradition, and of their use in new language games that make new forms of life possible.

To be able to think about the politics of radical democracy through the notion of tradition, it is important to emphasize the composite, heterogeneous, open, and ultimately indeterminate character of the democratic tradition. Several possible strategies are always available, not only in the sense of the different interpretations one can make of the same element, but also because of the way in which some parts or aspects of tradition can be played against others. This is what Gramsci, perhaps the only marxist to have understood the role of tradition, saw as a process of disarticulation and rearticulation of elements characteristic of hegemonic practices.[21]

Recent attempts by neoliberals and neoconservatives to redefine concepts such as liberty and equality and to disarticulate the idea of liberty from that of democracy demonstrate how within the liberal democratic tradition different strategies can be pursued, making available different kinds of intimations. Confronted by this offensive on the part of those who want to put an end to the articulation that was established in the nineteenth century between liberalism and democracy and who want to redefine liberty as nothing more than an absence of coercion, the project of radical democracy must try to defend democracy and to expand its sphere of applicability to new social relations. It aims to create another kind of articulation between elements of the liberal democratic tradition, no longer viewing rights in an individualist framework but as "democratic rights." This will create a new hegemony, which will be the outcome of the articulation of the greatest possible number of democratic struggles.

What we need is a hegemony of democratic values, and this requires a multiplication of democratic practices, institutionalizing them into ever more diverse social relations, so that a multiplicity of subject-positions can be formed through a democratic matrix. It is in this way—and not by trying to provide it with a rational foundation— that we will be able not only to defend democracy but also to deepen it. Such a hegemony will never be complete, and anyway, it is not desirable for a society to be ruled by a single democratic logic. Relations of authority and power cannot completely disappear, and it is important to abandon the myth of a transparent society, reconciled with itself, for that kind of fantasy leads to totalitarianism. A project of radical and plural democracy, on the contrary, requires the existence of multiplicity, of plurality, and of conflict, and sees in them the *raison d'être* of politics.

Radical Democracy, a New Political Philosophy

If the task of radical democracy is indeed to deepen the democratic revolution and to link together diverse democratic struggles, such a task requires the creation of new subject-positions that would allow the common articulation, for example, of antiracism, antisexism, and anticapitalism. These struggles do not spontaneously converge, and in order to establish democratic equivalences, a new "common sense" is necessary, which would transform the identity of different groups so that the demands of each group could be articulated with those of others according to the principle of democratic equivalence. For it is not a matter of establishing a mere alliance between given interests but of actually modifying the very identity of these forces. In order that the defense of workers' interests is not pursued at the cost of the rights of women, immigrants, or consumers, it is necessary to establish an equivalence between these different struggles. It is only under these circumstances that struggles against power become truly democratic.

Political philosophy has a very important role to play in the emergence of this common sense and in the creation of these new subject-positions, for it will shape the "definition of reality" that will provide the form of political experience and serve as a matrix for the construction of a certain kind of subject. Some of the key concepts of liberalism, such as rights, liberty, and citizenship, are claimed today by the discourse of possessive individualism, which stands in the way of the establishment of a chain of democratic equivalences.

I have already referred to the necessity of a concept of democratic rights, rights which, while belonging to the individual, can only be exercised collectively and presuppose the existence of equal rights for others. But radical democracy also needs an idea of liberty that transcends the false dilemma between the liberty of the ancients and the moderns and allows us to think individual liberty and political liberty together. On this issue, radical democracy shares the preoccupations of various writers who want to redeem the tradition of civic republicanism. This trend is quite heterogeneous, and it is therefore necessary to draw distinctions among the so-called communitarians who, while they all share a critique of liberal individualism's idea of a subject existing prior to the social relations that form it, have differing attitudes toward modernity. On the one hand, there are those like Michael Sandel and Alasdair MacIntyre, inspired mainly by Aristotle, who reject liberal pluralism in the name of a politics of the common good; and, on the other hand, those like Charles Taylor and Michael Walzer, who, while they criticize the epistemological presuppositions of liberalism, try to incorporate its political contribution in the area of rights and pluralism.[22] The latter hold a perspective closer to that of radical democracy, whereas the former maintain an extremely ambiguous attitude toward the advent of democracy and tend to defend premodern conceptions of politics, drawing no distinctions between the ethical and the political which they understand as the expression of shared moral values.

It is probably in the work of Machiavelli that civic republicanism has the most to offer us, and in this respect the recent work of Quentin Skinner is of particular interest. Skinner shows that in Machiavelli one finds a conception of liberty that, although it does not postulate an objective notion of the good life (and therefore is, according to Isaiah Berlin, a "negative" conception of liberty), nevertheless includes ideals of political participation and civic virtue (which, according to Berlin, are typical of a "positive" conception of liberty). Skinner shows that the idea of liberty is portrayed in the *Discourses* as the capacity for individuals to pursue their own goals, their "humors" (*humori*). This goes together with the affirmation that in order to ensure the necessary conditions for avoiding coercion and servitude, thereby rendering impossible the use of this liberty, it is indispensable for individuals to fulfill certain public functions and to cultivate required virtues. For Machiavelli, if one is to exercise civic virtue and serve the common good, it is in order to guarantee oneself a certain degree of personal liberty which permits one to pursue one's own ends.[23] We encounter in this a very modern conception of individual liberty articulated onto an old conception of political liberty, which is fundamental for the development of a political philosophy of radical democracy.

But this appeal to a tradition of civic republicanism, even in the privileging of its Machiavellian branch, cannot wholly provide us with the political language needed for an articulation of the multiplicity of today's democratic struggles. The best it can do is provide us with elements to fight the negative aspects of liberal individualism while it remains inadequate to grasp the complexity of politics today. Our societies are confronted with the proliferation of political spaces which are radically new and different and which demand that we abandon the idea of a unique constitutive space of the constitution of the political, which is particular to both liberalism and civic republicanism. If the liberal conception of the "unencumbered self" is deficient, the alternative presented by the communitarian defenders of civic republicanism is unsatisfactory as well. It is not a question of moving from a "unitary unencumbered self" to a "unitary situated self"; the problem is with the very idea of the unitary subject. Many communitarians seem to believe that we belong to only one community, defined empirically and even geographically, and that this community could be unified by a single idea of the common good. But we are in fact always multiple and contradictory subjects, inhabitants of a diversity of communities (as many, really, as the social relations in which we participate and the subject-positions they define), constructed by a variety of discourses and precariously and temporarily sutured at the intersection of those subject-positions. Thus the importance of the postmodern critique for developing a political philosophy aimed at making possible a new form of individuality that would be truly plural and democratic. A philosophy of this sort does not assume a rational foundation for democracy, nor does it provide answers, in the way of Leo Strauss, to questions concerning the nature of political matters and the best regime. On the contrary, it proposes to remain within the cave and, as Michael Walzer puts it, "to interpret to one's fellow citizens the world of meanings that we share."[24] The liberal democratic tradition is open to many interpretations, and the politics of radical democracy is but one strategy among others. Nothing guarantees its success, but this project has set out to pursue and deepen the democratic project of modernity. Such a strategy requires us to abandon the abstract universalism of the Enlightenment, the essentialist conception of a social totality, and the myth of a unitary subject. In this respect, far from seeing the development of postmodern philosophy as a threat, radical democracy welcomes it as an indispensable instrument in the accomplishment of its goals.

NOTES

1. Jürgen Habermas, "Modernity—An Incomplete Project," in *The Anti-Aesthetic: Essays on Postmodern Culture*, ed. Hal Foster (Port Townsend, Wash.: Bay Press, 1983).

2. Jean-François Lyotard, *Immaterialität und Postmoderne* (Berlin, 1985).

3. Richard Rorty, "Habermas and Lyotard on Postmodernity," in *Habermas and Modernity*, ed. Richard J. Bernstein (Oxford: Polity Press, 1985), 161-75.

4. Richard Rorty, "Postmodernist Bourgeois Liberalism," *Journal of Philosophy*, 80 (October 1983), 585.

5. Ernesto Laclau and Chantal Mouffe, *Hegemony and Socialist Strategy: Towards a Radical Democratic Politics* (London: Verso, 1985).

6. I am referring not only to poststructuralism but also to other trends like psychoanalysis, post-Heideggerian hermeneutics and the philosophy of language of the second Wittgenstein, which all converge in a critique of rationalism and subjectivism.

7. Claude Lefort, *The Political Forms of Modern Society* (Oxford: Polity Press, 1986), 305.

8. Claude Lefort, *Essais sur le Politique* (Paris: Editions du Seuil, 1986), 29.

9. On this issue see the insightful analysis of Gianni Vattimo, "La crisi dell 'umanismo,'" in *La fine della modernita*, (Milan: Garzanti Editore, 1985), chap. 2.

10. Carole Pateman, "Removing Obstacles to Democracy" (Paper presented to the International Political Science Association meeting, Ottawa, Canada, October 1986, mimeographed).

11. Recent interpretations of Aristotle try to dissociate him from the tradition of natural law and to underline the differences between him and Plato on this issue. See, for instance, Hans-Georg Gadamer's remarks in *Truth and Method* (New York: Crossroad, 1984), 278-89.

12. Paul Ricoeur, *Du texte à l'action* (Paris: Editions du Seuil, 1986), 248-51.

13. Gadamer, *Truth and Method*, 33-39.

14. Hannah Arendt, *Between Past and Future* (New York: Viking Press, 1968).

15. Richard Rorty, *Consequences of Pragmatism* (Minneapolis: University of Minnesota Press, 1982), 167.

16. John R. Searle, "The Word Turned Upside Down," *The New York Review of Books*, 27 October 1983, 78.

17. Michael Oakeshott, *Rationalism in Politics* (London: Methuen, 1967), 123.

18. Ibid, 124.

19. Gadamer, *Truth and Method*, 250.

20. Ludwig Wittgenstein, *Philosophical Investigations* (Oxford: Blackwell, 1953).

21. On this issue see my article "Hegemony and Ideology in Gramsci," in *Gramsci and Marxist Theory*, ed. Chantal Mouffe (London: Routledge and Kegan Paul, 1979), 168-204.

22. I refer here to the following studies: Michael Sandel, *Liberalism and the Limits of Justice* (Cambridge: Cambridge University Press, 1982); Alasdair MacIntyre, *After Virtue* (Notre Dame, Ind.: University of Notre Dame Press, 1984); Charles Taylor, *Philosophy and the Human Sciences*, Philosophical Papers, 2 (Cambridge: Cambridge University Press, 1985); Michael Walzer, *Spheres of Justice* (New York: Basic Books, 1983).

23. Quentin Skinner, "The Idea of Negative Liberty: Philosophical and Historical Perspectives," in *Philosophy in History*, eds. R. Rorty, J. B. Schneewind, and Q. Skinner (Cambridge: Cambridge University Press, 1984).

24. Walzer, *Spheres of Justice*, xiv.

Postmodernism and Politics

Stanley Aronowitz

Modernism and modernity refer to similar, but nonidentical, aspects of twentieth-century life. The first, modernism, concerns movements that seek to strip representations of their life-world referents, the immediate narratives forming the core of our everyday, taken-for-granted worlds of life experience. Political and economic modernity, on the other hand, has to do with growth-oriented planning and production, with a pluralist political system in which class politics is replaced by interest-group struggles, and with a strong bureaucracy that can regulate relations among, and between, money and human capital. Most postmodernist discourse is directed toward the deconstruction of the myths of *modernism* while leaving *modernity* as the best context within which its eclectic and diverse activities may flourish.

I

By now, nearly everyone agrees that the shift in sensibility that Nietzsche announced about a century ago has finally arrived. Postmodernism, the name given to this shift, is marked by the renunciation of foundational thought, of rules governing art, and of the ideological "master discourses" liberalism and Marxism. A major change in the political and cultural problematic, it is in turn related to other changes that have taken place since World War II. These can be summarized as follows:

1. Production in our now global economy is dispersed and deter-

ritorialized. This is true for production of traditional commodities such as steel, cars, and clothing, as well as for the communications and information industries, which have partly replaced the old use values as crucial sources of investment, profit, and hegemony. Relatedly, the economic dominance of Western Europe and the United States has been challenged by countries like Japan, Korea, and Malaysia, representative of new regional power. Of course, this does not spell the end of American production. In fact, certain industries have "revived," but on different foundations. "Mini" mills have replaced centralized steel production; some Japanese auto corporations have built plants in the United States, at times on a nonunion, paternalistic basis; low-wage apparel manufacturing survives on immigrant labor, both inside and outside the official economy. But the once commanding American lead in electronics has passed to the Pacific region, and the dominance over the crucial automobile industry has been lost.

2. The nation-state is alive, but by no means well. Having swept the third world in the immediate postwar period, nationalism appears to be in retreat. It lives as a vital force in the advanced capitalist countries only as a reactionary response to transnationalism, which, however, abjures Western hegemony ideologically even as it submits to it. Problems arise, meanwhile, out of the need to accommodate transnational corporations devoid of the older loyalty to nations of origin. For globalized production signifies transnational, if not truly international, ownership. The corporate "metastates" play on the differences between the old and new powers, moving opportunistically from one to the other. Thus, in economic terms at least, the transnationals enter into the balance of world power. "Productivism" in this setting becomes a program of mostly defeated national or state capitalisms that seek vainly to revive the old liberalism as a means for economic revival and political hegemony.[1]

3. National politics sinks into deeper crisis. Duly chosen by the electorate, the state regime is delegated the task of solving problems such as deficient investment, prodigious unemployment of "human" capital, international trade disruptions, and problems in world power arrangements, that is, products of market inequities. These tasks, in most late capitalist societies, are removed from political contention: parties and movements may oppose prevailing policies but not the state functions themselves, or the underlying discourse of

economic growth that propels them.[2] Yet as the state assumes larger responsibilities for the social order, the economy, and the functions necessary for transnational commerce and politics, it is also impoverished, principally in terms of revenues.[3] Austerity becomes the chief instrument of policy for Social Democrats and conservatives alike. Economic stability is purchased at the price of lower wages and cuts in the social wage. The parliamentary Left pledges to administer this austerity with a human face, while the Right pushes authoritarian measures that create wider income inequality. The major political forces promise neither social change nor economic affluence for the immense majority.

4. The moral foundation of these regimes is thus in question. Politicians are distinguished by powerlessness, especially in controlling the national economy. We expect nothing from them and their parties today except the maintenance of the status quo. The Right wins because it promises to return the country to the days when things were better, claiming that the "free" market is the mechanism whereby prosperity can be achieved. Few accept this, but because the Left promises nothing, there is a general willingness to gamble. Deterritorialization of production itself entails radically new patterns of everyday life. It means, for one thing, that we have lost a sense of place. The moral basis of traditional culture in Western Europe and the United States is also undermined by the very fact that they are now consumer societies through and through.

5. Political life, then, is no longer rooted in a conception of a qualitatively better world. Even social movements—which in the 1970s accused the political parties, left and right, of operating without vision—have ceased articulating their utopias and sunk into *Realpolitik*. Since the 1960s, they have been postmodern because they rejected the assumptions of modernity: reliance on formal democratic processes, growth politics based on an unalloyed support for industrialism, and, of course, sexual and power hierarchies. However, when they assume electoral power, on instrumental grounds, they are obliged to soften their intransigent antimodernism. The ecological slogan "save the earth" is inherited from nineteenth-century *Naturphilosophie* but, expressed as a political program, becomes postmodern in its demand for direct democracy, that is, popular control unmediated by the state over natural and social resources. Where radical modernism seeks to "seize" state power to advance the devel-

opment of the productive forces, postmodern political movements ask that these productive forces be partly dismantled. Postmodern politics demands deterritorialization and regionalization (not the same thing) of political and economic institutions.[4] Since the modern state is marked by its extreme centralizing tendencies (especially in Europe) and this is perceived as a logical development of modernity, postmodern movements oppose statism, including its socialist form, and demand the minimalist, central state.

6. The ecology movement, one kind of postmodern politics, is divided on deterritorialization or regionalism. Some argue that the community is the best site of economic, political, and cultural life, and that communitarian social relations would then be horizontal, as opposed to the vertical (hierarchical) configuration of power that is inherent in static versions of social rule. Regionalism, another position, argues for local governance defined geographically by way of a reading of the ecological environment. Both programs retain the primacy of the political insofar as they seek forms of power based on a conception of *scarcity*, a scarcity no longer of economic resources but of the ecosystem itself.

7. Terrorism is another major kind of postmodern politics. Like ecopolitics, it repudiates the retreat of other radicals into defending parliamentary democracy as the last hope of humankind in the wake of authoritarian state forms, East and West. Terrorism must be understood here in its two moments. First, acts of violence against those who "represent" legitimate power—the historical act preferred by some anarchists and nationalists—originated in the premodern revolt against modernity; but contemporary terrorism of this type results from the disillusionment of the generation of the sixties with conventional radical politics. Socialism, it is thought, either surrendered the will to create a kind of politics totally different from bourgeois democratic parliamentarism, or concluded that Soviet state socialism represented a new historical advance for humankind. Dissatisfied with these alternatives, terrorists revolted (rather like their anarchist forebears) against the smooth, repressive, democratic state of late capitalism and the state socialisms of the Communists.

Baudrillard calls attention to a second form of political terrorism: consumer society, privatization, withdrawal of the masses from participation in the sham of parliamentary democracy. This is surely more damaging than any deed against the symbols of hierarchical power, for it deprives global capitalism of the legitimacy that can only be procured through mass participation in the national state.[5] Not only have more people chosen to withhold their ballot, but public life withers in all late-capitalist and state-socialist societies. Social and political theory, however, remains split on exactly what this refusal means. Should we be relieved that politics and culture are finally liberated from their modernist foundations, or should we—like Habermas for example—doggedly retain the hope that propositions of universal validity can guide social life?

II

Recall Habermas's distinction between communicative action and discourse: communicative action refers to truth arrived at through the perfection of speech acts whose grammatical and semantic aspects have been fully explored to eliminate distortion (actually a variant on Peirce's theory of the relation of truth to the scientific community). In this view, postmodernity is thus cowardice, or to put it in a less militant way, postmodernity reveals a kind of exhaustion of a Marxist paradigm that can no longer credibly maintain its own truth claims.[6] But whereas Marxism, which presents itself as postliberal, may have reached the end of the line, modernity, according to Habermas, has not. He admonishes us to recognize its unfinished tasks: the rule of reason.[7] Rather than follow rules of governance based on power or discursive hegemonies, we are exhorted to create a new imaginary, one that would recognize that a politics based on power endangers human survival. Habermas privileges those societies able to resolve social conflicts, at least provisionally, so as to permit a kind of collective reflexivity. Characteristically, Habermas finds that the barriers to learning are not found in the exigencies of class interest, but in distorted communication.[8] The mediation of communication by interest constitutes here an obstacle to reflexive knowledge. "Progressive" societies are those capable of learning— that is, acquiring knowledge that overcomes the limits of strategic or instrumental action.

I have invoked Habermas's objection to postmodernism to highlight one of the latter's ineluctable features, the rejection of universal reason as a foundation for human affairs. Reason in this sense is a series of rules of thought that any ideal, rational person might adopt if his/her purpose was to achieve propositions of universal validity. Postmodern thought, on the contrary, is bound to discourse, literally narratives about the world that are admittedly partial. Indeed, one of the crucial features of discourse is the intimate tie between knowledge and interest, the latter being understood as a "standpoint" from which to grasp "reality." Putting these terms in quotation marks signifies the will to abandon scientificity, science as a set of propositions claiming validity by any given competent investigatory. What postmodernists deny is precisely this category of impartial competence. For competence is constituted as a series of exclusions—of women, of people of color, of nature as a historical agent, of the truth-value of art.

Fredric Jameson differs, of course, from Habermas in his criticism of postmodernism when he identifies it as the cultural logic of late capitalism. Yet his critique is actually another version of universal reason. Jameson does not establish the validity of Marxism by defending it against postmodernity, but by invoking its categories to explain the phenomenon. Thus he preserves the most stunning element of Marxist theory, its explanatory power. He places postmodernism in the context of the transformations of capitalism, hence avoiding the more or less tepid waters that prevent art criticism from explaining the phenomena it describes.

Chantal Mouffe and Ernesto Laclau, though professed post-Marxists, have curiously remained tied to the scientific paradigm insofar as they do not refuse ascriptive explanation. Working within Gramsci's concept of hegemony, they want to develop the Foucauldian relation of knowledge to power. While distancing themselves from the economic categories of Marxism, they greet postmodernism as one path toward the definition of new historical agents. To be sure, agency in their discourse is no longer rooted in anything that might be described as "social relations," much less "relations of production," but is rather to be found in the permutations and combinations of language. They are caught, therefore, in the logical contradiction of supporting social movements while arguing that agency can be found only in discursive formations.

For Mouffe and Laclau, as for Lyotard, postmodernist politics consists in the effort to combine the shift in the object of knowledge from society to language with the identification of new political agents that might replace class, However, even if these agents are situated in a discursive, rather than social, field, the form of Marxism is retained while its categories are not. This goes against Habermas's attempt to move the ground of politics from class struggle to disinterested communication among competent speakers, and against Jameson's insistence that postmodernism can be understood only if placed in the context of a developmental theory of capitalist periodicity. Mouffe and Laclau argue for postmodernism as a way to generate a new politics of interest which they call radical democracy. In fact, however, this concept cannot be conceived in an antifoundational framework. For radical democracy as a political stance must surely be *an ethical a priori*, if it is not to be seen as a manifestation of the unfolding of the history of class struggles or, in Adam Przeworski's terms, the struggles over class formation.[9] If one abandons here the idea that social forces are situated in a determinate relation to the means of material production, one is left with the assertion of radical democracy as the outcome of the practices of social movements. Now, we may legitimate this viewpoint by arguing that "subject-positions" parallel class positions, in which case my contention that Mouffe and Laclau have not strayed very far from Marxism is justified. Or radical democracy must be a demand adduced from empirical, historical examination of the actual practices of social movements for which democratic struggles have apparently been the vehicle of intervention. In that case, the phrase radical democracy argues, not for a new imaginary, but for the existing imaginary as the future imaginary: social movements constituted in subordinate subject-positions always fight for self-determination as the ground of their practices, and thus there is no need to justify by means of transcendent categories.

There is, finally, a third possibility. We may borrow from Croce the ethical standard of freedom, liberty, and democracy, which, in this instance, then becomes a restatement of the rule of reason over human affairs. For it asserts that bondage can only be justified by a frankly elitist statement about the rational character of subordination on the basis of racial or eugenic superiority, degrees of civilization, and so forth. But then radical democracy as a political stance would not avoid the essentialism it attributes to Marxism; it merely substitutes ethics for history.

Lyotard and Baudrillard try to avoid explanation in their respective accounts of the postmodern condition. By describing, rather than explaining, they obviously depart from their respective Marxist roots. But their descriptions of contemporary culture and politics (or, in Baudrillard's terms, the "end of politics") actually bear the ineradicable stamp of Critical Theory. In Baudrillard, for example, the villain remains consumer society, technology, the absence of a public in which critical debate about important issues can take place, and so forth. This is not far from Marcuse's "Great Refusal," to the extent that he retains the idea of historical agency at all. However, the refuseniks here are not the intellectuals who insist on the relevance of history, philosophy, and art to a contemporary world that disdains high culture. On the contrary, it is those who withdraw their participation from society, who engage in a politics of antipolitics and ask only to be freed from its obligations, obligations that are, in any case, simulacra of citizenship. The refusal of the privatized masses is, for Baudrillard, not evidence of apathy but of a politics that views the democratic state as a ruse.

Now, Baudrillard's discursive terrorism should not be mistaken for an attack on the ethical foundations of politics. On the contrary, he is reaffirming such ethics. Terrorism is directed against the cynicism of the democratic state which, however much it promises the freedom to participate in governance, delivers merely an *ersatz* public sphere, an imitation of public life. Of course, this leads to the conclusion that the end of politics is derived from the end of the social. For Baudrillard, all that exists is power that "casts a shadow" on the masses, creates an imitation of real public life—which at any rate does not exist or may never have existed.

What makes his position a politics is the claim that the masses are withdrawing "without knowing it" from the social and political areas in which power legitimates itself. Refusals are no longer directed against capitalism, imperialism, and other targets of traditional Marxism, but are instead, along the lines of Foucault, aimed at power as such. The intellectual cannot pretend to offer programs, strategies, or tactics for a putative political or social movement, since the referents are empty shells. Hence the conclusion that power as such is the enemy, that any talk of reform, even revolution, is a diversion from the real task—to annihilate the legitimacy of the state, and the parties of order (including Communists and Social Democrats). The task, in other words, is to shift the discourse to exposure of the whole game. Baudrillard thus takes on the appearance of a postmodern prophet but is really a funeral director of modernism, a parent he despises but is nevertheless symbiotically tied to.

Obviously, none of the political forms and ideologies are perfect representations of a postmodern politics, but it generally includes an effort of theory to find a pathway back to reason, even as it takes on the coloring of the refusal of reason as presently constituted by the state and the political parties of order. There the similarities among post-Marxist and postmodernist political theorists end. Baudrillard identifies no new historical actors to replace those that have been found to be either exhausted or engaged in sham, whereas Mouffe and Laclau post the alternative of radical democracy as the cutting edge of agency. What makes the latter discourse postmodern is its explicit refusal to ground itself in history or in the universalization of particular actors. Consequently, once the Marxist problematic is gone, radical democracy appears as a cultural posit whose only other alternative is nihilism.

But if, as I have suggested, radical democracy is ethically grounded, its postmodernist claim is shaky. The Mouffe and Laclau argument rests on the basis that politics (the state) can only be constituted by the interplay of discursive formations if it is to avoid the authoritarianism inherent in Marxist or liberal essentialism.[10] Radical democracy, then, presents itself as a consequence of the shift from social relations ensconced in a definite conception of human nature to discursive relations which presuppose that political action is rooted only in the struggle for hegemony, in other words, that power makes its own demands. Yet radical democracy does not *necessarily* entail deterritorialization, only the construction of decisions from below. "Below" could encompass geographically situated communities such as factories, offices, and neighborhoods, or communities not rooted in a sense of place.

Conceivably, the space of this politics could be situated in the intentional communities attempted by various countercultures. These are postmodern because they deny evolutionist ideology. They assume that the existing state of affairs may last indefinitely and, even if overturned, may not make room for freedom as long as the new society remains statist and ideologically committed to social hierarchy (as opposed to economic equality). Mass politics signifies for them the end of public discourse, in which there is face-to-face communication and decisions are arrived at by consciously applying the rules of evidence and argument. There is no question of seeking or securing a "mass base," for the masses are among the variables of the scientific paradigm that is the modern state: past historical actors such as the working class have lost their autonomous voice. Postmodern politics, then, takes as its objective the pragmatic willingness of ruling groups to accommodate the demands of organized movements that, in turn, frame their own politics entirely in terms set externally by the ruling class. This assessment provides the basis for the terrorist alternatives, but also for the countercultures.

Even if utopian thought seeks to transform the present by articulating an alternative future, its power lies in its lack of respect for politics as the art of the possible, in its insistence that realism consists in the demand for the impossible. Utopianism is discursive terrorism to the degree that it challenges the prevailing historical and instrumental rationality of bourgeois culture.

III

The referent of postmodern thought is practice, whether in science or human conduct. Its task is not to provide an axiomatic structure to guide thinking but to perform "reading" upon scientific, cultural, and social texts. The function of reading becomes either to reveal the immanence of the text, explicating its antinomies and contradictions (put more historically, its *tendency*), or similarly to unpack its latency—the degree to which it conforms, despite protestations to the contrary, to a first principle, or a priori logic.

The application of epistemological relativism to political theory results in a pluralist paradigm that explicitly "refutes" theories of power built on structural foundations. Instead of, for example, the primacy of the accumulation process, with its concomitant class differentiation and struggle, we are offered an image analogous to a parallelogram of forces contending as a democratic *polis* in a "marketplace," where power distribution occurs but does not obey any definite laws. We deconstruct "givenness" to show the cracks the sutures have patched, to demonstrate that what is taken as privileged discourse is merely a construction that conceals power and self-interest. "Who governs" is thus in the final account a purely empirical question, although power tends to accrue to those possessing superior economic resources. Rather than searching for "laws," the postmodern theorist is committed to framing propositions that together constitute a working model tailored to an empirically verifiable situation, the ideal situation being the small or medium-sized city, the government agency, the specific labor union or corporation. The "case study" approach is construed, now continuously, now not, on the basis of foundational agnosticism or antifoundationalism. And, notwithstanding its greater Foucauldian analysis of "history" framed as discourse, it resembles its American case study cousin.

I, too, take knowledge as a practice, but this does not exhaust the set of practices that constitutes discourse. There are practices that participate directly in, or confront, hegemonic power. Discourse/action constitutes the object of political inquiry,[11] politics as a menu of interventions within the problematic of power, whose effectivity is differentiated by both discursive positions and control of the means of production and coercion. This field, therefore, is not limited to the specificity of knowledge as discourse. Economy, state, and parties are nonsubsumable fields that have been conditioned by postmodernity.

But postmodern politics is not exhausted by practices on the Left. Right-wing postmodernism has never been so public: witness the flagrant disregard for legislative mandates and sanctions by the Reagan, Nixon, and other administrations of late-capitalist societies. In effect, the popular mandate, a cardinal principle of modernist political ideology, becomes subversive to the postmodern state when it is not rendered superfluous.

Such considerations have been theorized by Samuel Huntington and others. Huntington's attack, launched under the aegis of protecting democratic civilization, is a symptom of the fact that politics is today in a period of radical transition. The degeneration of official democracy has never before been more evident, and it is this rapid decline that gives rise to the Left defense of political modernity, especially by post-Marxists. It is too early to judge the debate about whether the radical revision of modernity or its transcendence seems appropriate to the political conjuncture. Rather, my brief map may help to clarify what is at stake in the argument.

This much is clear: the idea of the end of politics is unacceptable, even if descriptions of the *fact* of the degeneration of the public sphere are absolutely accurate. For agency is constituted in the gap between the promises of modern democratic society and its subversion by the various right-wing states. Politics renews itself primarily in extraparliamentary forms, which—given the still potent effectivity of the modern state form, if not its particular manifestations of governance—draw social movements into its orbit. Some call this co-optation, but it is more accurate to understand it as a process related to the economic and cultural hegemony of late capitalism, which draws the excluded not only by its dream work, but by the political imaginary that still occupies its own subjects.

Democracy remains prior to socialism, because of its having been denied to third-world societies and because it remains unfulfilled in the first and second worlds. For example, the struggle for trade-union rights in Korea, Brazil, South Africa, and, in recent years, in the United States and the United Kingdom, is eloquent testimony to the claim that modernity has not yet exhausted itself, that these apparently "elementary achievements" of industrial capitalist societies cannot be taken for granted. So, too, traditional individual and collective liberties have not yet become commonplace in revolutionary societies such as China, the Soviet Union, and Eastern European countries, while they remain a problem in recently "democratized" countries like the Philippines and Argentina. What has become crystal clear in the past decade is that the easy assumptions of modernist political ideology—that a free market and a democratic state go hand in hand—are simply not true. For we have learned from events in Eastern European and certain Latin American countries that, in this postmodern era, economic, political, and cultural relations are not synchronous, and that each sphere is relatively autonomous.

Nor can it be safely assumed, as both liberal and Marxist theorists are wont to do, that it is the economic, in the last instance at least, that comes to prevail. To be sure, as the Brazilian, Polish, and South African examples amply demonstrate, the struggle for democracy often presupposes the formation of a powerful working class movement that sees itself not merely as a force for self-betterment through specifically trade-union action, but also as a *national* movement. And, only in this sense—by the merger of the class movement and the national movement—does nationalism retain a progressive content. Otherwise, as I have noted, nationalism as a democratizing ideology is not necessarily democratic. On the contrary, it may become, as it has in Israel and its neighbors, an instrument of domination, both of capital and of one nation over another.

As the Soviet example shows, the success of a development strategy may or may not entail the formation of a free market. Nor does the development of a large working class entail the organization of a *movement* that links class justice to democratic political forms. Although such movements have animated recent struggles for democracy in Korea, South Africa, and Brazil, we await similar developments in Malaysia, Taiwan, Venezuela. In these instances, capital formation has proceeded without the decisive intervention of workers' movements, which, of course, has led to severe exploitation of labor. Where workers have organized to challenge the absolute power of capital, as in Venezuela, they are quickly incorporated on the basis of privileged arrangements, such as has occurred in the oil industry.

The concomitant emergence of new democratic and class movements still seems to depend in many cases on the link between intellectuals' and workers' organizations. As Touraine argues in his study of the Polish Solidarity movement, such connections are not made on the basis of the classic Leninist model of party formations, in which workers are hegemonized by intellectuals armed with Marxist science. On the contrary, we now see significant elements of the working class who are "educated," not only in the sense of basic literacy, but also in political and organizational alternatives. The political intellectuals—who are found in the universities and the Church and among independent professions such as law, medicine, and literature—contend, as Gramsci theorized, for moral and intellectual leadership—not necessarily of the nation as a whole, but of the vast technical and intellectual strata that populate all state-driven industrializing societies. Least of all groups do these intellectuals lead the workers. Rather, we ought to speak of an *alliance* of necessary democratic ingredients. The bourgeois-democratic stage is not set for a socialist revolution. Instead, socialism is to be understood as an extension of the democratic revolution. In nearly all situations, "democracy" is apprehended in three inseparable aspects; its parliamentary forms, which, however, are viewed not as an end for which the movement strives but as one (vital) component. The intellectuals understand political freedom, especially in securing individual rights of expression. Workers naturally demand the unconditional right to join unions of their own choosing and, above all, the rights to assemble freely and to strike. These various demands are not incommensurable, but they cannot be conflated, even under the rubric of "human rights." This is why we ought to speak of an alliance, rather than in strictly Gramscian terms. For embedded in Gramsci's idea of hegemony is the assumption that intellectuals as a social category do not bring to the social movement any interests of their own. This explicit denial of intellectuals as a "class" is rooted in the notion of an intellectual as a person of "ideas," who represents national culture but is not directly linked to its economic and political life. For Gramsci, as for Lenin, intellectuals affiliate with various classes, playing the role of cultural mediator on behalf of these classes. Gramsci recognizes that although intellectuals are vital actors in the historical process, their importance stems from their function, not from their position within the social structure.

In the recent explosion of democratic movements, especially in the countries of the semiperiphery, intellectuals relate to workers' and peasants' movements in two ways: as technical intellectuals of these movements, that is, by producing literature, performing bureaucratic tasks, advising leaders on policy, etc.; and as participants in alliance organizations directed toward the middle classes, of which they are a part. Whereas modernist social movements relied on intellectuals to interpret their goals and programs, as much to themselves as to the social formation, the social movements in postmodern politics constitute themselves. If this model is not (yet) completely fulfilled everywhere (as in the Brazilian peasant movement, which relied heavily on urban intellectual support), the tendency is definitely away from the traditional liberal or Leninist hegemonies. In this sense, the new social movements are *self-produced*, not only with regard to their appearance on the historical stage (the Luxemburgist "spontaneous mass movement"), but also with respect to their ideology, which is not merely "trade unionist" in content but clearly radical democratic. Here, the term *radical* entails a conception of democracy that goes beyond the parliamentary forms, even as it embraces the notion of representative government. More to the point, the social movements are (unevenly) internationalist and communitarian. They speak *for* their own local aspirations, *against* the power of the multinationals that control their labor power, *and also against* the national state that increasingly speaks for itself, as well as a segment of local capital. At the same time, these movements are increasingly aware that their own claims are bound up with those of others, whether within national borders or beyond. "Socialism," then, is not being brought to the workers of the semiperiphery from the outside, by intellectuals. In many instances, it is the name given to economic democracy, not to the centralization of ownership and control by the state. Even in revolutionary societies like Nicaragua, such policies are no longer proposed, much less implemented. Nicaragua has adopted, instead, a model of the garrison state under the weight of United States intervention, while its economy remains largely in private hands.

As a modernizing strategy, socialism fails in an international economy dominated by capitalist commodity relations. As *war communism*, it can be employed as a temporary expedient during civil war, but in the long term the new movements demand that it be articulated with their own democratic goals. This is by no means identical with the European doctrine of social democracy formulated as the alternative to both liberal and state capitalism at the turn of the century. Social democracy became, against the will of its left wing, a second modernizing strategy. In effect, it argued that state planning, the welfare state, and parliamentary democracy plus the limited nationalization of essential industries constituted a viable program for modernization. As we know retrospectively, its successes presupposed the subordination of the colonial world and the abatement of imperialist rivalries. Luxemburgism, which never won the support of a significant section of the workers' movement after 1912, assumed modernity and proposed what might be called *generalized* democracy in an unarticulated form. Postmodern politics resumes this theme with the crucial amendment that the state, held by Marxist theory to be the bearer of the new social order, even if it is destined to wither away, retains a limited function as the guarantor of democratic rights. For radical democrats, social ownership, the state, and the legislative system are no longer understood as transitional forms to a higher order specified by history, but as important, albeit subordinate, elements of a plural social formation in which the movement plays a crucial and independent part.

Only the most myopic observer can regard Solidarity or the South African Union of Mineworkers as traditional trade unions. Like the Sao Paolo metalworkers, they are characterized by a whole network of cultural affinities. The union is not primarily an instrumental organization; it is the name given to their communities. In some cases, these movements affiliate themselves with political parties that represent their (parliamentary) political demands, just as the trade union negotiates with employers. The point, however, is to grasp what lies beyond and prior to these functional elements, and to see the difference between their democracy and that of the social democratic or communist movements rooted in the older legacy. In the new movements, the union is the repository of the broad social vision; it is linked to the neighborhoods, as well as to the workplace. In short, it is a cultural as well as an economic, form.

I want to insist, finally, that the development of these new social movements, in both late-capitalist societies, and the industrializing societies of the communist and third worlds, *transforms* the meaning of the term *democracy* so that the claim, advanced by a theorist such as Habermas, that modernity has not been exhausted is surely not identical with the ideology of the new movements. What is postmodern about these movements consists in this: that they freely borrow the terms and programs of modernity but place them in new discursive contexts. Therefore, we must be careful in comparing the actions and voices of the new movements with what we already have at hand in the history of the Western Left. The new social movements speak in postmodern voices; they enter the national and international political arena speaking a language of localism and regionalism, a discourse that, although internationalist, does not appeal to traditional class solidarity as its primary line of attack, but addresses power itself as an antagonist. In this consists the originality of the postliberal and post-Marxist movements.

Notes

1. Witness the emergence of the new entrepreneurial spirit in the United States and the United Kingdom and the concomitant hysteria concerning high labor costs, which, it is held, have priced goods made within these countries out of the international markets. The cry to compete accompanies the genuine internationalization of production in nearly all the major capital and consumer goods industries.

2. The work of Walter Dean Burnham is particularly apposite here. Almost alone among mainstream students of politics, he has called attention to the crisis of American political parties. See Walter Dean Burnham, *The Current Crisis of American Politics* (Oxford: Oxford University Press, 1982).

3. Of course, one would not want to ignore the huge military budget in the United States. But in the postwar era, high spending has not always been a zero-sum game

with respect to transfer payments. The key intervening variable is the refusal of financial institutions to bear the growth of the debt in the wake of the decline of traditional social movements.

4. The distinction between the two is important. Deterritorialization simply entails the disaggregation of production from large centers such as Detroit, Pittsburgh and New York, although it often accompanies greater centralization of ownership. Conservative ecologists praise aspects of this development on environmental grounds (reduction of pollution and congestion) and conflate it with regionalization, which always implies the creation of a greater measure of local self-sufficiency; in other words, the internationalization and nationalization of the division of labor. Regionalist arguments, at best, combine this perspective with the effort to combat the alienation that is often attributed to the domination of nature.

5. Two pamphlets by Baudrillard express succinctly his antipolitical arguments. Jean Baudrillard, *In the Shadow of the Silent Majorities* and *Simulations* (New York: Semiotext(e), 1985).

6. Jürgen Habermas, *Communication and the Evolution of Society* (Boston: Beacon Press, 1979).

7. Jürgen Habermas, "Modernity—An Incomplete Project," in *The Anti-Aesthetic: Essays on Postmodern Culture*, ed. Hal Foster (Port Townsend, Wash.: Bay Press, 1983), 3-16.

8. Jurgen Habermas, *Theory of Communicative Action*, vol. 1, trans. Thomas McCarthy (Boston: Beacon Press, 1984).

9. Adam Przeworski, "Proletariat into Class" *Politics and Society 6, no. 2 (1976).*

10. See Ernesto Laclau and Chantal Mouffe, *Hegemony and Socialist Strategy* (London: Verso, 1985).

11. See note 1.

Politics and the Limits of Modernity
Ernesto Laclau

The theme of postmodernity, which first appeared within aesthetics, has been displaced to ever wider areas until it has become the new horizon of our cultural, philosophical, and political experience. In the latter realm, to which I shall here limit my analysis, postmodernity has advanced by means of two converging intellectual operations whose complex interweavings and juxtapositions have, however, also contributed to a large extent to obscuring the problems at hand. Both operations share, without doubt, one characteristic: the attempt to establish *boundaries*, that is to say, to separate an ensemble of historical features and phenomena (postmodern) from others also appertaining to the past and that can be grouped under the rubric of modernity. In both cases the boundaries of modernity are established in radically different ways. The first announces a weakening of the metaphysical and rationalist pretensions of modernity, by way of challenging the *foundational* status of certain narratives. The second challenges not the ontological status of narrative as such, but rather the current validity of *certain* narratives: those that Lyotard has called metanarratives (*meta-recits*), which unified the totality of the historical experience of modernity (including science as one of its essential elements) within the project of global, human emancipation.

In what follows, I shall consider the status of metanarratives and offer as basic theses: 1) that there has been a radical change in the thought and culture of the past few decades (concerning which there would be no inconvenience in considering it as the entry to a sort of postmodernity), which, however, passes neither through a crisis nor, much less, to an abandonment of metanarratives; 2) that the very idea of the abandonment of metanarratives is logically contradictory for it reproduces within postmodern discourse the "logic of founda- tions" that supposedly characterized modernity; and 3) that the deci- sive change relates to the new status of the discursive and the new language games practiced around narratives — of all sorts, metanarra- tives included. The very idea of a boundary between modernity and postmodernity marked by the outmodedness of metanarratives pre- supposes a theoretical discourse in which the *end* of something is thinkable, which is to say, transparent and intellectually graspable. What does it mean for something to "end"? It may be conceived, in a teleological sense, as the attainment of its highest form; in a dialec- tical sense, as its transformation into its contrary; in the movement of the eternal return, as a moment in the periodic becoming of forms; or as an annihilation that manifests its radical contingency. This is to say that a discourse is required that can conceive and construct the separation — even temporal separation — of two entities. To merely proclaim the end of something is an empty gesture.

Even worse, the uncritical introduction of the category *end* into a discourse, to substitute an effective "making an end" for the volun- tarist transparency of a simply announced and postulated end, means to smuggle back in what was to have been jettisoned. This can happen in two ways. First, insofar as something ends, something rad- ically different must commence. In such a case, it is impossible to avoid the category of the "new" and the idea of an innovative van- guard, which is precisely what the discourse of postmodernity pur- ports to have left behind. On the other hand, to postulate the outmo- dedness of metanarratives (without taking into consideration what happens to other narrative species) is to achieve rather modest intel- lectual gains in comparison with the objectives sought. The logic of identity, of full presence, is simply displaced, fully intact, from the field of totality to the field of multiplicity of atomized narratives.

If there is a sense of postmodernity, that is, an ensemble of pre- theoretical references that establish certain "family resemblances" among its diverse manifestations, this is suggested by the process of erosion and disintegration of such categories as "foundation," "new," "identity," "vanguard," and so on. What the "situation of postmodern- ity" challenges is not so much the discrimination and choice between social and cultural identities but the status and logic of the construction of those identities. Consequently, drawing up the limits of modernity involves a more complex and evolving operation than merely setting boundaries. Postmodernity cannot be a simple *rejection* of modernity; rather, it involves a different modulation of its themes and categories, a greater proliferation of its language games.

Some of these games, which avoid conceiving the tradition with which they play in terms of rejection or affirmation of the radical novelty of the present, have long been inscribed in the intellectual history of this century. What Heidegger has called the "de-struction of the history of ontology" is an example:

> The answer (to the question of Being) is not properly conceived if what it asserts propositionally is just passed along, especially if it gets circulated as a free-floating result, so that we merely get informed about a "stand point" which may perhaps differ from the way this has hitherto been treated. Whether the answer is a "new" one remains quite a superficial problem and is of no importance. Its positive character must lie in its being *ancient* enough for us to learn to conceive the possibilities which the "ancients" have made ready for us.[1]

This excludes the possibility of a simple rejection. Instead, it attempts to trace the genealogy of the present, dissolve the apparent obviousness of certain categories that are the trivialized and hardened sedimentations of tradition, and in this way bring to view the original problem to which they constitute a response. So, too, in Heidegger:

> If the question of Being is to have its own history made transparent, then this hardened tradition must be loosened up, and the concealments which it has brought about by taking the question of Being as our clue, we are to destroy the traditional content of ancient ontology until we arrive at those primordial experiences in which we achieved our first ways of determining the nature of Being—the ways which have guided us ever since.[2]

This same argument can be extended to the most diverse theoretical discourses. Consider, for example, the category of "class" within marxism. Central to the series of recent exchanges are the following questions: Is it classes or social movements that constitute the fundamental agents of historical change in advanced industrial societies? Or, is the working class in the process of disappearing? But these questions are quite secondary because, whatever answers they elicit, they *presuppose* what is fundamental: the obviousness and transparency of the category "class." The "de-struction" of the history of marxism, in Heidegger's sense, involves showing that a category such as "class," far from being obvious, is already a synthesis of determinations, a particular response to a more primary question of social agency. Because the contemporary situation poses this problem again in much more complex terms than were available to Marx, it is necessary to understand his response as a partial and limited synthesis, while appreciating more clearly the original sense of his questions. The sense of an intellectual intervention emerges only when it is possible to reconstitute the system of questions that it seeks to answer. On the other hand, when these questions are taken as simply obvious, their sense is obscured if not entirely lost. It is precisely the limitation of the responses that keeps alive the sense of a question.

In sketching out the limits of modernity, we must be agreed on what, in modernity, is being put to the test. If we question the specific values of the social/political/intellectual project that began globally with the Enlightenment, the narrative of its crisis requires the affirmation of *other* values; this, however, does not change the ontological status of the category of *value* as such. In this regard, it is important to point out that the critics of modernity have not even tried to introduce different values. When the theorists of the eighteenth century are presented as the initiators of a project of "mastery" that would eventually lead to Auschwitz, it is forgotten that Auschwitz was repudiated by a set of values that, in large part, also stem from the eighteenth century. So, too, when criticism is directed at the category of totality implicit in metanarratives, only the possibility of reuniting the partial narratives into a global emancipatory narrative comes under fire; the category of "narrative" itself is left completely unchallenged. I would like to argue that it is precisely the *ontological status* of the central categories of the discourses of modernity, and not their *content*, that is at stake; that the erosion of this status is expressed through the "postmodern" sensibility; and that this erosion, far from being a negative phenomenon, represents an enormous amplification of the content and operability of the values of modernity, making it possible to ground them on foundations much more solid than those of the Enlightenment project (and its various positivist or Hegelian-Marxist reformulations).

Language and Reality

Postmodernity does not imply a *change* in the values of Enlightenment modernity but rather a particular weakening of their absolutist
character. It is therefore necessary to delimit an analytic terrain from
whose standpoint this weakening is thinkable and definable. This terrain is neither arbitrary nor freely accessible to the imagination, but
on the contrary it is the historical sedimentation of a set of traditions
whose common denominator is the collapse of the immediacy of the
given. We may thus propose that the intellectual history of the twentieth century was constituted on the basis of three illusions of immediacy (the referent, the phenomenon, and the sign) that gave rise to
the three intellectual traditions of analytical philosophy, phenome-
nology, and structuralism. The crisis of that illusion of immediacy did
not, however, result solely from the abandonment of those categories but rather from a weakening of their aspirations to constitute full
presences and from the ensuing proliferation of language games
which it was possible to develop around them. This crisis of the absolutist pretensions of "the immediate" is a fitting starting point for
engaging those intellectual operations that characterize the specific
"weakening" we call postmodernity. Each of these three intellectual
traditions might serve as an equally valid point of departure for our
analysis; in what follows, however, I shall base my argument on the
crisis in structuralism.

As is well known, structuralism was constituted around the new
centrality it accorded to the linguistic model. If we want to concentrate on the crisis of "immediacy," which originally pretended to
characterize the notion of the sign, we should concentrate not so
much on the invasion of new ontic areas by the linguistic model but
on the internal transformation of the linguistic model itself. The
crisis consisted precisely in the increasing difficulty of defining the
limits of language, or, more accurately, of defining the specific identity of the linguistic object.

In this respect, I could mention three fundamental stages in the
structuralist tradition. The first is associated with Saussure, who, as it
is well known, tried to locate the specific object of linguistics in what
he called *langue*, an abstraction from the ensemble of language phenomena based on a set of oppositions and definitions, the most

important of which are: langue/parole, signifier/signified, syntagm/
paradigm. The two basic principles that oversaw the constitution of
the linguistic object were the propositions that there are no positive
terms in language, only differences, and that language is form not
substance. Both principles were central to the category of *value*,
which acquired increasing importance vis-à-vis *signification* in the
subsequent evolution of the structuralist tradition.

The increasing refinement of linguistic formalism soon led, however, to an understanding that Saussurean theory was based on a set
of ambiguities that could only be covered over by recourse to principles that contradicted its basic postulates. Take the distinction
between signifier and signified: if language is all form and not substance, and if there is a perfect isomorphism between the order of
the signifier and that of the signified, how is it possible to establish
the difference between the two? Saussure could only do so by
recourse to the idea of substance, phonic in one case, conceptual in
the other. As for the distinction between *langue* and *parole*—
between language as collective "treasure" and its use by each individual speaker—this distinction can be maintained *only* if one
assumes a subject exterior to the linguistic system. Consequently,
one of the fundamental oppositions of this system was required to be
externally defined, thus confining linguistic formalism within a new
limit. Beyond this point it was impossible to posit a "linguistics of
discourse," if by discourse we mean a linguistic unit greater than the
sentence. Saussure had spoken of semiology as a general science of
signs in social life, but so long as *langue* remained anchored in the
materiality of the *linguistic* sign, such a project could not proceed
beyond a vaguely metaphorical and programmatic level.

From this point on, post-Saussurean structuralism emphasized linguistic formalism in its bid to transcend the ambiguities and incon-
sistencies of Saussure's own work. This, then, is the second phase, in
which Hjelmslev, for example, broke with the strict isomorphism
between the order of the signifier and the order of the signified by
defining units smaller than the sign, whose distinctive features are no
longer isomorphic. In this manner, he was able to establish the difference between the two orders on purely formal grounds. Furthermore, the critique that had been taking place, of the Cartesianism
inherent in the category of the subject, made it possible to progres-
sively show that the linguistic interventions of individual speakers

reveal patterns and regularities conceivable only as *systems of differences*. This enabled the linguistic model to be expanded to the field of discourse.

There was, however, one further development. Once linguistic formalism had radically eradicated substance, there was no way of distinguishing between those systems of differential positions proper to speech and the "extralinguistic" or "extradiscursive" actions to which they are linked, for both speech and actions are differential positions within operations of much larger scope. But if this development expanded the value range of the "linguistic model," the linguistic *object* tended to lose its specificity. In this second moment of the radicalization of structuralism, the stable character of the relation between signifier and signified had not, however, been questioned; only the structural isomorphism between the two had been broken. The boundaries of linguistics had been expanded, but the immediacy and the characteristic of full presence of its objects were only reaffirmed.

When the presence and self-evidence of these objects have faded, we can detect the transition to a third moment, which, following a certain tradition, we can denominate poststructuralism. At issue now was the fixed link between signifier and signified. The quasi-Cartesian transparency that structural formalism had established between the purely relational identities of the linguistic system served only to make them more *vulnerable* to any new system of relations. In other words, as the ideal conditions of closure were defined more precisely, it was increasingly more difficult to hold to the *closed* character of the system. From this point the radical questioning of the immediacy and transparency of the sign takes place, the sundry variants of which are well known: the critique of the denotation/connotation distinction in the later Barthes, the affirmation of the primacy of the signifier and the increasing centrality of the "real" vis-à-vis the symbolic in Lacan, the emphasis on the constitutive character of *difference*, and the critique of the metaphysics of presence in Derrida.

The crisis of the immediacy of the sign appears to be dominated by a double movement: while the signified was ever less closed within itself and could be defined only in relation to a specific context, the limits of that context were increasingly less well defined. In effect, the very logic of limit was increasingly more difficult to define. For Hegel, for example, the perception of a limit was the perception of what is beyond it; the limit, then, lies within the conceivable. Structuralism's radical relationalism would thus be subsumable under the category of the infinite regress. This point could be generalized: the most diverse forms of contemporary thought are permeated by the relational character of identities in conjunction with the impossibility of intellectual mastery over the context. Consider the various contortions of Husserl's ego/splits, and his efforts to affirm the transcendental constitutivity of the subject: the weakening of the distinction betwen semantics and pragmatics in Wittgensteinian and post-Wittgensteinian philosophy; the character of Kuhn's paradigms; the unresolved problems in the transition from *epistemes* to *dispositifs* in Foucault; the pragmatic turn of dogmaless empiricism in Quine. Some of these examples, especially Husserl's, are attempts to break the impasse by means of an essentialist reaffirmation of closure. However, in the majority of cases, the realization of the openness of context has been the point of departure for a radical antiessentialist critique.

Let us turn our attention, at this point, to the various dimensions opened up by the unfixed character of the signifier/signified relation, that is, of all identity. In the first place, its effect is polysemic: if a plurality of signifieds is joined in an unstable fashion to certain signifiers, the necessary result is the introduction of equivocality (in the Aristotelian sense). But if one can affirm that this instability does not depend entirely on the equivocality of the signifier but on the contexts in which the signifier is used, it is no longer a question of *equivocality* but of *ambiguity* and *unfixity*, in the strict sense of the terms. For example, when I say "down the hill" or "the soft down on his cheek"[3] the term *down* is equivocal: its meaning varies in relation to different contexts, although in each context its meaning is perfectly clear. On the other hand, if I speak about "democracy" in the political context of Western Europe during the cold war years, the ambiguity of the term proceeds from the context itself, which is constituted to some extent by the simultaneous presence of communist and anticommunist discourses. The term, therefore, is radically ambiguous and not simply polysemous. It is not a matter of its meaning one thing in communist discourse and another in anticommunist discourse; this, of course, may happen, but if that were the sole distinguishing circumstance, we would be left with a plurality of perfectly well-defined contexts and, consequently, with a case of simple equivocalness. Something very different, however, takes place: since both discourses are antagonistic and yet operate largely in the same argumentative context, there is a loosening of the relational systems that constitute the identity of the term. Thus, the term becomes a floating signifier. This radical ambiguity, which subverts the fixity of the sign, is precisely what gives the context its openness.

Three consequences follow from the above. First, that the concept of discourse is not linguistic but prior to the distinction between the linguistic and the extralinguistic. If I am building a wall and I tell someone "hand me a brick" and then place it on the wall, my first act is linguistic and the second is behavioral, but it is easy to perceive that they are both connected as part of a total operation, namely, the construction of the wall. This relational moment within the total operation is neither linguistic nor extralinguistic, for it includes both types of actions. If, on the other hand, we think about it positively, the concepts that apprehend it must be prior to the linguistic/extra-linguistic distinction. This instance of ground is called discourse and is therefore coterminous with the "social." Because every social action has a *meaning*, it is constituted in the form of discursive sequences that articulate linguistic and extralinguistic elements.[4]

A second consequence is that the relational character of discourse is precisely what permits the generalization of the linguistic model within the ensemble of social relations. It is not that reality is language, but that the increasing formalization of the linguistic system brought about the definition of a set of relational logics that embrace more than the linguistic narrowly defined. The act of placing a brick on a wall is not linguistic, but *its relation* to the linguistic act of previously asking for the brick is a particular discursive relation: a syntagmatic combination of the two acts. The relational logics of the social widen considerably, which opens up the path toward a new conceptualization of objectivity.

The third consequence clearly derives from the two previous ones. The radical relationalism of social identities increases their vulnerability to new relations and introduces within them the effects of ambiguity to which we referred above.

These three consequences give us a framework that makes possible an approximation to the postmodern experience. If something has characterized the discourses of modernity, it is their pretension to intellectually dominate the foundation of the social, to give a rational context to the notion of the totality of history, and to base in the latter the project of a global human emancipation. As such, they have been discourses about essences and fully present identities based in one way or another upon the myth of a transparent society. Postmodernity, on the contrary, begins when this fully present identity is threatened by an ungraspable exterior that introduces a dimension of opacity and pragmatism into the pretended immediacy and transparency of its categories. This gives rise to an unbreachable abyss between the real (in the Lacanian sense) and concepts, thus weakening the absolutist pretensions of the latter. It should be stressed that this "weakening" does not in any way negate the contents of the project of modernity; it shows only the radical vulnerability of those contents to a plurality of contexts that redefine them in an unpredictable way. Once this vulnerability is accepted in all its radicality, what does not necessarily follow is either the abandonment of the emancipatory values or a generalized skepticism concerning them, but rather, on the contrary, the awareness of the complex strategic-discursive operations implied by their affirmation and defense.

The narration of the beginnings of postmodernity—as with all beginnings—involves a multiple genealogy. In the next section, I shall attempt to trace this in relation to a particular tradition—marxism—which constituted both one of the highest points of the emancipatory narratives of modernity and one of their first crises. Whence the emergence of a post-marxism or a postmodern marxism resulting from the new relational contexts in which the categories of classical marxism were involved. Subject to increasing tensions, these categories became involved in newer and ever more complex language games.

Capitalism, Uneven Development, and Hegemony

Let us clarify the sense of our genealogical question; the narrative that is being sought does not attempt to establish the *causes* of a certain process, if by causes we mean that which possesses all the internal virtualities that bring about an effect. If that were the case, we would have simply inscribed the past anew onto the rationalistic transparency of a conceptually graspable foundation. On the contrary, it is rather a question of narrating the *dissolution* of a foundation, thus revealing the radical contingency of the categories linked to that foundation. My intention is *revelatory* rather than *explanatory*.

I shall begin with a central tenet of marxism: that capitalism exists only by dint of the constant transformation of the means of production and the increasing dissolution of preexisting social relations. The history of capitalism, therefore, is, on the one hand, the history of the progressive destruction of the social relations generated by it and, on the other, the history of its border with social forms exterior to it. Actually, it is a question of two borders that the very logic of capitalism must constantly recreate and redefine. Such a situation engenders two conceptual alternatives: either the movement of these borders is a process of contingent struggle whose outcome is largely indeterminate, or it is History brought to a predetermined and predeterminable end by a cunning Reason, which works on the contradictions of that History. It is clear that a philosophy of history can *only* be formulated along the lines of the second alternative. And there is little doubt that classical marxism followed those lines. Suffice it to mention the preface to *A Contribution to the Critique of Political Economy*.[5]

Let us consider this latter alternative in relation to the radically relational character of identity discussed above. If the limits of the system can be subverted by a reality exterior to it, then, insofar as every identity is relational, the new relations of exteriority cannot but transform the identities. Identities can remain stable only in a closed system. Is there any compatibility, then, between the idea of historical agents—particularly the working class—as identities defined within the capitalist system, and the fact that the system always acts upon a reality exterior to it? Yes, if one accepts the solution put forth by classical marxism: that the relation of exteriority can be *internally* defined, since every exterior relation is destined *a priori* to succumb as a result of capitalist expansion. The internal logic of capital thus comes to constitute the rational substrate of History and the advent of socialism is thought to be made possible only by the results of the *internal* contradictions of capitalism.

If this were all, little would be left to say and the attempts to trace within marxist discourses the genealogy of a post-marxism would be doomed to failure. But this is not the whole story. In fact, emergent within marxism are diverse discourses in which the relation between the "internal" and the "external" has become increasingly complex and has begun to deconstruct the categories of classical marxism. The language games played around these categories became ever more difficult and risky: "classes," for example, were conceived as constituted by relational complexes quite removed from those originally attributed to them.

The history of marxism has met with several such nodal moments of ambiguity and discursive proliferation. However, those phenomena grouped under the rubric of "uneven and combined development" must be singled out for special consideration because of the variety and centrality of the effects they have produced. In a recently published book,[6] I have described the basic lines of the emergence and expansion of this concept of uneven and combined development, and so I shall only summarize its distinctive features here. At the beginning, this concept attempted only to characterize an exceptional context. The Russian bourgeoisie, having entered history belatedly and consequently having been rendered incapable of taking on the democratic tasks of overthrowing czarist absolutism, gave way to the working class who assumed these tasks. But the tasks "proper" to the working class are socialist and not democratic. Therefore, how does one define the "exceptionality" of one class taking over another class's tasks? The *name* given to this taking over was "hegemony," but the *nature* of the relation it implied was far from being clear. Was the relation between the working class and the democratic tasks it took on *internal* or *external* to its nature as class? And what do we make of the fact that this uneven development soon ceased to have an exceptional character? The social upheavals proper to the age of imperialism necessitated ever more complex articulatory practices as a result of their operation in ever less orthodox historical contexts. Trotsky came to understand uneven and combined development as the historical law of our era. But what, then, is *normal* development supposed to be?

At this point I can return to some of the points made earlier. Every (social or other type of) identity is relational and vulnerable to the subversion of any exteriority. This implies that the combination of tasks proper to uneven development cannot but modify the nature of the social agents that enact them. Such was clearly the case in the emergence, during the era of popular fronts, of such entities as "the masses," the "national," the "popular," etc., excluded from marxist discourse in the heyday of the Second International. But this also implied, necessarily, that the suturing, foundational, and metaphysical value of classist categories had been radically questioned. That is, if classist identities are subverted by an exteriority, by new relational and articulatory contexts, they cannot be the *foundation* of History. The pragmatism and the contingency pass from the task to the agents, and the ground of possibility of a philosophy of History is dissolved.

This radical questioning of the logic of foundations is precisely the weakening effect that I and my colleague Chantal Mouffe found to be intrinsic to postmodern experience. And by exploring those points in the marxist tradition in which the weakening effect operates, we can trace the genealogy of a post-marxism. Let's look at two examples: Sorel and Gramsci. Sorel was clear on two issues: that the logic of capitalist development did not move in the direction that Marx predicated, and that the participation of the working class in the democratic political system led to its integration within that system. The first process weakened the logic of capital as the foundation of History; the second produced the same effect of weakening by showing that the social identity of the working class was vulnerable to the new system of relations by virtue of that class's very political participation. Sorel's response to this is well known: on the one hand, he posited a theory of myth that implied a radical relationalism, for only violence and the total severance of relations between the working class and the political system permitted a proletarian identity, and on the other, the absolute rejection of the underlying rationality of History, insofar as social relations assume structural coherence only when patterned by myth.

Gramsci presents us with an identical relationalism that leads, however, to the opposite solution. Sorel rejected all relations of exteriority and proposed a pristine proletarian identity. Gramsci, on the contrary, fully explored the multiplicity of relational ensembles which developed in the Italy of his time, thus systematically expanding the field of hegemonic relations, but as a result of that he had to acknowledge that the political subjects were not the classes but what he denominated as collective wills. Where Sorel saw all participation within the political system as a loss of identity, Gramsci conceived of hegemonic articulations as a process of creating identities. Both, however, posited the same relational, and ultimately ungrounded, character of identities.

If we situate these two examples in a broader historical perspective, the direction our genealogical exploration should take is more easily discerned. The systematic discovery of discursive areas in the marxist tradition saw the emergence of new entities and categories that, rather than prolong the basic concepts of classical marxism through their cumulative enrichment, added a logically unintegratable *supplement* to them, in the manner of what Derrida has called the "logic of supplementarity"—that hingelike discursive play that renders opposition ambiguous. I do not think it is an exaggeration to argue that the fundamental terminological additions to marxism, from Lenin to Gramsci, constitute supplements in this very sense. The genealogy of marxism, then, coincides with the deconstruction of its myth of origins.

This myth is continually nourished by a multitude of operations that tend to conceal its fissures. These operations find their crudest form in the glorious and invincible marxism-Leninism à la Soviet, but it at least has the virtue of being visible, in the conspicuous clumsiness of the bureaucrat; the *trahison des clercs* shows a greater sophistication, which operates, however, in the service of concealment. All of Lukács's sophistication is reduced to mediations that make the highest forms of "bourgeois" culture compatible with a transparent notion of class not much different from that held by a member of the Soviet Academy of Science. More recently, a highly capable group of German theorists wasted a great deal of their time, as well as that of their readers, in the alchemistic quest of trying to derive the concept of the State from the concept of Capital. When it comes to *the last instance*, the convictions of the "refined" materialist are not much different from those of the vulgar materialist. What all this means is that the history of marxism loses its plurality; the language games within that history and its relation to our period are defined and codified beforehand. Marxism is accepted or rejected *in toto*; Marx's texts are not read as one reads texts by Freud, Hegel, or Plato, that is, by questioning them from the perspective of our own problems and present situation.

Rather, a final revelation is awaited that will allow us to distance ourselves from the reality we live and to inhabit a different history, an illusory one to be sure. But when we take up our current problems, our engagement with them is merely impressionistic and pragmatic. Most frequently, the ultimate act of servility and faith in the unity of marxism is to abandon it completely; but this serves only to maintain the myth of its coherence and unity.

This attitude has become so generalized that the preceding arguments probably sound a bit outdated. This indifference to the marxist tradition, however, leads to an important loss as regards the constitution of a radical politics. In the first place, there is an impoverishment of the tradition. If the isolated struggles cannot be inserted within a wider horizon that "totalizes" an ensemble of an experience, the result is the impossibility of constructing a radical imaginary. Furthermore, an abstract, nondeconstructive rejection of a tradition in no way implies going beyond it. This brings us back to our original problem: to affirm the end of something means nothing unless we specify the form in which it ends. Both Spinoza's philosophy and Hitlerism have historically come to an *end* in some sense, but the different forms in which we conceive their end and closure impinge upon us, with respect to not only how we determine our relation to the past but also how we define our present.

Let us return to our arguments concerning the destruction of a tradition, in the Heideggerian sense. To set the limits of an answer is to re-create the original meaning of the question. To set the historical limits of marxism is to reestablish a living dialogue with that tradition, to endow it with a certain contemporaneity against the *timelessness* that its orthodox defenders attribute to it. In this sense, "post-marxism" is not an "ex-marxism," for it entails an active involvement in its history and in the discussion of its categories. But this involvement does not imply a dogmatic affirmation of its unity and coherence; rather, it requires specification of its plurality. By tracing our current problems within the marxist tradition—in the writings of Luxemburg, Bauer, Sorel, or Gramsci, in which many violently repressed intuitions brought about deconstructive effects—it becomes possible to construct a discourse that can creatively appropriate the past. Historical amnesia is a recipe for parochialism at best. At worst, it leads to the appropriation of one's struggles by antagonistic discourses.

Here, however, it is necessary to be more precise: if we are to *reconstruct* radical tradition (because this is precisely what this is about), not as a necessary departure from a point of origin, but as the genealogy of the present, it is clear that marxism cannot be its only point of reference. The plurality of current social struggles, emerging in a radically different and more complex world than could have been conceived in the nineteenth century, entails the necessity of breaking with the provincial myth of the "universal class." If one can talk about universality, it is only in the sense of the relative centralities constructed hegemonically and pragmatically. The struggles of the working class, of women, gays, marginal populations, third-world masses, must result in the construction of their own reappropriations of tradition through their specific genealogical efforts. This means, of course, that there is no *a priori* centrality determined at the level of structure, simply because there is no rational foundation of History. The only "rationality" that History might possess is the relative rationality given to it by the struggles and the concrete pragmatic-hegemonic constructions. Sorel's and Gramsci's basic intuitions ought to be radically developed with this in mind. Only thus, by lowering the ontological pretensions of marxist categories and treating them not as the ground of History but as pragmatic and limited syntheses of a historical reality that subverts and surpasses them, will it be possible to entertain their current validity. This puts us squarely within the discussion around postmodernity from the point of view of marxism. Two central problems are at stake. The first is that of the consequences of the collapse of the discourse of foundation from the point of view of a radical political discourse: does not this collapse lead to political nihilism, to the impossibility of giving a foundation to the political practice and critique? The second refers to the unity of the emancipatory project as conceived by the Enlightenment: does not the plurality and dispersion of the current social struggles imply its necessary abandonment as a global project?

The Process of Arguing and Common Sense

The collapse of the myth of foundations deprives History and society of an ultimate meaning, of an absolute point of departure for political reasoning in the sense of a Cartesian cogito. In classical ontological terms, this means that the social is groundless; if we accept the relational character of all identity, the ideal conditions of closure for a system are never achieved and therefore all identity is more or less a floating signifier. This lack of closure modifies the nature and importance of political argument in two important senses. In the first place, if an ultimate ground is posited, political argument would consist in *discovering* the action of a reality external to the argument itself. If, however, there is no ultimate ground, political argument increases in importance because, through the conviction that it can contribute, it itself *constructs*, to a certain extent, the social reality. Society can then be understood as a vast argumentative texture through which people construct their own reality.[7]

However, in a second sense, this transition from argument as discovery to argument as social construction entails a necessary modification of the *type of argument*. On the one hand, if we could take as a point of departure a foundation of the social operating as *cogito*, the argument would be of a logical or algorithmic type insofar as it would constitute a forum of judgment beyond appeal. Without such a forum, however, the argument would have the tendency to prove the *verisimilitude* of an argument rather than its truth, thus becoming pragmatic and open-ended. This brings us back to the Aristotelian notion of *phronesis*. Let us suppose that we are trying to determine if an enemy is to attack by land or by sea. Recourse to an algorithm would be to no avail; we could, however, reason that one possibility is *more likely* than the other. This greater likelihood is, in turn, determined by other arguments used on other occasions. The ensemble of arguments constitutes the texture of a group's *common sense*. And this common sense, extended in time, is what constitutes a *tradition* (of struggle, of exercise of power, etc.). Now, since this tradition is by definition open-ended—that is, ungrounded in any ultimate algorithmic certainty—it is responsive to the diverse argumentative practices that take place in society. One argument answers another, but in this process of counterargumentation, the argument itself, that is, its own identity, is itself modified in one way or another.

Here is the basis for our answer to the first question. Abandonment of the myth of foundations does not lead to nihilism, just as uncertainty as to how an enemy will attack does not lead to passivity. It leads, rather, to a proliferation of discursive interventions and arguments that are necessary, because there is no extradiscursive reality that discourse might simply reflect. Inasmuch as argument and discourse constitute the social, their open-ended character becomes the source of a greater activism and a more radical libertarianism. Humankind, having always bowed to external forces—God, Nature, the necessary laws of History—can now, at the threshold of postmodernity, consider itself for the first time the creator and constructor of its own history. The dissolution of the myth of foundations—and the concomitant dissolution of the category "subject"—further radicalizes the emancipatory possibilities offered by the Enlightenment and marxism.

Another objection could be raised to this withdrawal of foundations: wouldn't this eliminate any motivation for action? Are we not then in the situation, evoked by Sartre, of a chooser with no motive to choose? This, however, is not a valid objection, for the lack of foundations leads only to the affirmation that "human" as such is an empty entity, but social agents are never "humans" in general. On the contrary, social agents appear in concrete situations and are constituted by precise and limited discursive networks. In this sense, lack of grounding does not abolish the meaning of their acts; it only affirms their limits, their finitude, and their historicity.

Global Emancipation and Empty Signifiers

I shall now take up the second problem of whether the dispersion and plurality of social struggles dissolve the global character of the emancipatory project. To be sure, one cannot smuggle in the unity and totality of a project once one has rejected its foundation. But is unity of foundation the only form of totalizing practice in society? Are there not also totalizing effects on the level of what we have called pragmatic hegemonic practices? Remember that any identity is ambiguous insofar as it is unable to constitute itself as a precise difference within a closed totality. As such, it becomes a floating signifier whose degree of emptiness depends on the distance that separates it from its fixedness to a specific signified. (Earlier, we used "democracy" as an example of such a signifier.) This degree of fixity of a signifier varies in inverse proportion to the extent of its circulation in a given discursive formation. The ambiguity of the signifier "democracy" is a direct consequence of its discursive centrality; only those signifiers around which important social practices take place are subject to this systematic effect of ambiguity. (The same argument could be made for the "imprecision" of populist symbols.)

In reality, effective ambiguity does not arise only from the attempts to fix signifiers to antagonistic discourses, although this latter case is

teresting to us. It may have a multiplicity of sources, and it
ascribed to the phenomenon of symbolic representation. A
is emptied when it is disengaged from a particular signified
nes to symbolize a long chain of equivalent signifieds. This
ment and expansion of the signifying function constitute the

elationship between a foundation and what it founds is quite
t from a symbolic representation and that which is symbol-
foundational logic there is a necessary, determining relation
n the founding agency and the founded entity; in symbolic
ntation, on the other hand, no such internal motivation exists
chain of equivalent signifieds can be extended indefinitely.
mer is a relation of delimitation and determination, i.e., fixa-
e latter is an open-ended horizon.

the contraposition between foundation and horizon that I
nables us to understand the change in the ontological status of
patory discourses and, in general, of metanarratives, in the
on from modernity to postmodernity. A formation that is uni-
totalized in relation to a horizon is a formation without foun-
it constitutes itself as a unity only as it delimits itself from that
it negates. The discourses of equality and rights, for example,
ot rely on a common human essence as their foundation; it
s to posit an egalitarian logic whose limits of operation are
y the concrete argumentative practices existing in a society. A
n, then, is an empty locus, a point in which society symbolizes
its very groundlessness, in which concrete argumentative practices
operate over a backdrop of radical freedom, of radical contingency.
The dissolution of the myth of foundations does not dissolve the
phantom of its own absence. This absence is—at least in the last third
of the nineteenth century—the condition of possibility for affirming
the historical validity of our projects and their radical metaphysical
contingency. This double insertion constitutes the horizon of postmodern freedom, as well as the specific metanarrative of our age.

NOTES

1. Martin Heidegger, *Being and Time*, trans. Linda Russell (Oxford: Oxford University Press, 1985), 40.

2. Ibid., 22.

3. The example is from J. Lyons, *Introduction to Theoretical Linguistics* (Cambridge: Cambridge University Press, 1968), 69.

4. It would not be correct to argue, given the functional character of the discursive, that every discursive sequence presupposes language; this is no doubt true, but language in turn also presupposes vocal chords. Thus, rather than define the abstract conditions of existence of something, we should define the structural totality in which these conditions are articulated.

5. That there are, here and there, hints of a different perspective in Marx's work is undeniable; for example, the well-known letter to Vera Zasulich on the possibilities opened up by the Russian peasant communes. But they were only hints; there can be no doubt that his thinking moved in the opposite direction.

6. Ernesto Laclau and Chantal Mouffe, *Hegemony and Socialist Strategy: Towards a Radical Democratic Politics* (London: Verso, 1985).

7. As I said above, this argumentative fabric is not solely verbal; it is also interlaced with nonverbal actions to which it gives rise. Thus, every nonverbal action has meaning, and, reciprocally, every verbal argument has a performative dimension.

Social Criticism without Philosophy: An Encounter between Feminism and Postmodernism

Nancy Fraser and Linda Nicholson

Feminism and postmodernism have emerged as two of the most important political-cultural currents of the last decade.[1] So far, however, they have kept an uneasy distance from one another. Indeed, so great has been their mutual wariness that there have been remarkably few extended discussions of the relations between them.[2]

Initial reticences aside, there are good reasons for exploring the relations between feminism and postmodernism. Both have offered deep and far-reaching criticisms of the institution of philosophy. Both have elaborated critical perspectives on the relation of philosophy to the larger culture. And, most central to the concerns of this essay, both have sought to develop new paradigms of social criticism that do not rely on traditional philosophical underpinnings. Other differences notwithstanding, one could say that, during the last decade, feminists and postmodernists have worked independently on a common nexus of problems: they have tried to rethink the relation between philosophy and social criticism so as to develop paradigms of "criticism without philosophy."

On the other hand, the two tendencies have proceeded, so to speak, from opposite directions. Postmodernists have focused primarily on the philosophy side of the problem. They have begun by elaborating antifoundational metaphilosophical perspectives and from there have gone on to draw conclusions about the shape and character of social criticism. For feminists, on the other hand, the question of philosophy has always been subordinate to an interest in social criticism. So they have begun by developing critical political perspectives and from there have gone on to draw conclusions about the status of philosophy. As a result of this difference in emphasis and direction, the two tendencies have ended up with complementary strengths and weaknesses. Postmodernists offer sophisticated and persuasive criticisms of foundationalism and essentialism, but their conceptions of social criticism tend to be anemic. Feminists offer robust conceptions of social criticism, but they tend, at times, to lapse into foundationalism and essentialism.

Thus, each of the two perspectives suggests some important criticisms of the other. A postmodernist reflection on feminist theory reveals disabling vestiges of essentialism, while a feminist reflection on postmodernism reveals androcentrism and political naïveté.

It follows that an encounter between feminism and postmodernism will initially be a trading of criticisms. But there is no reason to suppose that this is where matters must end. In fact, each of these tendencies has much to learn from the other; each is in possession of valuable resources that can help remedy the deficiencies of the other. Thus, the ultimate stake of an encounter between feminism and postmodernism is the prospect of a perspective that integrates their respective strengths while eliminating their respective weaknesses. It is the prospect of a postmodernist feminism.

In what follows, we aim to contribute to the development of such a perspective by staging the initial, critical phase of the encounter. In the first section, we examine the ways in which one exemplary postmodernist, Jean-François Lyotard, has sought to derive new paradigms of social criticism from a critique of the institution of philosophy. We argue that the conception of social criticism so derived is too restricted to permit an adequate critical grasp of gender dominance and subordination. We identify some internal tensions in Lyotard's arguments; and we suggest some alternative formulations that allow for more robust forms of criticism without sacrificing the commitment to antifoundationalism. In the second section, we examine some representative genres of feminist social criticism. We argue that, in many cases, feminist critics continue tacitly to rely on the sorts of philosophical underpinnings that their own commitments, like those of postmodernists, ought, in principle, to rule out. And we identify some points at which such underpinnings could be abandoned without any sacrifice of social-critical force. Finally, in a brief conclusion, we consider the prospects for a postmodernist feminism. We discuss some requirements that constrain the development of such a perspective, and we identify some pertinent conceptual resources and critical strategies

Postmodernism

Postmodernists seek, *inter alia*, to develop conceptions of social criticism that do not rely on traditional philosophical underpinnings. The typical starting point for their efforts is a reflection on the condition of philosophy today. Writers like Richard Rorty and Jean-François Lyotard begin by arguing that *Philosophy* with a capital *P* is no longer a viable or credible enterprise. From here, they go on to claim that philosophy and, by extension, theory, more generally, can no longer function to *ground* politics and social criticism. With the demise of foundationalism comes the demise of the view that casts philosophy in the role of *founding* discourse vis-à-vis social criticism. That "modern" conception must give way to a new "postmodern" one in which criticism floats free of any universalist theoretical ground. No longer anchored philosophically, the very shape or character of social criticism changes; it becomes more pragmatic, ad hoc, contextual, and local. And with this change comes a corresponding change in the social role and political function of intellectuals.

Thus, in the postmodern reflection on the relationship between philosophy and social criticism, the term *philosophy* undergoes an explicit devaluation; it is cut down to size, if not eliminated altogether. Yet, even as this devaluation is argued explicitly, the term *philosophy* retains an implicit structural privilege. It is the changed condition of philosophy that determines the changed character of social criticism and of engaged intellectual practice. In the new postmodern equation, then, philosophy is the independent variable, while social criticism and political practice are dependent variables. The view of theory that emerges is not determined by considering the needs of contemporary criticism and engagement. It is determined, rather, by considering the contemporary status of philosophy. As we hope to show, this way of proceeding has important consequences, not all of which are positive. Among the results are a certain underestimation and premature foreclosure of possibilities for social criticism and engaged intellectual practice. This limitation of postmodern thought will be apparent when we consider its results in the light of the needs of contemporary feminist theory and practice.

Let us consider as an example the postmodernism of Jean-François Lyotard, since it is genuinely exemplary of the larger tendency. Lyotard is one of the few social thinkers widely considered postmodern who actually uses the term; indeed, it was Lyotard himself who introduced it into current discussions of philosophy, politics, society, and social theory. His book, *The Postmodern Condition*, has become the *locus classicus* for contemporary debates, and it reflects, in an especially acute form, the characteristic concerns and tensions of the movement.[3]

For Lyotard, postmodernism designates a general condition of contemporary Western civilization. The postmodern condition is one in which "grand narratives of legitimation" are no longer credible. By "grand narratives" he means, in the first instance, overarching philosophies of history like the Enlightenment story of the gradual but steady progress of reason and freedom, Hegel's dialectic of Spirit coming to know itself, and, most important, Marx's drama of the forward march of human productive capacities via class conflict culminating in proletarian revolution. For Lyotard, these "metanarratives" instantiate a specifically modern approach to the problem of legitimation. Each situates first-order discursive practices of inquiry and politics within a broader totalizing metadiscourse that legitimates them. The metadiscourse narrates a story about the whole of human history which purports to guarantee that the "pragmatics" of the modern sciences and of modern political processes—the norms and rules that govern these practices, determining what counts as a warranted move within them—are themselves legitimate. The story guarantees that some sciences and some politics have the *right* pragmatics and, so, are the *right* practices.

We should not be misled by Lyotard's focus on narrative philosophies of history. In his conception of legitimating metanarrative, the stress properly belongs on the "meta" and not the "narrative." For what most interests him about the Enlightenment, Hegelian, and Marxist stories is what they share with other, nonnarrative forms of philosophy. Like ahistorical epistemologies and moral theories, they aim to show that specific first-order discursive practices are well formed and capable of yielding true and just results. *True* and *just* here mean something more than results reached by adhering scrupulously to the constitutive rules of some given scientific and political games. They mean, rather, results that correspond to Truth and Justice as they really are in themselves independent of contingent, historical social practices. Thus, in Lyotard's view, a metanarrative is meta in a very strong sense. It purports to be a privileged discourse capable of situating, characterizing, and evaluating all other discourses, but not itself infected by the historicity and contingency that render first-order discourses potentially distorted and in need of legitimation.

In *The Postmodern Condition*, Lyotard argues that metanarratives, whether philosophies of history or nonnarrative foundational philosophies, are merely modern and dépassé. We can no longer believe, he claims, in the availability of a privileged metadiscourse capable of capturing once and for all the truth of every first-order discourse. The claim to meta status does not stand up. A so-called metadiscourse is in fact simply one more discourse among others. It follows for Lyotard that legitimation, both epistemic and political, can no longer reside in philosophical metanarratives. Where, then, he asks, does legitimation reside in the postmodern era?

Much of *The Postmodern Condition* is devoted to sketching an answer to this question. The answer, in brief, is that in the postmodern era legitimation becomes plural, local, and immanent. In this era, there will necessarily be many discourses of legitimation dispersed among the plurality of first-order discursive practices. For example, scientists no longer look to prescriptive philosophies of science to warrant their procedures of inquiry. Rather, they themselves problematize, modify, and warrant the constitutive norms of their own practice even as they engage in it. Instead of hovering above, legitimation descends to the level of practice and becomes immanent in it. There are no special tribunals set apart from the sites where inquiry is practiced. Rather, practitioners assume responsibility for legitimizing their own practice.

Lyotard intimates that something similar is, or should be, happening with respect to political legitimation. We cannot have, and do not need, a single, overarching theory of justice. What is required, rather, is a "justice of multiplicities."[4] What Lyotard means by this is not wholly clear. On one level, he can be read as offering a normative vision in which the good society consists in a decentralized plurality of democratic, self-managing groups and institutions whose members problematize the norms of their practice and take responsibility for modifying them as situations require. But paradoxically, on another level, he can be read as ruling out the sort of large-scale, normative political theorizing that, from a "modern" perspective at least, would be required to legitimate such a vision. In any case, his justice of multiplicities conception precludes one familiar, and arguably essential, genre of political theory: identification and critique of macrostructures of inequality and injustice that cut across the boundaries separating relatively discrete practices and institutions. There is no place in Lyotard's universe for critique of pervasive axes of stratification, for critique of broad-based relations of dominance and subordination along lines like gender, race, and class.

Lyotard's suspicion of the large extends to historical narrative and social theory as well. Here, his chief target is Marxism, the one metanarrative in France with enough lingering credibility to be worth arguing against. The problem with Marxism, in his view, is twofold. On the one hand, the Marxian story is too big, since it spans virtually the whole of human history. On the other hand, the Marxian story is too theoretical, since it relies on a *theory* of social practice and social relations that claims to *explain* historical change. At one level, Lyotard simply rejects the specifics of this theory. He claims that the Marxian conception of practice as production occludes the diversity and plurality of human practices. And the Marxian conception of capitalist society as a totality traversed by one major division and contradiction occludes the diversity and plurality of contemporary societal differences and oppositions. But Lyotard does not conclude that such deficiencies can and should be remedied by a better social theory. Rather, he rejects the project of social theory *tout court*.

Once again, Lyotard's position is ambiguous, since his rejection of social theory depends on a theoretical perspective of sorts, of its own. He offers a postmodern conception of sociality and social identity, a conception of what he calls "the social bond." What holds a society together, he claims, is not a common consciousness or institutional substructure. Rather, the social bond is a weave of crisscrossing threads of discursive practices, no single one of which runs continuously throughout the whole. Individuals are the nodes or "posts" where such practices intersect and, so, they participate in many simultaneously. It follows that social identities are complex and heterogeneous. They cannot be mapped onto one another or onto the social totality. Indeed, strictly speaking, there is no social totality and *a fortiori* no possibility of a totalizing social theory.

Thus, Lyotard insists that the field of the social is heterogeneous and nontotalizable. As a result, he rules out the sort of critical social theory that employs general categories like gender, race, and class. From his perspective, such categories are too reductive of the complexity of social identities to be useful. And there is apparently nothing to be gained, in his view, by situating an account of the fluidity and diversity of discursive practices in the context of a critical analysis of large-scale institutions and social structures.

Thus, Lyotard's postmodern conception of criticism without philosophy rules out several recognizable genres of social criticism. From the premise that criticism cannot be grounded by a foundationalist philosophical metanarrative, he infers the illegitimacy of large historical stories, normative theories of justice, and social-theoretical accounts of macrostructures that institutionalize inequality. What, then, *does* postmodern social criticism look like?

Lyotard tries to fashion some new genres of social criticism from the discursive resources that remain. Chief among these is smallish, localized narrative. He seeks to vindicate such narrative against both modern totalizing metanarrative and the scientism that is hostile to all narrative. One genre of postmodern social criticism, then, consists in relatively discrete, local stories about the emergence, transformation, and disappearance of various discursive practices treated in isolation from one another. Such stories might resemble those told by Michel Foucault, though without the attempts to discern larger synchronic patterns and connections that Foucault sometimes made.[5] And like Michael Walzer, Lyotard evidently assumes that practitioners would narrate such stories when seeking to persuade one another to modify the pragmatics or constitutive norms of their practice.[6]

This genre of social criticism is not the whole postmodern story, however. For it casts critique as strictly local, ad hoc, and ameliorative, thus supposing a political diagnosis according to which there are no large scale, systemic problems that resist local, ad hoc, ameliorative initiatives. Yet Lyotard recognizes that postmodern society does contain at least one unfavorable structural tendency that requires a more coordinated response. This is the tendency to universalize instrumental reason, to subject *all* discursive practices indiscriminately to the single criterion of efficiency or "performativity." In Lyotard's view, this threatens the autonomy and integrity of science and politics, since these practices are not properly subordinated to performative standards. It would pervert and distort them, thereby destroying the diversity of discursive forms.

Thus, even as he argues explicitly against it, Lyotard posits the need for a genre of social criticism that transcends local mininarrative. And despite his strictures against large, totalizing stories, he narrates a fairly tall tale about a large-scale social trend. Moreover, the logic of this story, and of the genre of criticism to which it belongs, calls for judgments that are not strictly practice-immanent. Lyotard's story presupposes the legitimacy and integrity of the scientific and political practices allegedly threatened by "performativity." It supposes that one can distinguish changes or developments that are *internal* to these practices from externally induced distortions. But this drives Lyotard to make normative judgments about the value and character of the threatened practices. These judgments are not strictly immanent in the practices judged. Rather, they are "metapractical."

Thus, Lyotard's view of postmodern social criticism is neither entirely self-consistent nor entirely persuasive. He goes too quickly from the premise that philosophy cannot ground social criticism to the conclusion that criticism itself must be local, ad hoc, and untheoretical. As a result, he throws out the baby of large historical narrative with the bathwater of philosophical metanarrative and the baby of social-theoretical analysis of large-scale inequalities with the bathwater of reductive Marxian class theory. Moreover, these allegedly illegitimate babies do not in fact remain excluded. They return, like the repressed, within the very genres of postmodern social criticism with which Lyotard intends to replace them.

We began this discussion by noting that postmodernists orient their reflections on the character of postmodern social criticism by the falling star of foundationalist philosophy. They posit that, with philosophy no longer able credibly to ground social criticism, criticism itself must be local, ad hoc, and untheoretical. Thus, from the critique of foundationalism, they infer the illegitimacy of several genres of social criticism. For Lyotard, the illegitimate genres include large-scale historical narrative and social-theoretical analyses of pervasive relations of dominance and subordination.[7]

Suppose, however, one were to choose another starting point for reflecting on postfoundational social criticism. Suppose one began, not with the condition of philosophy, but with the nature of the social object one wished to criticize. Suppose, further, that one defined that object as the subordination of women to and by men. Then, we submit, it would be apparent that many of the genres rejected by postmodernists are necessary for social criticism. For a phenomenon as pervasive and multifaceted as male dominance simply cannot be adequately grasped with the meager critical resources to which they would limit us. On the contrary, effective criticism of this phenomenon requires an array of different methods and genres. It requires, at minimum, large narratives about changes in social organization and ideology, empirical and social-theoretical analyses of macrostructures and institutions, interactionist analyses of the micropolitics of everyday life, critical-hermeneutical and institutional analyses of cultural production, historically and culturally specific sociologies of gender. . . . The list could go on.

Clearly, not all of these approaches are local and "untheoretical." But all are nonetheless essential to feminist social criticism. Moreover, all can, in principle, be conceived in ways that do not take us back to foundationalism, even though, as we argue in the next section, many feminists have so far not wholly succeeded in avoiding that trap.

Feminism

Feminists, like postmodernists, have sought to develop new paradigms of social criticism that do not rely on traditional philosophical underpinnings. They have criticized modern foundationalist epistemologies and moral and political theories, exposing the contingent, partial, and historically situated character of what have passed in the mainstream for necessary, universal, and ahistorical truths. And they have called into question the dominant philosophical project of seeking objectivity in the guise of a "God's eye view" which transcends any situation or perspective.[8]

However, whereas postmodernists have been drawn to such views by a concern with the status of philosophy, feminists have been led to them by the demands of political practice. This practical interest has saved feminist theory from many of the mistakes of postmodernism: women whose theorizing was to serve the struggle against sexism were not about to abandon powerful political tools merely as a result of intramural debates in professional philosophy.

Yet even as the imperatives of political practice have saved feminist theory from one set of difficulties, they have tended, at times, to incline it toward another. Practical imperatives have led some feminists to adopt modes of theorizing that resemble the sorts of philosophical metanarrative rightly criticized by postmodernists. To be sure, the feminist theories we have in mind here are not "pure" metanarratives; they are not ahistorical normative theories about the transcultural nature of rationality or justice. Rather, they are very large social theories, theories of history, society, culture, and psychology, that claim, for example, to identify causes and/or constitutive features of sexism that operate cross-culturally. Thus, these social theories purport to be empirical rather than philosophical. But, as we hope to show, they are actually "quasi metanarratives." They tacitly presuppose some commonly held but unwarranted and essentialist assumptions about the nature of human beings and the conditions for social life. In addition, they assume methods and/or concepts that are uninflected by temporality or historicity and that therefore function *de facto* as permanent, neutral matrices for inquiry. Such theories, then, share some of the essentialist and ahistorical features of metanarratives: they are insufficiently attentive to historical and cultural diversity; and they falsely universalize features of the theorist's own era, society, culture, class, sexual orientation, and/or ethnic or racial group.

On the other hand, the practical exigencies inclining feminists to produce quasi metanarratives have by no means held undisputed sway. Rather, they have had to coexist, often uneasily, with counter-exigencies that have worked to opposite effect, for example, political pressures to acknowledge differences among women. In general, then, the recent history of feminist social theory reflects a tug-of-war between forces that have encouraged and forces which have discouraged metanarrative-like modes of theorizing. We can illustrate this dynamic by looking at a few important turning points in this history.

When, in the 1960s, women in the New Left began to extend prior talk about "women's rights" into the more encompassing discussion of "women's liberation," they encountered the fear and hostility of their male comrades and the use of Marxist political theory as a support for these reactions. Many men of the New Left argued that gender issues were secondary because they were subsumable under more basic modes of oppression, namely, class and race.

In response to this practical-political problem, radical feminists, such as Shulamith Firestone, resorted to an ingenious tactical maneuver: Firestone invoked biological differences between women and men to explain sexism. This enabled her to turn the tables on her Marxist comrades by claiming that gender conflict was the most basic form of human conflict and the source of all other forms, including class conflict.[9] Here, Firestone drew on the pervasive tendency within modern culture to locate the roots of gender differences in biology. Her coup was to use biologism to establish the primacy of the struggle against male domination rather than to justify acquiescence to it.

The trick, of course, is problematic from a postmodernist perspective, since appeals to biology to explain social phenomena are essentialist and monocausal. They are essentialist insofar as they project onto all women and men qualities that develop under historically specific social conditions. They are monocausal insofar as they look to one set of characteristics, such as women's physiology or men's hormones, to explain women's oppression in all cultures. These problems are only compounded when appeals to biology are used in conjunction with the dubious claim that women's oppression is the cause of all other forms of oppression.

Moreover, as Marxists and feminist anthropologists began insisting in the early 1970s, appeals to biology do not allow us to understand the enormous diversity of forms that both gender and sexism assume in different cultures. And in fact, it was not long before most feminist social theorists came to appreciate that accounting for the diversity of the forms of sexism was as important as accounting for its depth and autonomy. Gayle Rubin aptly described this dual requirement as the need to formulate theory that could account for the oppression of women in its "endless variety and monotonous similarity."[10] How were feminists to develop a social theory adequate to both demands?

One approach that seemed promising was suggested by Michelle Zimbalist Rosaldo and other contributors to the influential anthropology collection, *Woman, Culture and Society*, published in 1974. They argued that common to all known societies was some type of separation between a "domestic sphere" and a "public sphere," the former associated with women and the latter with men. Because in most societies to date women have spent a good part of their lives bearing and raising children, their lives have been more bound to "the domestic sphere." Men, on the other hand, have had both the time and mobility to engage in those out-of-the-home activities that generate political structures. Thus, as Rosaldo argued, whereas in many societies women possess some or even a great deal of power, women's power is always viewed as illegitimate, disruptive, and without authority.[11]

This approach seemed to allow for both diversity and ubiquity in the manifestations of sexism. A very general identification of women with the domestic and of men with the extradomestic could accommodate a great deal of cultural variation both in social structures and in gender roles. At the same time, it could make comprehensible the apparent ubiquity of the assumption of women's inferiority above and beyond such variation. This hypothesis was also compatible with the idea that the extent of women's oppression differed in different societies. It could explain such differences by correlating the extent of gender inequality in a society with the extent and rigidity of the separation between its domestic and public spheres. In short, the domestic/public theorists seemed to have generated an explanation capable of satisfying a variety of conflicting demands.

However, this explanation turned out to be problematic in ways reminiscent of Firestone's account. Although the theory focused on differences between men's and women's spheres of activity, rather than on differences between men's and women's biology, it was essentialist and monocausal nonetheless. It posited the existence of a "domestic sphere" in all societies and thereby assumed that women's activities were basically similar in content and significance across cultures. (An analogous assumption about men's activities lay behind the postulation of a universal "public sphere.") In effect, the theory falsely generalized to all societies a historically specific conjunction of properties: women's responsibility for early childrearing, women's tendency to spend more time in the geographical space of the home, women's lesser participation in the affairs of the community, a cultural ascription of triviality to domestic work, and a cultural ascription of inferiority to women. The theory thus failed to appreciate that, whereas each individual property may be true of many societies, the conjunction is not true of most.[12]

One source of difficulty in these early feminist social theories was the presumption of an overly grandiose and totalizing conception of theory. Theory was understood as the search for the one key factor that would explain sexism cross-culturally and illuminate all of social life. In this sense, to theorize was by definition to produce a quasi metanarrative.

Since the late 1970s, feminist social theorists have largely ceased speaking of biological determinants or a cross-cultural domestic/public separation. Many, moreover, have given up the assumption of monocausality. Nevertheless, some feminist social theorists have continued implicitly to suppose a quasi metanarrative conception of theory. They have continued to theorize in terms of a putatively unitary, primary, culturally universal type of activity associated with women, generally an activity conceived as "domestic" and located in "the family."

One influential example is the analysis of "mothering" developed by Nancy Chodorow. Setting herself to explain the internal, psychological dynamics that have led many women willingly to reproduce social divisions associated with female inferiority, Chodorow posited a cross-cultural activity, mothering, as the relevant object of investigation. Her question thus became: How is mothering as a female-associated activity reproduced over time? How does mothering produce a new generation of women with the psychological inclination to mother and a new generation of men not so inclined? The answer she offered was in terms of "gender identity": female mothering produces women whose deep sense of self is "relational" and men whose deep sense of self is not.[13]

Chodorow's theory has struck many feminists as a persuasive account of some apparently observable psychic differences between men and women. Yet the theory has clear metanarrative overtones. It posits the existence of a single activity, "mothering," which, while differing in specifics in different societies, nevertheless constitutes enough of a natural kind to warrant one label. It stipulates that this basically unitary activity gives rise to two distinct sorts of deep selves: one relatively common across cultures to women, the other relatively common across cultures to men. And it claims that the difference thus generated between "feminine and masculine gender identity" causes a variety of supposedly cross-cultural social phenomena, including the continuation of female mothering, male contempt for women, and problems in heterosexual relationships.

From a postmodern perspective, all these assumptions are problematic because essentialist. But the second one, concerning "gender identity," warrants special scrutiny, given its political implications. Consider that Chodorow's use of the notion of gender identity presupposes three major premises. One is the psychoanalytic premise that everyone has a deep sense of self, which is constituted in early childhood through one's interactions with one's primary parent and which remains relatively constant thereafter. Another is the premise that this "deep self" differs significantly for men and for women but is roughly similar among women, on the one hand, and among men, on the other hand, both across cultures and within cultures across lines of class, race, and ethnicity. The third premise is that this deep self colors everything one does; there are no actions, however trivial, which do not bear traces of one's masculine or feminine gender identity.

One can appreciate the political exigencies that made this conjunction of premises attractive. It gave scholarly substance to the idea of the pervasiveness of sexism. If masculinity and femininity constitute our basic and ever-present sense of self, it is not surprising that the manifestations of sexism are systemic. Moreover, many feminists had already sensed that the concept of "sex-role socialization," an idea Chodorow explicitly criticized, ignored the depth and intractability of male dominance. By implying that measures such as changing images in textbooks or allowing boys to play with dolls would be sufficient to bring about equality between the sexes, this concept seemed to trivialize and co-opt the message of feminism. Finally, Chodorow's depth-psychological approach gave scholarly sanction to the idea of sisterhood. It seemed to legitimate the claim that the ties that bind women are deep and substantively based.

Needless to say, we have no wish to quarrel with the claim of the depth and pervasiveness of sexism, nor with the idea of sisterhood. But we do wish to challenge Chodorow's way of legitimating them. The idea of a cross-cultural, deep sense of self, specified differently for women and men, becomes problematic when given any specific content. Chodorow states that women everywhere differ from men in their greater concern with "relational interaction." But what does she mean by this term? Certainly not any and every kind of human interaction, since men have often been more concerned than women with some kinds of interactions, for example, those having to do with the aggrandizement of power and wealth. Of course, it is true that many women in modern Western societies have been expected to exhibit strong concern with those types of interactions associated with intimacy, friendship, and love, interactions that dominate one meaning of the late twentieth-century concept of "relationship." But surely this meaning presupposes a notion of private life specific to modern Western societies of the last two centuries. Is it possible that Chodorow's theory rests on an equivocation on the term *relationship*?[14]

Equally troubling are the aporias this theory generates for political practice. While "gender identity" gives substance to the idea of sisterhood, it does so at the cost of repressing differences among sisters. Although the theory allows for some differences among women of different classes, races, sexual orientations, and ethnic groups, it construes these as subsidiary to more basic similarities. But it is precisely as a consequence of the request to understand such differences as secondary that many women have denied an allegiance to feminism.

We have dwelt at length on Chodorow because of the great influence her work has enjoyed. But she is not the only recent feminist, social theorist who has constructed a quasi metanarrative around a putatively cross-cultural, female-associated activity. On the contrary, theorists like Ann Ferguson and Nancy Folbre, Nancy Hartsock, and Catharine MacKinnon have built theories around notions of "sexaffective production," "reproduction," and "sexuality," respectively.[15] Each claims to have identified a basic kind of human practice found in all societies that has cross-cultural explanatory power. In each case, the practice in question is associated with a biological or quasi-biological need and is construed as functionally necessary to the reproduction of society. It is not the sort of thing, then, whose historical origins need be investigated.

The difficulty here is that categories like sexuality, mothering, reproduction, and sex-affective production group together phenomena that are not necessarily conjoined in all societies, while separating from one another phenomena that are not necessarily separated. As a matter of fact, it is doubtful whether these categories have any determinate cross-cultural content. Thus, for a theorist to use such categories to construct a universalistic social theory is to risk projecting the socially dominant conjunctions and dispersions of her own society onto others, thereby distorting important features of both. Social theorists would do better to construct genealogies of the *categories* of sexuality, reproduction, and mothering before assuming their universal significance.

Since around 1980, many feminist scholars have come to abandon the project of grand social theory. They have stopped looking for *the* causes of sexism and have turned to more concrete inquiry with more limited aims. One reason for this shift is the growing legitimacy of feminist scholarship. The institutionalization of women's studies in the United States has meant a dramatic increase in the size of the community of feminist inquirers, a much greater division of scholarly labor, and a large and growing fund of concrete information. As a result, feminist scholars have come to regard their enterprise more collectively, more like a puzzle whose various pieces are being filled in by many different people than a construction to be completed by a single, grand theoretical stroke. In short, feminist scholarship has attained its maturity.

Even in this phase, however, traces of youthful quasi metanarratives remain. Some theorists who have ceased looking for *the* causes of sexism still rely on essentialist categories like "gender identity." This is especially true of those scholars who have sought to develop "gynocentric" alternatives to mainstream androcentric perspectives, but who have not fully abandoned the universalist pretensions of the latter.

Consider, as an example, the work of Carol Gilligan. Unlike most of the theorists we have considered so far, Gilligan has not sought to explain the origins or nature of cross-cultural sexism. Rather, she set herself the more limited task of exposing and redressing androcentric bias in the model of moral development of psychologist Lawrence Kohlberg. Thus, she argued that it is illegitimate to evaluate the moral development of women and girls by reference to a standard drawn exclusively from the experience of men and boys. And she proposed to examine women's moral discourse on its own terms in order to uncover its immanent standards of adequacy.[16]

Gilligan's work has been rightly regarded as important and innovative. It challenged mainstream psychology's persistent occlusion of women's lives and experiences and its insistent but false claims to universality. Yet, insofar as Gilligan's challenge involved the construction of an alternative "feminine" model of moral development, her position was ambiguous. On the one hand, by providing a counterexample to Kohlberg's model, she cast doubt on the possibility of any single, universalist developmental schema. On the other hand, by constructing a female countermodel, she invited the same charge of false generalization she had herself raised against Kohlberg, though now from other perspectives such as class, sexual orientation, race and ethnicity. Gilligan's disclaimers notwithstanding,[17] to the extent that she described women's moral development in terms of a different voice; to the extent that she did not specify which women, under which specific historical circumstances, have spoken with the voice in question; and to the extent that she grounded her analysis in the explicitly cross-cultural framework of Nancy Chodorow, her model remained essentialist. It perpetuated in a newer, more localized fashion traces of previous, more grandiose quasi metanarratives.

Thus, vestiges of essentialism have continued to plague feminist scholarship even despite the decline of grand theorizing. In many cases, including Gilligan's, this represents the continuing subterranean influence of those very mainstream modes of thought and inquiry from which feminists have wished to break away.

On the other hand, the practice of feminist politics in the eighties has generated a new set of pressures that have worked against metanarratives. In recent years, poor and working-class women, women of color, and lesbians have finally won a wider hearing for their objections to feminist theories that fail to illuminate their lives and address their problems. They have exposed the earlier quasi metanarratives, with their assumptions of universal female dependence and confinement to "the domestic sphere," as false extrapolations from the experience of the white, middle-class, heterosexual women who dominated the beginnings of the second wave. For example, writers like Bell Hooks, Gloria Joseph, Audre Lord, Maria Lugones, and Elizabeth Spelman have unmasked the implicit reference to white Anglo women in many classic feminist texts; likewise, Adrienne Rich and Marilyn Frye have exposed the heterosexist bias of much mainstream feminist theory.[18] Thus, as the class, sexual, racial, and ethnic awareness of the movement has altered, so has the preferred conception of theory. It has become clear that quasi metanarratives

hamper, rather than promote, sisterhood, since they elide differences among women and among the forms of sexism to which different women are differentially subject. Likewise, it is increasingly
apparent that such theories hinder alliances with other progressive
movements, since they tend to occlude axes of domination other
than gender. In sum, there is growing interest among feminists in
modes of theorizing that are attentive to differences and to cultural
and historical specificity.

In general, then, feminist scholarship of the 1980s evinces some
conflicting tendencies. On the one hand, there is decreasing interest
in grand social theories as scholarship has become more localized,
issue-oriented, and explicitly fallibilistic. On the other hand, essentialist vestiges persist in the continued use of ahistorical categories
like "gender identity" without reflection as to how, when, and why
such categories originated and were modified over time. This ten-
sion is symptomatically expressed in the current fascination, on the
part of U.S. feminists, with French psychoanalytic feminisms: the
latter propositionally decry essentialism even as they performatively
enact it.[19] More generally, feminist scholarship has remained insufficiently attentive to the *theoretical* prerequisites of dealing with diversity, despite widespread commitment to accepting it politically.

By criticizing lingering essentialism in contemporary feminist
theory, we hope to encourage such theory to become more consistently postmodern. This is not, however, to recommend merely *any*
form of postmodernism. On the contrary, as we have shown, the version developed by Jean-François Lyotard offers a weak and inadequate conception of social criticism without philosophy. It rules out
genres of criticism, such as large historical narrative and historically
situated social theory, that feminists rightly regard as indispensable.
But it does not follow from Lyotard's shortcomings that criticism
without philosophy is in principle incompatible with criticism with
social force. Rather, as we argue next, a robust, postmodern-feminist
paradigm of social criticism without philosophy is possible.

Toward a Postmodern Feminism

How can we combine a postmodernist incredulity toward metanarratives with the social-critical power of feminism? How can we con-

ceive a version of criticism without philosophy that is robust enough to handle the tough job of analyzing sexism in all its "endless variety and monotonous similarity"?

A first step is to recognize, *contra* Lyotard, that postmodern critique need forswear neither large historical narratives nor analyses of societal macrostructures. This point is important for feminists, since sexism has a long history and is deeply and pervasively embedded in contemporary societies. Thus, postmodern feminists need not abandon the large theoretical tools needed to address large political problems. There is nothing self-contradictory in the idea of a postmodern theory.

However, if postmodern-feminist critique must remain "theoretical," not just any kind of theory will do. Rather, theory here would be explicitly historical, attuned to the cultural specificity of different societies and periods and to that of different groups within societies and periods. Thus, the categories of postmodern-feminist theory would be inflected by temporality, with historically specific institutional categories like "the modern, restricted, male-headed, nuclear family" taking precedence over ahistorical, functionalist categories like "reproduction" and "mothering." Where categories of the latter sort were not eschewed altogether, they would be genealogized, that is, framed by a historical narrative and rendered temporally and culturally specific.

Moreover, postmodern-feminist theory would be nonuniversalist. When its focus became cross-cultural or transepochal, its mode of attention would be comparativist rather than universalist, attuned to changes and contrasts instead of to "covering laws. " Finally, postmodern-feminist theory would dispense with the idea of a subject of history. It would replace unitary notions of "woman" and "feminine gender identity" with plural and complexly constructed conceptions of social identity, treating gender as one relevant strand among others, attending also to class, race, ethnicity, age, and sexual orientation.

In general, postmodern-feminist theory would be pragmatic and fallibilistic. It would tailor its methods and categories to the specific task at hand, using multiple categories when appropriate and forswearing the metaphysical comfort of a single "feminist method" or "feminist epistemology." In short, this theory would look more like a tapestry composed of threads of many different hues than one woven in a single color. The most important advantage of this sort of theory would be its usefulness for contemporary feminist political practice. Such practice is increasingly a matter of alliances rather than one of unity around a universally shared interest or identity. It recognizes that the diversity of women's needs and experiences means that no single solution—on issues like child care, social security, and housing—can be adequate for all. Thus, the underlying premise of this practice is that, whereas some women have some common interests and face some common enemies, such commonalities are by no means universal; rather, they are interlaced with differences, even with conflicts. This, then, is a practice made up of a patchwork of overlapping alliances, not one circumscribable by an essential definition. One might best speak of it in the plural as the practice of "feminisms." In a sense, this practice is in advance of much contemporary feminist theory. It is already implicitly postmodern. It would find its most appropriate and useful theoretical expression in a postmodern-feminist form of critical inquiry. Such inquiry would be the theoretical counterpart of a broader, richer, more complex, and multilayered feminist solidarity, the sort of solidarity that is essential for overcoming the oppression of women in its "endless variety and monotonous similarity."

NOTES

1. This essay is from the forthcoming anthology, *The Institution of Philosophy: A Discipline in Crisis?* eds. Avner Cohen and Marielo Dascal (Totowa, N.J.: Rowman & Littlefield, 1988). We are grateful for the helpful suggestions of many people, especially Johathan Arac, Ann Ferguson, Marilyn Frye, Nancy Hartsock, Alison Jaggar, Berel Lang, Thomas McCarthy, Karsten Struhl, Iris Young, Thomas Wartenberg, and the members of SOFPHIA. We are also grateful for word-processing help from Marina Rosiene.

2. Exceptions are Jane Flax, "Postmodernism and Gender Relations in Feminist Theory," *Signs: Journal of Women in Culture and Society* 12, no. 4 (1987), 621-43; Sandra Harding, *The Science Question in Feminism* (Ithaca, N.Y.: Cornell University Press, 1986) and "The Instability of the Analytical Categories of Feminist Theory," *Signs: Journal of Women in Culture and Society* 11, no. 4 (1986), 654-64; Donna Haraway, "A Manifesto for Cyborgs: Science, Technology and Socialist Feminism in the 1980's," *Socialist Review* 80 (1983), 65-107; Alice A. Jardine, *Gynesis: Configurations of Women and Modernity* (Ithaca, N.Y.: Cornell University Press, 1985); Jean-François Lyotard, "Some of the Things at Stake in Women's Struggles," trans. Deborah J. Clarke, Winifred Woodhull, and John Mowitt, *Sub-Stance*, no. 20 (1978), 9-17; Craig Owens,

"The Discourse of Others: Feminists and Postmodernism," in *The Anti-Aesthetic: Essays on Postmodern Culture*, ed. Hal Foster (Port Townsend, Wash.: Bay Press, 1983).

3. Jean-François Lyotard, *The Postmodern Condition: A Report on Knowledge*, trans. G. Bennington and B. Massumi (Minneapolis: University of Minnesota Press, 1984).

4. In addition to Ibid., see Jean-François Lyotard and Jean-Loup Thebaud, *Just Gaming* (Minneapolis: University of Minnesota Press, 1987); also Lyotard "The Differend," trans. George Van Den Abbeele, *Diacritics* (Fall 1984), 4-14.

5. See, for example, Michel Foucault, *Discipline and Punish: The Birth of the Prison*, trans. Alan Sheridan (New York: Vintage Books, 1979).

6. Michael Walzer, *Spheres of Justice: A Defense of Pluralism and Equality* (New York: Basic Books, 1983).

7. It should be noted that, for Lyotard, the choice of Philosophy as a starting point is itself determined by a metpolitical commitment, namely, to antitotalitarianism. He assumes, erroneously in our view, that totalizing social and political theory necessarily eventuates in totalitarian societies. Thus, the "practical intent" that subtends Lyotard's privileging of philosophy (and which is in turn attenuated by the latter) is anti-Marxism. Whether it should also be characterized as "neoliberalism" is a question too complicated to explore here.

8. See, for example, the essays in *Discovering Reality: Feminist Perspectives on Epistemology, Metaphysics, Methodology, and Philosophy of Science*, ed. Sandra Harding and Merrill B. Hintikka (Dordrecht, Holland: Reidel, 1983).

9. Shulamith Firestone, *The Dialectic of Sex* (New York: Bantam, 1970).

10. Gayle Rubin, "The Traffic in Women," in *Toward an Anthropology of Women*, ed. Rayna R. Reiter (New York: Monthly Review Press, 1975), 160.

11. Michelle Zimbalist Rosaldo, "Woman, Culture and Society: A Theoretical Overview," in *Woman, Culture and Society*, ed. Michelle Zimbalist Rosaldo and Louise Lamphere (Stanford: Stanford University Press, 1974), 17-42.

12. These and related problems were soon apparent to many of the domestic/public theorists themselves. See Rosaldo's self-criticism, "The Use and Abuse of Anthropology: Reflections on Feminism and Cross-cultural Understanding," *Signs: Journal of Women in Culture and Society* 5, no. 3 (1980), 389-417. A more recent discussion, which points out the circularity of the theory, appears in Sylvia J. Yanagisako and Jane F. Collier, "Toward a Unified Analysis of Gender and Kinship" in *Gender and Kinship: Toward a Unified Analysis*, ed. Jane F. Collier and Sylvia J. Yanagisako (Stanford: Stanford University Press, forthcoming 1988).

13. Nancy Chodorow, *The Reproduction of Mothering: Psychoanalysis and the Sociology of Gender* (Berkeley: University of California Press, 1978).

14. A similar ambiguity attends Chodorow's discussion of "the family." In response to critics who object that her psychoanalytic emphasis ignores social structures, Chodorow has rightly insisted that the family is itself a social structure, one frequently slighted in social explanations. Yet, she generally does not discuss families as historically specific social institutions whose specific relations with other institutions can be analyzed. Rather, she tends to invoke "the family" in a very abstract and general sense defined only as the locus of female mothering.

15. Ann Ferguson and Nancy Folbre, "The Unhappy Marriage of Patriarchy and Capitalism," in *Women and Revolution*, ed. Lydia Sargent (Boston: South End Press, 1981), 313-38; Nancy Hartsock, *Money Sex and Power: Toward a Feminist Historical Materialism* (New York: Longman, 1983); Catherine MacKinnon, "Feminism, Marxism,

Method, and the State: An Agenda for Theory," *Signs: Journal of Women in Culture and Society* 7, no. 3 (Spring 1982), 515-44.

16. Carolin Gilligan, *In a Different Voice: Psychological Theory and Women's Development* (Cambridge, Mass.: Harvard University Press, 1982).

17. Ibid., 2.

18. Marilyn Fry, *The Politics of Reality: Essays in Feminist Theory* (Trumansburg, N.Y.: The Crossing Press, 1983); Bell Hooks, *Feminist Theory from Margin to Center* (Boston: South End Press, 1984); Gloria Joseph, "The Incompatible Ménage à Trois: Marxism, Feminism and Racism," in *Women and Revolution*, ed. Lydia Sargent (Boston: South End Press, 1981), 91-107; Audre Lord, "An Open Letter to Mary Daly," in *This Bridge Called My Back: Writings by Radical Women of Color*, ed. Cherrie Moraga and Gloria Anzaldua (Watertown, Mass: Persephone Press, 1981), 94-97; Maria C. Lugones and Elizabeth V. Spelman, "Have We Got a Theory for You! Feminist Theory, Cultural Imperialism and the Demand for the Woman's Voice," *Hypatia, Women's Studies International Forum* 6, no. 6 (1983), 578-81; Adrienne Rich, "Compulsory Heterosexuality and Lesbian Existence," *Signs: Journal of Women in Culture and Society* 5, no. 4 (Summer 1980), 631-60; Elizabeth Spelman, "Theories of Race and Gender: The Erasure of Black Women," *Quest* 5, no. 4 (1980/81), 36-62.

19. See, for example, Hélène Cixous, "The Laugh of the Medusa," trans. Keith Cohen and Paula Cohen in *New French Feminisms*, ed. Elaine Marks and Isabelle de Courtivron (New York: Schocken Books, 1981), 245-261; Hélène Cixous and Catherine Clément, *The Newly Born Woman*, trans. Betsy Wing (Minneapolis: University of Minnesota Press, 1986); Luce Irigaray, *Speculum of the Other Woman* (Ithaca, N.Y.: Cornell University Press, 1985) and *This Sex Which is Not One* (Ithaca, N.Y.: Cornell University Press, 1985); Julia Kristeva, *Desire in Language: A Semiotic Approach to Literature and Art*, ed. Leon S. Roudiez (New York: Columbia University Press, 1980) and "Women's Time," trans. Alice Jardine and Harry Blake, *Signs: Journal of Women in Culture and Society* 7, no. 1 (Autumn 1981), 13-35. See also the critical discussion by Ann Rosalind Jones, "Writing the Body: Toward an Understanding of l'Écriture féminine," in *The New Feminist Criticism: Essays on Women, Literature and Theory*, ed. Elaine Showalter (New York: Pantheon Books, 1985); Toril Moi, *Sexual/Textual Politics: Feminist Literary Theory* (London: Methuen, 1985).

Tooth and Claw: Tales of Survival and *Crocodile Dundee*
Meaghan Morris

"The moment of *survival* is the moment of power."

Elias Canetti

In a passage of *Cinema 1: The Movement-Image*, Gilles Deleuze makes a casual distinction between the path of commercial success in contemporary cinema and the movement of cinema's "soul." The distinction clarifies a historical claim that a "crisis of the action-image" seized postwar American cinema: "the greatest commercial successes always take that route, but the soul of the cinema no longer does." For Deleuze, cinema's soul craves *thought*; and in the aftermath of the Second World War, thought begins to undo the system of actions, perceptions, and affects that had supported classic cinema. One of the reasons, and one of the results, is that we can now scarcely believe that "a global situation can give rise to an action which is capable of modifying it."[1]

My point of departure is to see in this casual moment another instance of *thought* veering away from the problems posed to criticism by cinema's "big, fat, commercial successes" (Paul Hogan).[2] *L'image-mouvement* and *l'image-temps* invent a philosophy of time, rather than a theory of film or of popular culture, and for Deleuze, no useful problem may be posed by those blockbuster cycles, which, from *Star Wars* to *The Wild Geese* to *The Road Warrior* to *Rambo* to *Crocodile Dundee* (not to mention the small, fat commercial successes of Chuck Norris and Charles Bronson films), have had quite a bit to say in the aftermath of the Vietnam War about action, its capacity to modify a global situation, and "our" capacity for belief. More surprising is the relative lack of attention paid to such films in recent debates about postmodernity—with its concern for the bases of valid actions ("moves"), the multinational against the local, and the conditions of credibility.

Indeed, an avoidance of cinema in general structures some founding texts of postmodern debate: historic essays by Habermas, Lyotard, and Jameson, which have helped create for contemporary theory its own version of cinema's blockbuster—the state-of-the-globe, state-of-the-arts, Big Speculation.[3] There is a *genial disinterest* exemplified by the Habermas-Lyotard debate: it is clear that these texts do not emerge from a cultural sphere in which the latest Muppet movie might be taken to be an "event"; while Lyotard's venture into film theory, *L'acinéma*, is confined to classic experimentalist problems. Fredric Jameson is quite right to note a convergence of commitment to the art-revering values of high modernism, uniting these otherwise fiercely opposed protagonists in a common belief in the powers of critical culture.[4] Then there is the use of *functional allusions* to cinema: the addition of "film" to a general list of cultural practices surveyed or the parabolic exegesis of an exemplary instance (the "nostalgia film" in Jameson's essay), which confirms and extends a prior argument.

From these morsels of analysis, little enough can be said about the complexities of cinema—but more important, the complexities of cinema have had little to say to the analyses. Yet, surely—to emphasize but one issue, the famous "mixing" of high and popular culture so often said to characterize a postmodern condition—if one cultural form alone could suffice to shake the sense of classical dichotomies (avant-garde/kitsch, avant-garde/modernist, innovation/tradition, experiment/cliché, high/low, elite/popular), would not cinema be that form? And, if one institution could invoke relations between modernity and modernization, technology and ideology, economics and politics and culture, wouldn't cinema surely be that institution? Why, then, for the founding texts of postmodern debate, did cinema not occupy a position at least as privileged as that accorded to architecture?

With these questions in mind, I want to put forward some working assumptions for reading the politics of action, location, and credibility in Peter Faiman/Paul Hogan's *Crocodile Dundee*. However I am not interested in producing an essentialist reading of *Crocodile Dundee* as a "postmodern film," although it might be possible to do so—stressing its folksy, common-sense populism, its use of parody and pastiche, its comedy of cultural (in)difference, and the pragmatics of its well-made move in the game of international cinema. What I prefer to do instead is to take postmodernism not as a cultural logic (a reflection of which I might read in the film), but as a repertoire of critical terms. The notion of repertoire does not imply that my choice of terms, or text, is arbitrary. As I have suggested, *Crocodile Dundee* is one of a number of recent films about action and belief, and the relationship of both to global situations. I want to read it as an intersection point of some fables of survival, read against the context of the apocalyptic rhetoric pervading postmodernism.

At the same time, the problem of whether a global situation can give rise to an action capable of modifying it is also the problem of the "action" of a text upon the social signifying systems that make it possible and that constitute its materials. I shall take from the repertoire the notion of "appropriation" to analyze a privileged mode of action in and by the film—the critical modification of cultural, and cinematic, codes. Appropriation often functions, especially in recent art criticism, as a vague essentialist wave in the general direction of intertextuality. As I define it here (in order to question the term, and its place in the postmodern repertoire, later), *appropriation* is a critical interpretation, produced in some textual practices, of the intertextuality that is a constitutive principle of all text making. This interpretation is made explicit by a sign of appropriation: a type of *mise en abyme* (of the code and/or the enunciation) that generates some kind of explicit commentary on the modifying power, or desired effects, of its own action on other textual elements, other texts.[5] By doing so, it presupposes some problem of power to be regulated in and by that action (in the sense that parody, for example, implies a *status* problem). In this sense, I want to take appropriation as an object of commentary in *Crocodile Dundee*, as well as a means of modification by which the film solves certain "action" problems.

My emphasis is not simply determined either by the film's practice, which makes it easy to assimilate to an aesthetics of recoding, or by its economic strategy of surviving as an Australian film in the global market by means of that recoding. It is also determined by the film's allusions to colonialism. As the Indian art critic Geeta Kapur points out,[6] the term *appropriation* resounds with the history of Western imperialism: and *Crocodile Dundee* is a *postcolonial* comedy of survival, with remnants of the British land-taking, appropriative regime (bushmen, aborigines, Darwinian "natural" perils) emerging into the "multinational" cultural space of American-media modernity.

The Call of the Crocodile-Poacher

The whole world wonders now why the call for designs outside of Australia itself was ever made. This is but proof of what is so often said of these people: they are mere imitators. Originality is unknown. They are positively unable to originate. Everything is a copy with some small alteration, usually a disadvantage to the subject.

Jessie Ackermann, *Australia From A Woman's Point of View*, 1913

SUE: *I'm always all right when I'm with you, Dundee ... God that sounds corny. Why do you always make me feel like Jane in a Tarzan comic?*

DUNDEE *(feeble imitation of Tarzan's call):*
AARGH-AARGH!

Crocodile Dundee, *1986*

Sue Charlton (played by Linda Kozlowski) in *Crocodile Dundee* is not the first American woman journalist to brave the wilds of remote Australia and live to tell the tale. Jessie Ackermann, a dauntless organizer for the Women's Christian Temperance Union, made four visits to Australia around the turn of the century, traveled widely, and wrote a critical account of her experiences. Ackermann's brisk American faith that innovation and pioneering make a nation produced one of the sharpest (though not "original") statements of a powerfully active myth—that the one distinctive feature of Australian culture is its *"positive unoriginality."* That Ackermann was referring, in the passage quoted above, to a call for designs of the national capital city (Canberra), and thus to a symbolic founding gesture, suggests the rich potential of this myth for a variety of uses. Today, it can still be a tragic flaw requiring bureaucratic interventions in culture, or an ironic virtue, placing Australia in a privileged postmodern position as a playground of simulation.

This is, of course, a myth (in Barthes's sense of the term), and a very complicated one. It naturalizes historic, hegemonic operations. It generalizes to "these people" the dilemmas of a colonial intelligentsia. It internalizes, in its classic Australian form, global material structures and effects of imperialism as "national" psychic problems.

It universalizes the modernist imperative of originality. And it rarely (except in its ironic mode) examines the eye of the beholder. It functions, that is to say, in much the same way as many accounts of postmodernism, as a global (rather than national), cultural "condition."

By the mid-1980s, positive unoriginality and its effects on foreign beholders had become a focus of bitter political conflict for the Australian film industry. For almost a decade in journalism and in public reports, the film industry had been represented as a creature on the verge of extinction. The prognostic varies with circumstances, but the problem remains the same: how to ensure survival for a frail young thing beset by local perils, international (American) predators, and deadly shades from the past rising up to harrow the present. Most of this rhetoric (including the hopes and fears of a Hollywood invasion) can be derived from the structural fragility of a small industry dependent on government support—and thus on party-political whim, national economic fluctuations, and bureaucratic maneuver—in a country of sixteen million people with expensively American tastes in film. From this economically menacing environment, and from myths of cultural insecurity, three theories of unoriginality and national cinema emerge.

One assumes that unoriginality is a "bad thing," a by-product of "cultural imperialism." In this context, that notoriously imperfect term refers not only to the usual dominance of Hollywood norms in the programming of pleasures, and dominance of the American majors in the Australian film market (a 78 percent share of theatrical rentals in 1985), but also to memories of disastrous meddling by American studio interests in Australian film production.

Not surprisingly, an argument with these reference points often combines a call for collective originality with a realist aesthetic ("cultural exactitude"), an essentialist model of audience (the eye of the beholder as site of national perception), and a politics of primary anti-Americanism. Thus, filmmaker Bob Ellis on Hollywood's power for monstrous alien-ation: "I have seen so many people coming back with those strange Peter Allen accents talking about warmth and love and having a nice day, and it is like the end of *The Invasion of the Body Snatchers*. You run towards the car, you open the door and everybody is turning into eggs."[7] To this horrid prospect, Ellis opposes an ideal of native accent, *positive authenticity*—well articulated by Bruce Beresford's *Breaker Morant* (1980).

But Ellis's allusion to that canonical Australian text, *The Invasion of the Body Snatchers*, exposes the vulnerability of his cultural nationalism (and the closed concept of culture it must at some level assume) to a second theory of unoriginality: cheerful acceptance that it is a natural and necessary thing in modern times. Film is an industry in a Western megaculture, and Australia is simply part of it. Ideals of "originality," independence, and authenticity are sentimental anachronisms, inappropriate to the *combinatoire* of industrial cinema; performance, in film, is all, and performance is by nature "inauthentic." Imitation today is true realism, because "the broad base of Australian culture, from McDonald's to prime-time television and everything in between, is comparable to the American" (Tony Ginnane, producer).[8] The eye of the beholder, wherever it is placed, is always American anyway. This is an ideal of *positive unspecificity* (give or take a decorative use of landscape, aborigines, wildlife, and so on). An exemplary text might be Richard Franklin's 1981 coproduction *Roadgames*, starring Jamie Lee Curtis, Stacy Keach, and a dingo.

At the box office, neither theory was ever a roaring commercial success. A third possibility emerged—to displace the originality/authenticity and imitation/unspecificity couples. It salvages some of the cultural assertiveness of one and all the economic pragmatism of the other. It rejects both hostility to Hollywood (*The Invasion of the Body Snatchers* really is part of Australian culture) and outright denials of Australian contexts. It takes the "eye of the beholder" as a figure for seeing double: survival and specificity can both be ensured by the revision of American codes by Australian texts, in a play that can be seen quite differently by various audiences and individual eyes therein. Furthermore, it has a tradition: parody (like the in-joke) has always been a favorite ploy of Australian colonial culture. A characteristic example would be the revision of the road-movie genre by the Kennedy-Miller *Mad Max* films.

This is a theory of fully *positive* unoriginality, a context in which, for critics, the privileged metaphors of postmodernism can come into play—image scavenging, borrowing, stealing, plundering, and (for the more sedate) recoding, rewriting, reworking. But it wasn't merely the *zeitgeist*, or global trends in criticism, that fostered this cultural logic.

From 1980 to 1986, most Australian films were funded under a special modification of the federal Income Tax Assessment Act, called *Division 10BA*. Essentially a government-run tax avoidance scheme, 10BA was an alarming success. In fiscal year 1983/84, the revenue cost to the Australian government was estimated by Treasury at $100 million and rising. The concessions were drastically reduced, the risks spiraled for investors, and they began to demand substantial preselling of films.[9] In the context of Australia's tiny domestic market, this meant preselling films overseas, most desirably in the United States. Preselling has aesthetic consequences: favoring themes thought "familiar" to Americans, using imported (usually American) actors to attract foreign audiences—and, consequently, shaping narratives to validate their "role." That is to say, the financial organization of the industry gradually shifted "credibility" away from the rhetoric of national authenticity.

Crocodile Dundee was funded under 10BA, and is true to its logic. The cultural strategy is scarcely concealed: Dundee, the provincial crocodile-poacher, flagrantly acts as a figural *mise en abyme* of the film's relation to a Hollywood canon and to Australian mythology. Moreover, *Crocodile Dundee* is an *export-drive* allegory: the small, remote community of Walkabout Creek, with its fumbling exotica industry (emblematic of Australia's place in the global cinema economy), manages to export its crocodile-poacher and, with a little help from the American media, market him brilliantly in New York. The subsequent real success of the film—an example of the pre-cession of the simulacrum that might delight Jean Baudrillard—can then be taken by some producers as a call for others to follow.

Crocodile Dundee, however, did make some innovations; it overturned the assumptions of a decade of debate. According to insistent publicity reports, the film was deliberately *not* presold, to avoid initial interference, and it made a profit in unpopulous Australia before beginning its American release. This makes its career (like that of Paul Hogan) the stuff of media legend; the art of combining economic pragmatism with cultural assertion in positive unoriginality ironically acquires a nationalist aura. The strategy of appropriation in the film can also be read in these terms.

Unlike the romantic, virtuoso variations played by the *Mad Max* films, only rarely interrupted (most often in *The Road Warrior*) by comic Australian asides, *Crocodile Dundee*'s use of appropriation aims explicitly at what Jessie Ackermann calls "some small alteration, usually a disadvantage to the subject." The "subjects" (American models) are comically altered, and disadvantaged, by the narrative. For example, three American references (or, signs of appropriation) define the hero's cultural mission and his *savoir-pouvoir-faire*: "Davy Crockett," "Jungle Jim," and "Tarzan." Each of these reiterates frontier codes, and also reconciles, for Australian consumption, the old bush mythos with the imported media culture of the 1950s. So their function is initially confirmatory and sentimental. But in each case, an imbalance is created by a failure to fit the model.

Dundee is compared to Davy Crockett in disgruntlement by Sue after the crocodile attack, when his attention to her haunches makes him more like the croc than the wholesome Crockett.[10] His New York rival calls Dundee "Jungle Jim" at the airport, before his first battle with an escalator. It is a demeaning reference—not just to Dundee as rustic, but by assimilation to the aging Weissmuller. Jungle Jim is a failed frontier figure: so Dundee's charm in beating the escalator prepares for his success in the urban jungle, at the expense of the younger "native." His real New York name (first given to him by the prostitutes) is "Tarzan." When formally baptized by Sue, after saving her from the mugger, he smiles, thumps his chest, and fluffs the line she gives him—trying Tarzan's yodel, he comes out with a mangled gurgle.

One function of all three references, as *mises en abyme* of the code, is to affirm the mock-heroic novelty of Dundee's idiom in relation to the slightly tired American models (or straight media repeats, like *I Love Lucy*) by which he is made intelligible. On the one occasion when the hero gives himself an American name, "Fred Astaire"—as he lurches exuberantly around a tin-pot pub, with Sue as his Ginger Rogers—he uses it to invent a self-promoting bush ballad. Self-promotion is Dundee's job as a tourist commodity, and his *raison d'être* as hero (his nickname makes him "more colorful for the tourist industry"). In this context, appropriation is a competitive activity; a seizing of not only comic advantage but also mythic power (capital).

A schematic comparison of the first and last scenes of the film must suffice to suggest how the strategy of seizure works in the overall narrative structure. Most reviews of the film assume that it has two parts, one for Australia and one for New York, and that it plays for two potential audiences. In fact, two obvious cuts slice the film into three parts, juxtaposing contrasted "sceneries" (city/outback/city) in the dramatic manner of wonderful-world travelogues. The first part, though usually ignored, is crucial. A prelude to the credits, it is internally structured by contrasts; two urban locations, New York and Sydney, and two urban *spaces*—office and hotel room, the high-rise control points of a media regime. The action linking these commercial spaces (center and periphery of the *Newsday* empire) is a communicative one: a telephone call between editor and reporter, stay-at-home lover and wandering lady.

The call initiates a *hunt*, a quest for a story for *Newsday*—with Dundee as an object for promoting a global circuit of power. It also states a disjunction between business and pleasure arising from sexual equality: Richard is torn between his roles as editor and lover, whereas Sue prefers work to love. At the same time, the fictional enunciative setting is defined initially as urban, as well as international. Far from being differently addressed, "Australian" and "American" audiences are rhetorically conjoined in the vast network of media simultaneity. But at this point, both space and communication are controlled (from "above") by Americans.

The last scene takes place underground. Sue is again on a hunt for Dundee, but her goal has changed. She isn't chasing him on *Newsday*'s business, but for her own pleasure—the power circuit has been broken, and Sue's gender confusion solved, by Dundee's manly charm. The subway should be "her" place, rather than his, but to reach him, she adapts to its dense, American urban space an Australian rural "medium" of communication over vast distance: an echoing coo-ee call, and then the bush telegraph—the public transfer of private information by word of mouth.[11] The New York subway has become another setting for an Australian country practice. The exotic "story" that *Newsday* sought has taken control of the narrative; the Australian in American space has power over action and speech. On the cue "sheep," Dundee literally *treads all over* this mass of Americans, as a sheepdog bounds over a mob (of sheep). As a finale, the sheep—now "Americans" to Australians, while acting as all "our" audience-doubles—flock to the reconciled couple (distance and difference overcome), to applaud Dundee/Hogan's performance, and confirm the happy ending.

Crocodile Dundee is more than an export-allegory, with Dundee as commodity, salesman, and company combined. It is a *takeover* fantasy of breaking into the circuit of media power in order to invade the place of control. As a 10BA polemic, the film's response to insular fears that Hollywood turns Australians into eggs seems to be a utopian call to turn Americans into sheep (as we all are assimilated, in one crucial scene, to a buffalo stunned by the hero's mesmeric gaze). It is an ambitious fairy tale, and an Oedipally ungrateful one. It thereby remains, of course, and for all the comic reversals, utterly admiring of the (brutalizing) structure of American power.

In this admiration, appropriation as positive unoriginality figures as a means of resolving the practical problems of a peripheral cinema, while reconciling conflicting desires for power and independence: symbolic nationalist victory is declared, but on internationalist (American) grounds. Unfortunately, perhaps, for Australian cinema, not all simulacra without originals produce a reality in their own image. Rather than leading local cinema out of the wilderness, *Crocodile Dundee*'s position may be more like that of Canetti's survivor who exults when everyone else is dead.[12]

Many critics stress that in the action-highlights of the film, Dundee does real or feigned battle with phantasmal Others of an equally fantasmal "white, male, working class"—beasts, blacks, deviants, uppity women, snobs. These are, in fact, symmetrically distributed in the two main locations: city-cowboy/pretentious yuppie; predatory animal/savage pimp; woman with a gun/transvestite; voyeur aborigine-/black mugger. But there is also a carefully preemptive distribution of friendly (or easily mesmerized) Others: the amiable bourgeois at Sam's dinner, the buffalo, the dogs, the prostitutes, the baritone society-lioness, the tribal aborigines, the chauffeur ("Tonto," for one outraged critic[13]), the black in the bar. Furthermore, the film combats political critics by placing itself "*post*"; it historicizes radicalism as obsolete opinion. It parodies, and again preempts, two possible rhetorical positions from which it could be, and has been, attacked: patronizing dismissal of its "crudity" (the posture of Richard the yuppie), and indignant protest (the stance of Sue's past husband, the "prize ratbag").

The reduction of the latter to, and by, a throwaway line of dialogue points to a significant omission from the list of phantasmal Others, which I shall read as a structuring absence in the film's politics of opinion. There are no urban intellectuals in Dundee's bestiary. The closest that Dundee gets to a cartoon New York egghead is the head-wrapped society matron, whose bothersome indeterminacy is quickly reduced *to* sexual difference by a brutally practical act. Otherwise, and crucial to a film so rhetorically concerned with legitimating "majority" opinion, and itself as majoritarian, the only intellectuality (and the only institution) admitted as credible is media power: that *force* of public "opinion."

I want to consider the Australian setting in the film that foregrounds a problem of opinion (the arms race, nuclear issues) and a political conflict (aboriginal land rights). Both involve struggles for survival (the human race, tribal culture). Together, they define something like the film's primal scene of appropriation.

The setting is the mythic Australian outback: for the Eurocentric discourses traversing the film, a perfect Other to the ultimate urban jungle; historically an "empty" (that is, violently depopulated) space for the enactment of colonialist fantasy. The perfection of the outback for this purpose is its supposed "remoteness" from cities (learning, modernity) and, unlike other legendary wastes, its "isolation" in the middle of a monster island—prime territory for Darwinian fancies of throwbacks, remnants, mutants, the (primitive) origin, and the (apocalyptic) end of life. The outback is an ideal site for the staging of knowledge conflicts. Its value is reversible: it can be invested with romantic, pretechnical wisdom (Roeg's *Walkabout*, Herzog's *Where The Green Ants Dream*) or surreal, degenerate ignorance (Kotcheff's *Outback*, a.k.a. *Wake In Fright*, Mulcahy's *Razorback*) and a zone of life-and-death struggle over what it means, *in extremis*, to be human (*The Road Warrior*, *Beyond Thunderdome*). The shuttle between opposites, the disintegration of categories, is the outback's power for metamorphosis: from the midst of it surges, usually, "the beast"—savage black, crazed white, man-eating pig, crocodile, dingo. It's from this space that what one neoconservative columnist calls the "muscular innocence"[14] of Mick Dundee—the survivor with no opinions—is born.

Sue, too, can be given a genealogy in her role as questioning American, outback Pandora ("gotta have an opinion, gotta have a voice"). She is a creature of 10BA descent: bred from a history of experiments in cultural hybridization and a long line, predating even 10BA, of imported figures in need of a narrative justification of their place in exportable bits of landscape. Occasionally, these figures are just colonial immigrants like all other whites (Edward Woodward in *Breaker Morant*, Kirk Douglas in *The Man From Snowy River*). More frequently, they are bearers of a hermeneutic function. They are asking, learning, looking for something, like William Holden seeking his son in *The Earthling*, or Richard Chamberlain pursuing ultimate mysteries in Weir's *The Last Wave*. Sue's curiosity in *Crocodile Dundee* (a woman and a reporter, "the biggest stickybeak in the world") is thus strongly overdetermined. In the exchange between Dundee's muscular innocence of politics and her enfeebled liberal conscience, the very *form* of "questioning" is a mode of American ignorance.

The discussion of Aborigines is divided into two dark nights in the outback. Each raises a problem of appropriation, framed in two different ways: bad (whites land-taking, blacks taking back the land) and good (reciprocal borrowing between cultures). On the first night, Sue begins by posing the ultimate global question: the arms race. Dundee refutes the need for general political statements ("gotta have a voice") by specific cultural contexts: "Who's going to hear it out here?" Foiled by outback eccentricity, Sue tries something "closer to home": Aboriginal land rights. He still doesn't state "his" opinion. Instead, he paraphrases Aboriginal belief—Aborigines don't own the land, they belong to it.

This is, in one sense, true. But it is a significantly partial truth. First, in the enunciative shift of paraphrase, Dundee takes the "place" of Aboriginal opinion (also construing it as unconflictual). While implying that a land-rights politics of reappropriation is un-Aboriginal, he discursively appropriates the right to Aboriginal speech. Of course, any enunciative shift "appropriates": appropriation in this sense is neither displaced identity, nor colonialist invasion, but a process that takes place in both—the discursive struggle for power to fix the terms of reference. The terms are fixed on this occasion with a homely reference to the timeless land, a dog with two fleas squabbling over ownership. Aboriginal land claims, however, are not made for "the land" in general, but for particular sites. Dundee effaces this distinction in a discourse on (European) romantic nature—and confirms its supremacy by casually throttling a snake.

In this scene, land appropriation as *politics* is dismissed on behalf of absent Aboriginal opinion. The second scene works as a comic counterbalance to the first: a real Aborigine appears, to demonstrate the value of *cultural* appropriation. With land rights consigned to irrelevance as a foreign city-girl confusion (and a "white" political argument), Sue's romanticism about "primitive culture" is then correspondingly ridiculed.

Nev (David Gulpilil) isn't really savage, like the snake and the croc. He isn't even tribal. Nev is a city boy, doing corroboree duty to please his Dad. When Sue tries to photograph him as an exotic bearer of primitive belief, he repositions himself as the subject of basic camera skills. Nev says nothing about land rights. Nev, in fact, is a model appropriator: the culturally mobile aborigine, a survivor in transit between tribal and modern life, evading museumification and the closure of authenticity. So, it turns out, is Dundee. Already assimilated to Aborigines by Wally's tourist pitch, and by didgeridoo strains on the soundtrack, Dundee now comes out as a tribal initiate and postmodern hero—a "white aborigine."[15] His dismissal of land-rights politics and his claim to represent Aboriginal knowledge are validated by kinship. Both men are children of the outback, products of metamorphosis, and brother cultural poachers.

Together these two scenes effect a remarkable management of opinion. An easily recognizable conservative political discourse ("these strangers with their protest talk don't know anything about blacks anyway, and couldn't last five minutes in the bush") is reconciled with a radically demythologizing critique of cultural authenticity. Indeed, the land-rights discussion is *framed* by that critique: from the first scenes in Walkabout Creek (the barmaid's deflation of Dundee's legend) to the closing scenes in New York (the chauffeur's Harlem Warlords boomerang trick), the film's comic action is to evade the confinements of myth: goanna or hot dog, "You can live on it, but it tastes like shit."

Again, appropriation acts rhetorically for the film not as violence and invasion but as negotiation and defusion of conflict. There is, however, a missing link in the evolution of this consensus. Hostility to Aboriginal land rights is not simply a function of racism, populist suspicion of privileges for minority groups, or of radical critiques of *le propre* and the pitfalls of sentimental humanism—any one of which can find its own satisfactions in the urbane figure of Nev. Hostility to land rights is a function of the pressure of mining companies—in particular, those seeking to mine uranium on Aboriginal land. Sue's posing of the land-rights issue as an *alternative* to the arms race to frame Dundee's opinions has already, therefore, a certain poignant effect. Nothing in the comedy that follows allows a hint to emerge that the outback—primal space of land appropriation and cultural exchange—might now also provide raw materials for global nuclear threat. Instead, a link between local and global, Australian Aboriginal and European, Northern Territory and New York, is supplied by a discourse on racial and sexual stereotypes, the frailties of liberalism, and the primacy of natural perils.

Much as, in the New York narrative, the society matron takes the place of the urban intellectual, in the outback Sue and Nev take the place of the uranium miner. Although both work together to confound the discourse of critical protest, their functions are slightly different. One obvious difference in the comedies of race and sex is that male Aboriginal modernity (cultural) is not satirized from Dundee's outback position, whereas white female modernity (political, like land rights) is. Another is constructed by a circuit of complicity linking two moments of reciprocal violation: the black peering at the lone white woman in the bush, and the white woman sneaking up to watch an all-male tribal ceremony.[16] The first invasion is resolved by Australian-male complicity between Dundee and Nev about Sue's naïveté (nothing was going to happen anyway); the second is resolved in cross-cultural-white complicity between Dundee and Sue about the Aborigines' innocence (something did happen, but the elders don't know). The effect of this is to distance the violation of tribal law and diminish its seriousness, while foregrounding Sue's frailties. Aboriginal opinion doesn't really matter, whereas Sue's opinions are wrong. That Sue's own political sense is, to say the least, vestigial—a remnant of an archaic phase of symbolic activity ("you name it, we marched")—is the perfect outback touch.

Hence, perhaps, the cornered air to much political criticism of the film. *Crocodile Dundee* is difficult to attack because it so successfully manipulates a media process, the commodification of *opinion*, that left-wing critics—having profited from it in the 1970s—now often refuse to admit (or else ascribe to a "new" condition). It doesn't follow, of course, that the millions who come out "feeling good" from *Crocodile Dundee* emerge as anti-land-rights fanatics; not only because of their critical activity, but because media opinion is a matter, not of contents, but, precisely, of *mood*. However, it does follow—to an extent that culturalist theories of consumer "appropri-ation" may allow us to forget—that the film takes an active part in a politics of opinion by splitting land rights from the nuclear, the cul-tural from the political, and consigning the tools to make connec-tions to a realm of discredited, and parochialized, critical knowledge.

Colonial *Candide*

These movies are comforting in this time of terrible pessimism and depression when we've reached a level of cynicism which leads us to appreciate your naive optimism and vigor. Since the best of your films have been set in your colonial period, they recall the frontier spirit which we have lost. We wish that we could return to the "good old days" when America seemed as robust and unsophisticated as Australia appears in these buoyant movies.

Kathleen Carroll, interview, 1982

It is no wonder that always and everywhere the image of the colonial is the very pattern of naiveté, or that naive work is presumed to speak to us figuratively from a far-off land.

William Routt, "On the Expression of Colonialism in Early Australian Film: Charles Chauvel and Naive Cinema," 1984

In a savage attack on *Crocodile Dundee*, Phillip Adams (pundit, advertiser, and chairman of the Australian Film Commission) mused on the marketing of innocence. In the past, "there was something dead clever about Hogan's professed naivety," but now, he thought, Hogan had fallen for the worn-out genre of "overstated antipodean reactions to northern hemispherical sophistication." In other words, Dundee was *truly* naïve, the innocent abroad, "colonial Candide."[17] Events proved, however, that Hogan had still been dead clever.

Naïveté is an attribute of the Other: there is no more blatant claim to cunning than the confession "I am naïve" (which can then be read ironically as a sign of naïveté). As a term to position the Other, it advances the speaker in knowledge and history. The naïve is rhetor-ically *distanced* from a subject-here-and-now (or, as in "I am naïve," displaced from *enunciation* to *enounced*). So it is commonly linked to nostalgia: home-longing, the invention of origins, nondifferential repetition, fullness, and, in William Routt's phrase, "something out-side of history, untouched and unchanging forever Caliban."[18]

According to Routt, the subject seeing naïveté claims to be innocent, whereas in fact, "the predatory gaze of sophistication is the condition of existence for *naïveté.*"

With these terms, *Crocodile Dundee* can easily be read as a cynical play on postmodern passion for the naïve and the nostalgic. While not precisely an instance of *la mode retro*, as analyzed by Fredric Jameson, it recycles cinema myths to appeal to, and create, nostalgia: for old-fashioned entertainment, for rural innocence, for naïve values of harmony and immediacy, for simple conservative virtues. Yet, it is also an exercise in predation; *Caliban's Revenge* rather than *Tarzan's New York Adventure* (says Hogan, "It's like the image Americans have of us, so why not give them one?"[19]). Who, where, is exploiting whom? What is more sophisticated, more . . . postmodern, than an innocent double game of *simulated* faux naïf?

This reading is certainly plausible. But Routt's stress on the circumstances allowing recognition of naïve style might also be applied to radical critiques of the postmodern taste for nostalgia. Most exponents and critics of postmodernism, as style or as cultural logic, seem to agree on the importance of nostalgia; either in naïveté as lost ideal or as simulacrum—for someone. In radical critiques, nostalgia usually implies neoconservatism and historical regression. I don't wish to play Caliban to such discussions by crushing their complexity, but I wish to use my readings of *Crocodile Dundee* to question some assumptions that make it plausible, first, to see nostalgia in predatory practice, and, second, to see appropriation as counterattack in postmodern scenarios of struggle.

If *Crocodile Dundee* were read (naïvely) against Fredric Jameson's argument about postmodernity, for example, one might see it only as a symptom of the "*insensible colonization of the present* by the nostalgia mode."[20] To see it as still another example of global yet American culture, albeit from a far-off land, would be to miss out on its local industrial strategy, and its political ambivalence about different kinds of "sensible" colonization past and present. That is to say, one would be left with something like a Paramount press-kit version of its meanings and functions, in the sense that the universality of a global-yet-American cultural logic would be accepted, and affirmed, in the moment of critique. The problem is partly a product of the form of blockbuster diagnostic: few films that negotiate any kind of relation to Hollywood's (colonizing) history can escape the impact of Jameson's generalizations. Behind his model of postmodernity lies what he calls "the nostalgia mode" *in cinema* that frames his concept of appropriation as a "cannibalizing" intertextuality, and completes a divorce between (modern) "real history" and (postmodern) "history of aesthetic styles," between history proper and nostalgic historicism.[21] Leaving aside the general problems with this kind of periodization, it seems to me that the notion of nostalgia that Jameson shares with other critics, who may not share his aesthetics, obscures more than it enlightens.

First, *nostalgia* may not really be such a useful term in the era of Star Wars for the actuality of appropriation as a territorializing mode. The outback maneuvers in *Crocodile Dundee* are situated in relation to not only colonial and nuclear politics but also contemporary practices of tourism, safari holidays, theme parks, and locality environmentalism, which can now conflict with mining as a reason for "conservation"; whereas the film's aggressive play for New York is a response to, and an action in, a long history of American cultural domination and of the export rationale in conservative Australian thinking. *Crocodile Dundee* is saturated in "real history": it may use myth, and ridicule of myth, to produce a position in real history, but it does not express a significant home-longing for the world of Davy Crockett (as compensation, or as replacement past).

Second, the term *nostalgia* in radical critique may simply reintroduce the apocalyptic guarantee of historical determinism by positing a limit—some final phase, some "apotheosis" of capital—*at* which an absolutist culture fabricates a past, the better to pervade in perpetuity the present, while brave remnants of "progressive" thought struggle to redeem the real past, and a better future. But this mode of romantic pessimism affirms the former and cripples the latter by effacing, like the terror of "the bomb," the indecisiveness of actual conflicts. That a film like *Crocodile Dundee* should bother to include a little sermon on the end of radicalism and the irrelevance of landrights claims is perhaps a greater testimony to the liveliness of both.

Perhaps it seems forced to play such a film against Jameson's arguments. *Crocodile Dundee*'s territory, after all, is as far from Warhol as it is from van Gogh (though not so far from the Bonaventura Hotel). The awkwardness is partly due to a mismatch with the *mood* of appropriation as nostalgia that Jameson's text derives from the high-art critical tradition enabling and regulating the genre of postmodern diagnostic. In this sense, it is exemplary in its use of cinema to supplement (frame) an argument defined by reference to art and architecture—two institutions (in Peter Burger's sense) that most tenaciously retain "originality" and "progress" (the rhetoric of "advanced work") as *problems* still validating the professional differentiation, the critical packaging, of products. In this context, "appropriation" and "nostalgia" are cover versions of those problems.

"What would it look like not to repress the concept of the copy?" asked Rosalind Krauss in 1981, during the recent art cycle of retreat and revival in the rhetoric of originality, choosing the photographic work of Sherrie Levine as her answer.[22] It would be facile to answer that the result might look like most cultural practices, mass or otherwise, since Gissing wrote *New Grub Street*—or like the everyday landscape of postcolonial countries. It is institutionally reasonable that a fiction of "the" copy repressed should have acted as a liberating device to retrieve not only a critical function for art (rewriting its history, commenting on popular culture) but also a critical function for critics.

Something different happens, however, when this art-institutional fiction is transposed to serve as key synecdoche (like Warhol's *Diamond Dust Shoes* for Jameson, or the myth of the simulacrum for Jean Baudrillard) in a general critique of contemporary culture. Art's old privilege as survival-principle (Canetti), and authentic voice of critique and protest, is salvaged, unpropitiously, in the effort to come to terms with the commodity erosion of that privilege, and to begin to think away from the terms its privilege imposed. Criticism swings between mourning and affirmation, installed in postmodern melancholia yet looking for radical options.

Commercial cinema fits awkwardly into this scenario, unless as a Caliban for commentary in art. It is unwieldy; its constitutive montage of materials, and its material involvement with architecture, make it hard to reify appropriation as *distinctive* technique in cinema. There is no repression of the copy, but also little place for retrieving optimism from reproducibility in any sense of the term. No professional imperative for originality and progress exists (although there may be admiration). Classically, cinema *auteurs*, like architects, have always emerged in action under social constraints, not in primal creativity. But unlike architects, they are not institutionally redeemed for art by the regimes of manifesto-writing and design exhibition that preside over "movements" (like postmodernism). Although film-makers may engage in both, the primary modes of film and *auteur* packaging are advertising, review-snippeting, trailers, magazine pro-files—always already in appropriation as the precondition, and not the postproduction, of meanings. One might say the same, of course, of all mass culture: all-pervasive, omni-active appropriation is strictly a nonevent. This may be one reason why work *about* mass culture, which nonetheless circulates as art (including film and video), emerges so often, in the postmodern field, packaged as critical response to melancholia, whereas the study of that culture really con-tributes little to the formulation, rather than illustration, of problems.

Another symptom of the evasion of mass-cultural problems is a development that seems to move away from the problematics of art-nostalgia: the tendency in much journalistic, as well as academic, crit-icism to enshrine *to appropriate* as the model verb of all and any action—to make, to do, to write, to read, to give, to take, to produce, to consume, to rob, to receive, to exploit, to resist, to revenge (though not to revolt). In accumulating so many functions, *appropri-ation* gains radical credibility: it outrages humanist commitments to stable property values, adds a little *frisson* of impropriety and risk by romanticizing as violation the intertextual *sine qua non* of all cul-tural activity, and semantically guarantees a politics to practitioners by installing predation as the universal rule of cultural exchange. As a reified token of rapacious relations, *appropriation* is a lexical minimyth of power, a promise, if not of freedom, then of survival. All energies become seizures, and we all get a piece of the action.

A robust affirmation of rapacity as the law of the cultural market-place is certainly more invigorating for criticism than what Deleuze (speaking of action cinema) calls "melancholy hegelian reflections on its own death." In radical criticism's own action-image crisis of doubt in the powers of critical action to modify, rather than intensify, the situation of postmodernity—the doubt that Jameson calls "the abolition of critical distance"—appropriation has worked overtime at theorizing just such a possibility of modification. It also appeals to a certain corporate-raider chic no doubt better adapted to the mood of the times than the industrious term *production*—which was over-worked in much the same way by criticism in the 1970s.

Yet close links remain between rapacity and melancholia in the use of appropriation as a buzzword in otherwise politically antagonistic discourses to raise the same or similar questions—the authority of history, the power of tradition, the status of cultural canons. The jargon of appropriation is what postmodernisms of reaction and resistance have held in common in their different responses (and what has helped to make them so hard to distinguish). It is a jargon that preserves a certain faith in a cultural logic of affluence, a belief that "we" are living in claustrophobia with a glut of riches that we can (depending on our politics) either sanctify or seize. Postmodernized radical criticism has ceased to talk about "impoverishment" by culture, preferring to speak of the wealth released in cumulative acts of appropriation. As Geeta Kapur points out, it is a term implying not only aggression but abundance.

It is hardly surprising, then, that the figure of the colonial should now so insistently reappear from all sides not as deprived and dispossessed by rapacity but as the naïve spirit of plenitude, innocence, optimism—and effective critical "distance." Primitivism for art is (like Dundee for action cinema, the outback for tourism) only an obvious conservative version of this figure. Resistant postmodernism has had its equivalents in "popular culture" on the one hand and idealized enclaves of colonized "others" (women, blacks, etc.) on the other. That the latter have often proved slow to seize their place in postmodernity suggests a problem with the premise of surfeit.

For Peter Sloterdijk, all cynicisms provide answers to "the question of survival, of self-preservation and self-assertion".[23] The dead cleverness of *Crocodile Dundee* is one such answer, and a fulsome one. It has a reconciliatory, cohesive force quite at odds with the analytic spirit usually claimed for bricolage-appropriation and yet a zestful, entrepreneurial optimism that differs (at least in its shameless *avowal* of competitive ambition) from the lugubrious celebration of a lost past predicated so often for (or by) the conservative postmodernism (or antimodernism) with which it nonetheless shares many elements of racial, sexual, and political hostility.

It may be best to refuse to assert another. Yet it seems to me that radicalism might better survive the boom in postmodern opinion (for which "appropriation" has become as commodified a catchphrase as Paul Hogan's "G'day") by venturing into that distance that has not been abolished but expanded to infinity by postmodern criticism: the gap between the politics of production, and of regimes of consumption, or rather, since that distinction is now engulfed, between the politics of culture and the politics of politics. This distance (so actively exploited in *Crocodile Dundee*) is presided over by the figure of appropriation and its subsidiaries—like the rhetorical gap between *mass* culture (what the industry does) and *popular* culture (what we do with it). How to invent—not discover or retrieve—some connections is now a major ethical and imaginative action problem for radical politics.

It isn't a matter of nostalgia for fundamentals. Today, the distance between cultural politics and political politics has become so great, so *sublime*, that radical criticism seems unable to comprehend it. In "appropriating" the appropriations of popular culture as prime model of political action, criticism doesn't so much abandon old terrains of "genuine" struggle, as Jameson might say, but, more seriously, loses credibility: it ceases to be able to say why cultural "struggle" should be so necessary. The politics traversing *Crocodile Dundee* are impeded by no such reticence and no such Panglossian faith in the basic benevolence of cultural activity.

For classical Pangloss, everything was for the best in the best of all possible worlds, and there were no effects without causes. For postmodern Pangloss, a multiplicity of causes compete with a variety of effects, so we had best make the best of everything in the only possible world. There is really no need for nostalgic returns to a theory of cause and effect, or of originality, to suggest that radical criticism nonetheless needs to invent, as well as appropriate, a few good gardening tools.

NOTES

1. Gilles Deleuze, *Cinema 1: The Movement-Image*, trans. Hugh Tomlinson and Barbara Habberjam (Minneapolis: University of Minnesota Press, 1986), 206.

2. Cited in John Baxter, "A Fistful of Koalas," *Cinema Papers* 57 (1986), 26-29.

3. The essays I am referring to are Jürgen Habermas, "Modernity—An Incomplete Project," in *The Anti-Aesthetic*, ed. Hal Foster (Port Townsend, Wash.: Bay Press, 1983); Jean-François Lyotard, *The Postmodern Condition*, with Foreword by Fredric Jameson, (Minneapolis: University of Minnesota Press, 1984); Fredric Jameson, "Postmodernism, or the Cultural Logic of Late Capitalism," *New Left Review* 146 (1984), 53-92; Andreas Huyssen, "Mapping the Postmodern," *New German Critique* 33 (1984), 5-52. Naturally, a great deal of work in film and media studies has drawn on these discussions. My comment concerns only the elision of cinema in these formulations of postmodernism, not the vast associated literature.

4. Jean-François Lyotard, "L'acinéma," *Wide Angle* 2 (1978), 52-59. Jameson, Foreword to Lyotard's *The Postmodern Condition*, xvi-xvii.

5. These terms are loosely adapted from Ross Chambers, *Story and Situation: Narrative Seduction and the Power of Fiction* (Minneapolis: University of Minnesota Press, 1984), 33.

6. With Laleen Jayamanne and Yvonne Rainer, "Discussing Modernity, 'Third World,' and *The Man Who Envied Women*," *Art & Text* 22/23 (1987), 41-51.

7. 1982 interview in P. Hamilton and S. Matthews, *American Dreams, Australian Movies* (Sydney: Currency Press, 1986), 157.

8. Ibid, 95.

9. 10BA initially offered a 150 percent write-off for film investment, with no tax payable on the first 50 percent of profits. In August 1983, the concessions were reduced to 133 percent: 33 percent, and then again, in September 1985, to 120 percent: 20 percent. *Film assistance: Future options: A discussion paper by the Australian Film Commission* (Winchester, Mass.: Allen & Unwin, 1987), 1-8. By 1985, the year of the actual filming of *Crocodile Dundee*, the level of guaranteed presale income required to attract investors had reached 65 percent. At the time of writing, the scheme was under review as no longer viable either for the industry or for the government.

10. For the pleasure of American deconstructionists, we might note that instead of playing Fess Parker, Dundee plays with Sue's *fesses*.

11. I must thank Julie Rose for pointing this out to me. The bush telegraph was once a way for settlers to warn bushrangers about the movements of police. In urban society today, it usually means gossip.

12. Elias Canetti, *Crowds and Power* (New York: Penguin 1973), 265. *Crocodile Dundee* is a particularly unfortunate model for future Australian cinema because of Paul Hogan's unusual status as a recognizable American commodity (through tourism commercials); because the Paramount budget for publicizing the film in North America rivaled its local production budget; and because its success on these terms (as well as its cultural conservatism) makes the task of sustaining and justifying support for local independent film even more difficult than before.

13. Frank Campbell, "The Golden Age of Hoges," *The Sydney Morning Herald*, 7 January 1987. For Campbell, the racial and sexual conservatism of the film makes it a "soft," not an anti, *Rambo*, mixing a cocktail of messages for audiences "which cannot afford to be seen taking them neat."

14. "The Shining Hero Inside Mick Dundee," *The Australian*, 20-21 December 1986. His innocence is compared to Sue's "left-liberal cant."

15. The white Aborigine has been one of the privileged figures of postmodern rhetoric in Australian art writing; see Paul Taylor, "The Art of White Aborigines," *Flash Art* 112 (May 1983), 48-50. It's also an old colonial metaphor ("miscegenation") of contradiction and reconciliation.

16. The reciprocal relation of Sue and Nev is underscored by the fact that Aboriginal women are nonexistent for the film. At one of *their* ceremonies, however, Sue might well be admitted whereas Dundee would not. At this level of the film's politics of opinion, it maintains the old anthropological myth of patriarchal control in Aboriginal societies.

17. "Sorry Hoges, but this time you've blown it," *The Australian*, 26 April 1986.

18. "On the Expression of Colonialism in Early Australian Film," in *An Australian Film Reader*, ed. A. Moran and T. O'Regan (Sydney: Currency Press, 1985), 62.

19. Cited in Baxter, "A Fistful of Koalas," 28.

20. Jameson, "Postmodernism," 67, my emphasis.

Tales of Survival and *Crocodile Dundee* 127

21. This divorce, rather than *la mode retro* or the film remake, is antihistorical: thanks to the notion of "style," it can't allow for mediation by *cinema* (that is, institutional and social as well as aesthetic) history constructed by films and by criticism.

22. "The Originality of the Avant-Garde: A Postmodernist Repetition," reprinted in R. Krauss, *The Originality of the Avant-Garde and Other Modernist Myths* (Cambridge, Mass.: MIT Press, 1985), 186.

23. Peter Sloterdijk, "Cynicism—The Twilight of False Consciousness," *New German Critique* 33 (1984), 195.

Visiting the Banana Republic
Paul Smith

Capitalism arose and took off its pajamas [and put on] gloriously comfortable minimalist trousers . . . pants truly essential to the wanderer's duffel—they make you feel at home anywhere in the world.[1]

In a general argument about what he sees as two kinds of postmodernist production, Hal Foster makes the point that there is one sort that is "aligned with neoconservative politics, [and another] related to poststructuralist theory." The first takes on the weight of its historical heritage in order to oppose or deny it and thus becomes "an a-history, in fact" or "a history of victors."[2] Foster claims that the other kind—building itself on the descriptions offered by poststructuralism of split subjectivity, failed representations, repressive and regressive cultural forms, and so on—takes the burden of historical analysis more seriously. This claim is clearly arguable, except perhaps when it responds to a kind of Apollonian severity in postmodern neoconservativism on the one hand and to a certain moment of Dionysiac pleasure in poststructuralism's heyday on the other. All the same, it might be pointed out that the neoconservative strategies of postmodernism have indeed taken history very seriously, conceiving it as *dangerous* and thence doing something about it, and that poststructuralist attention to history has in general constituted little more than a fashionable, breast-beating chorus of cries to "historicize."

Perhaps Foster's distinction is best annotated by his own later observation that these two kinds of postmodernism are finally at one with each other. Their oneness resides, of course, in the fact that their supposedly apparent autonomy is finally subsumed under the logic of capital. Foster rightly recalls the fact that even in the postmodern age it is still capital that structures and destructures social forms; or, to put it another way, capital deterritorializes and reterritorializes social forms in a way analogous to the process of imperial-

128

ist decolonization and economic recolonization.[3] This process con-
signs the critical discourses and art-practices of our time to working
with and among the constantly redisposed elements of a culture that
is more than ever the object of an ideology of asymptotic change, or
even of "revolution."[4] This is not to say, of course, that those discourses and practices do not in their turn add to the momentum of
postmodern change. Quite the contrary: one of the tasks of this article is to describe an instance of how the discourses of postmodernism—their conditions originally primed by capitalist structuring and
destructuring—are then reassumed for the use of capital itself.

A specific level of quotidian capitalist formations now can be
viewed, in part, as the result of capital's reappropriation of discourses
that first arose as the symptoms of radical aesthetic and/or theoretical
postmodernism. One everyday example of this phenomenon is in
rock-music video and its frequent recourse—within, to be sure, the
constraints of a highly formalized capital media enterprise such as
the MTV cable channel—to forms of representation and discursive
practice that had previously been unacceptable or merely marginal
to television. Music video's willingness in many instances to either
dispense or play with television's chronic reliance on formulaic narrative structures, visual centering, sound/image corroboration, and
so on now enables it to draw up and draw upon a vocabulary of postmodernism without embarrassment or seeming contradiction. The
tendency is perhaps best exemplified and concretized in MTV's reg-
ular "Art Break" slot in which, for ten or fifteen seconds, a camera
crosses the work of a postmodern artist like Richard Tuttle or David
Salle.

I want to look at another instance of this sort of reappropriation:
the chain-store and catalog business, Banana Republic Travel and
Safari Clothing Company. This company was started in 1978 by Patricia and Mel Ziegler, converts to entrepreneurism from the world of
art and writing.[5] By 1983 their company had become successful
enough to attract the attention of larger concerns and Banana Republic was bought by the clothing retail corporation called The Gap,
while the Zieglers still maintained autonomy and control over it.
Banana Republic has by now spawned about seventy stores across
the United States and also conducts an extensive mail-order business,
sending out over eight million catalogs a year. Each of the stores is
appointed uniquely but in such a way as to reflect (somewhat inex-

actly) the motifs in the company's name—travel and safari in Africa and other parts of the third world. Most of these stores are intended to be reminiscent, that is, of the colonial general store and/or the colonialist gentleman's mess. Similarly, the company's catalogs feature a kind of mimicry and perversion of late nineteenth-century colonialist travel-writing, mixed with a relatively familiar form of contemporary catalog sales rhetoric.[6]

The use of the phrase *banana republic* in this enterprise is somewhat inexact and contradictory: the most frequent area of reference in the company's decor and rhetoric (and, indeed, in its actual retail products) is the colonial and postcolonial world of British imperialism, rather than those areas of the globe submitted to American capital expansion in the early twentieth century and in relation to which the term *banana republic* is more often used. This anomaly is significant as part of the system of Banana Republic in that it is consistent with what I shall later describe as the company's postmodernist discourse, in which particular historical data are taken up and altered.

When asked about the origin of the company's name, Mel Ziegler explains that the phrase was used:

> because our merchandise came from countries where one regime
> had deposed another and declared all the old uniforms surplus. The
> new general could never be seen in the old general's uniform. . . .
> and [it was] part of a whimsy of creating an imaginary republic where
> I was Minister of Propaganda and Finance and Patricia was Minister
> of Culture.

These words are quite telling in a number of ways. They seem to invoke the term *banana republic* as a catchall and demeaning (that is, historically unspecific and racist) description for all and any nations that have emerged from direct colonial dependency into republican status and thence into, more specifically, economic dependency. Without much apparent self-consciousness Ziegler relies upon the confidence, endlessly reelaborated in the actual activities of his company, that even (or especially) in postcolonial times such nations are still the loci of the production of surplus for the capitalist economies of the North. Equally significant is Banana Republic's adoption of the term *surplus*—a word resonant within both Marxist and postmodernist discourses—as one of the founding terms in a patronizing, postcolonialist view of the South. More signal, perhaps, is the way in which the supposed humor of this demeaning

characterization of the third world is turned, by a wonderful cata-
chresis, to designate an "imaginary republic"—an apt, idealizing
metaphor for the American business organization. Importantly, the
original object of the humor is erased and elided here where this
postmodern capitalist enterprise names its primary areas of concern:
Finance, Culture, and Propaganda.

Banana Republics

The management of Banana Republic's parent corporation, The Gap,
is unusually reluctant to disclose financial details of its affiliates.
However, The Gap's organization as a whole made profits of about
$10.2 million in the first quarter of 1986 and had total revenues of
about $534 million from sales at more than six hundred stores across
the United States in 1985. Banana Republic itself may have accounted
for somewhere between $10 million and $15 million of the 1985
figure, without including catalog sales—although some estimates of
the company's total sales for 1985 go as high as $60 million.

While these figures might indicate that The Gap and its affiliates
are a relatively small force within the clothing retail industry (by way
of comparison, the retail leader, The Limited, made $145.3 million
profit on sales of over $2.4 billion in 1985), the growth of Banana
Republic itself has been quite phenomenal since 1978 when it first
set up shop with capital of only $1,500. The company's acquisition by
The Gap marked its change from a small, entrepreneurial business to
part of a large corporation fully integrated into the modes and channels of multinational capitalism.

The clothing retail business in the United States has traditionally
been highly competitive and was thus one of the sectors most
affected by the recessions of the seventies and by increased availability of cheap imported products. In what was, during the seventies, a
fairly general trend for American industries—and now a sufficiently
familiar story—domestic production of clothing was decimated as
distributors and retailers began to cut costs and increase trade volumes by involving themselves more directly in offshore production.
Capital flight, and other deindustrializing tactics at home, helped
restructure the business in the direction of vertical integration, with
companies such as The Limited and The Gap in the vanguard.[7]

Within such a context, Banana Republic would seem a particularly suitable kind of enterprise for a company like The Gap to appropriate. In fact, Banana Republic's original goal—to sell mostly non-U.S. surplus clothing by stressing its "authenticity," "genuineness," reliability, and, in short, its quality—adds a rhetorical element of respectability to industry operations, which, although immensely profitable, tended to suffer to some extent from a reputation for selling relatively unreliable and shoddy mass-market goods. In general, it would seem that this claim to quality by the Banana Republic has stayed in place over the last three or four years, but that the goods themselves are increasingly often manufactured by The Gap's production networks in the third world. This means that Banana Republic's processes of production and distribution are becoming more and more assimilated into those of its parent company—a development that can be taken as fairly typical of the postrecession capitalist reorganization in the eighties.

Perhaps the most immediately apparent characteristic of that reorganization has been the almost total removal of domestic participation in production because of the turn to the third world, and the concomitant conversion of domestic industrial jobs into so-called service jobs. These new modes of production and distribution can be dated roughly to the early seventies and to the increasing establishment of free production zones (FPZs) and export processing zones (EPZs) in the third world. These zones (growing steadily and rapidly in both number and size even now) are evidently one of the focal points in what is often called the new international division of labor. Clearly, the attraction of such zones resides not simply in their reserve supply of cheap labor but equally in the concessions made to capital interests by third-world governments eager for foreign revenue. Indeed, it can even be said that "the most important privilege granted to capital in free production zones is simply the lack of any restrictions on foreign investment and on capital transfers";[8] and in addition, American, Japanese, and European capital clearly benefits from such concessions as tax exemptions, development grants, antiunion legislation, low or nonexistent minimum wage requirements, and so on.

For the U.S. clothing industry, the process of production now tends typically to begin with the purchase of raw materials (mostly cotton) from countries such as India or China. Those fibers are more often than not processed (that is, dyed and woven) in Hong Kong before being sent to export processing zones — such as those in the Philippines, South Korea, Taiwan, Mauritius, Sri Lanka, etc. — for the actual manufacture of clothing. The U.S.-domestic part of the process is thence confined to the receiving, labeling, and distributing of goods — and, of course, the selling of them. If, as is sometimes the case with Banana Republic, the clothing imported consists of unretouched surplus items, it is usually cleaned in this country at the same time as it is labeled.

The advantages to capital at the level of distribution are almost as numerous as they are at the production stages. Product distribution can be domestically centralized and at least partially automated. More important, high-wage industrial jobs can be removed and the domestic wage-bill reduced, since distribution labor is mostly unskilled and can often be supplemented and/or replaced by automation. Equally, such service workers are generally not unionized and have minimal benefits and low job longevity. The clothing retail companies also strive for ever-lower inventories, since they now can rely on timely delivery and speedy turnover of goods when they are produced offshore.[9]

The economic and social effects of this process (which I have described only crudely here) are profound for both the Western and third-world nations involved. If, as seems correct, this newly organized mode of production and division of labor can be described as "capital's attempt to break through the historical barriers of the nation-state [and] to transcend capital within the limits of the capitalist mode of production itself,"[10] the upshot is unsurprising: the exacerbation on a different level of the chronic contradictions and inequalities of the capitalist system. That is, even as it comes closer to realization, the persistent capitalist dream of high rates of surplus-value in the cheap production of goods, of high-volume trade, of low labor requirements, combined with a decrease in the number of workers directly involved in domestic production and a concomitant increase in managerial control, produces not inconsiderable tensions, domestically as much as internationally.[11]

These tensions arise, of course, from the fact that as capital increasingly leaves traditional domestic industries, as investments are made in third-world production facilities, and as imports rise, the United States becomes (at least, on the books) a major debtor nation. One effect of all this is precisely to underscore the contradictions that arise within capital between transnational (business) and national (statist) interests. Even while the offshore concentration of capital increases profits, capital flight from the domestic economy causes a whole range of socioeconomic and political problems—ones that the United States has been experiencing especially acutely throughout the Reagan years: widespread unemployment, the radical restructuring of labor communities, hardship for smaller firms and their subsequent assimilation into multinational corporations, large-scale trends toward profit taking from speculation rather than production, internal division over protectionism and tariffs, military buildups to help restore the balance between capital and state forces, and so on.[12]

The corresponding conditions in third-world production and exporting areas are equally well known. Export processing zones and free production zones scarcely bring the kinds of benefits that may perhaps have once been sincerely expected. Average income in third-world countries tends not to reflect the rates of growth in capital influx and is, in any case, more than ever unevenly distributed between rural and urban areas. With a few exceptions—such as in Sri Lanka or Mauritius—increased gross national products have not generally entailed major increases in, or better management of, government services, and the concessions to capital in terms of legislation and rule-bending have effectively restricted any organized labor pressure for better conditions. The infamously low wages paid for long laboring hours, and the sweatshop conditions under which the work is usually carried out, remain not just an economic but a social problem that the governmental infrastructure of any advanced industrial country would be hard-pressed to ameliorate. That problem is compounded by others—such as the trend toward the feminization of the low-wage labor force, the breakdown of urban-rural development patterns, and the decline of traditional agricultural production—as the economies of the third world attempt to reconcile older social structures with the effects of capital domination.

Thus, the historical social forms of both the North and the South are broken down and rebuilt. The world is reterritorialized by the international division of labor at the same time as the American domestic map is redrawn in the process of deindustrialization. As economic and social divides are deepened both at home and away, the disjunctions in the distribution of wealth are everywhere increased.

Critical Mapping

For some time now, Marxist thought has been divided (to put it very crudely, but nonetheless to point to something real) between the two poles of, on the one hand, a criticism clinging hard to the classic conceptions of Marx's thought (to notions of the class struggle and the determining instance of the economic), and on the other hand, a "cultural" analysis that has moved farther and farther away from those founding contexts. Mediating instances are, of course, everywhere but can usually be seen to have an origin in either one or the other of the polar possibilities. The more or less orthodox Marxist tools, if used for an analysis of the kind of economic tale I have briefly and partially sketched out, are surely, to some extent, appropriate. Yet, my claim is that the very complexity and dispersion of the economic and other factors involved globally in that tale must be *equally* understood as a specifically postmodern condition, supported and enabled by the restructuring and reterritorializing of strictly noneconomic elements: representational strategies and ideological and cultural formations.

Although there is no doubt about the continuing, and even renewed, need for analysis of the economic, traditional Marxist tools and their emphasis on the narrative of modes of production are ill-prepared for the labyrinthine or antinarrative text of the postmodern. As Lyotard and many others have proposed, the "grand narratives" of the institutions of the Enlightenment have fallen into disuse; it now seems vain to expect these grand narratives to analyze a social text that has been forged precisely from their ruins. If the classical narrative of production will not suffice as a way of analyzing late twentieth-century capitalism, it is not because the term *production* is inadequate or questionable at this point—indeed, the need for analysis of the precise conditions of production is even more crucial in the postmodern era. Rather, it is, at least in part, because—during the last twenty years or so, in the work of structuralism and poststructuralism and in the era of the postmodern—we have learned to question not only the explanatory form of narrative itself but also the totalizing epistemologies that subvent it and that it subvents. At the same time, the right has learned how to theorize and manipulate narrative in a new and more insidious way than before, producing the neoconservative postmodern and such phenomena as Banana Republic. On the left, the narrative of production has undergone intense scrutiny from the likes of Althusser and Baudrillard: the former attempting to replace it with a more structural analysis and the latter trying to displace it altogether. More generally, contemporary critical thought, in its interrogation of systems of representation and thence of the question of history itself (history as representation), has cast the question of narrative in different terms. In that multifaceted critical context, the "scientific" status of the classical narrative of production and its attendant structures of knowledge become questionable, if not untenable. The objectivity and empirical viability of classic Marxism have been rendered vulnerable by whole critical methodologies and vocabularies.

Even in the realm of Marxist economic theory itself, the goal of fidelity to the terms of Marx's own analysis of nineteenth-century capital is either elusive or only partly attained because of the radical changes in capital development in the last decades. Theorists such as Ernest Mandel have, of course, made fairly convincing attempts to counter the often-heard claims that Marxist economics has nothing to say about late capitalism. However, Mandel's attachment to the orthodox narrative, demonstrated in his theories of capital cycles and "long wave" patterns of capitalist development,[13] is obliged to ignore many of the realities and the potential realities of late capitalism. As a telling example of this, one might take Mandel's argument, in *Late Capitalism*, that automation of the industrial base will not come about — and, indeed, that it is not among capital's goals. This claim is entirely dependent on Marx's account of the generation of surplus-value, whereby the formula for the mass of surplus-value can be arrived at only with the participation of human labor selling its time to capital. Mandel says that "the mass of surplus value itself necessarily diminishes as a result of the elimination of living labour from the production process in the course of the final stage of mechanization-automation" and that, indeed, "generalized automation . . . pose[s] an absolute barrier to the valorization of capital."[14]

The supporting quotations from Marx that Mandel brings to bear on this particular position underscore precisely one of the points at which the development of late capitalism exceeds or negates the master narrative. Where Marx asserts that systemic automation of the industrial processes would cause a revolution because of the removal of productive human labor,[15] late capitalism has nonetheless shown its ability to forestall such a possibility by the "refunctioning" and redefining of labor time—into, roughly speaking, service jobs and into consumption time and "leisure." Although Marxist economics seems unprepared to reconceptualize the processes of surplus-value production outside the parameters of the classic formulas, capitalism itself is daily forging a set of social conditions that clearly demands such a reconceptualization.

I have chosen what is, of course, but one moment in Mandel's sustenance of classic Marxist categories, and I don't want to suggest that his attempts to reassert the importance of fundamental categories such as mass and rate of surplus-value or his emphasis on long-term patterns of capital concentration are to be ignored or discarded. Rather, the subsuming of such categories and their analysis under the classic narrative of modes of production legislates against a thorough analysis of the ways, not only in which the mode of production has changed, but also in which it is newly and complexly articulated into (and from) contemporary modes of representation and ideological formations. Mandel's aim is to reinstate the hegemony within Marxism of a faith in the determining instance of the economic, and thence to be able to treat capitalist development entirely positivistically as an objective historical process of eventual regularity, carrying along with it predictable contradictions. Serving this aim is Mandel's reluctance to consider factors other than the economic as causative. For instance, at the beginning of the book on "long waves," he curtly dismisses what ought finally to be seen as overdetermining elements in an analysis of capitalist development: namely, "monetary, psychological, or purely inventive factors."[16] Even when he does discuss social forces other than the economic, they tend to be seen merely as by-products of the economic. Thus, in his chapter, "Ideology in the Age of Late Capitalism," we find a familiar argument pitting the truth of Marxist rationality against the false-consciousness fostered by the capitalist economic system.[17]

In the new international economic system, the ideologies that support and engender particular forms of domination can no longer be seen as mere mystifications. Rather, they subsist as material and effective structures in their own right, implicated into the systems of representation and forms of subjectivity in a way both quantitatively and qualitatively different from how they have chronically been thought of in Marxist theories of false-consciousness. Just as the theory of the fetishization of commodities is fundamentally challenged by capital's vastly enhanced ability to move funds electronically and to set up an unprecedented disjunction between the rate of movement of commodities themselves and that of money, so too the specular image of the camera obscura of ideology can no more "explain" subjection to the new international division of labor than it can account for the extraordinary complex of interpellative appeals made to the subject at all levels and in all locations. In other words, some of the tenets of traditional Marxism are subject not merely to the ravages of revisionist theorizing but more to the radical re-formations of capital itself.

Moreover, capital's tendency to effect a kind of mixed economy across the international division of labor without actual (or, at least, overt) territorial imperialism is another factor in this disjunction that inhibits the Marxist paradigms at this point (even though, admittedly, Marx often allowed that such a state of affairs could come to exist). Multinational capital formation—with its daily extension of capital's domination, and the deepening divide between rich and poor in both international and intranational contexts—no longer makes its claims through direct colonial subjugation of the subject, but rather by the hyperextension of interpellative discourses and representations generated with and from a specifically new form of capital domination. Thus, it is important to recognize that domination occurs intensively at the levels of discourse, representation, and subjectivity.

At such a historical moment, the objectifying analyses so often relying upon the theoretical base of the narrative of production and its relatively nondisjunct phenomena certainly need to increase their responsiveness to the changes in capital in the North—its formation, accumulation, and distribution. But, at the same time, there are other, interrelated tasks. First of all, there is the pointed need for analysis of socioeconomic conditions in the third world that will go beyond the usual paradigms of dependency theory and will look instead to the ways in which, for instance, representations of colonial and neocolonial power alter and change with the influx of foreign capital and commodities; or that will look at the ways in which social divisions are locally restructured (the divisions between male and female subjects of the EPZs, for example). However, this kind of analysis is not the aim of the present essay, which would suggest a further, though complementary, set of tasks.

Oppositional criticism has of late been concerned to align itself very firmly with questions of the third world. Although this is, I would stress, no bad thing, there has been a tendency to offer concern with such issues as a "seal of authority or guarantee of authenticity" for political commitment; third-world issues become, as women's issues before them, a bulwark to the left's political imaginary.[18] Rather, or in addition, it seems necessary right now—and consonant with a recognition of the demise of the grand narratives—to continue to concentrate on the specificity of the general disposition of capital and its effects on domestic structures in the major economies. But this is not simply a matter of describing and analyzing the economic conditions of the North—though that is indeed a large part of the task. It is also a matter of recognizing the ways in which social representations accompany, adapt to, and even formulate the nature of changes and trends in the capitalist economy. This seems especially crucial in a context in which capital's claims for the legitimation of contemporary social and economic structures are made largely at the level of the *consumer*, who is never the consumer of just a commodity but equally of the commodity's *text* and ideology. This more generalized notion of consumption is especially important in an instance such as that of Banana Republic, in which the commodity-text far exceeds the mere function of advertizing the commodity and instead legitimates both it and its underlying mode of production. The production of this commodity-text is indefeasibly bound up with more widespread and general shifts in the modalities of both representation and subjectivities.

One major attempt to grapple with these shifting modes is Fredric Jameson's influential article, "Postmodernism, or The Cultural Logic of Late Capitalism," which examines the wholesale changes in aesthetic production in the postmodernist period. Jameson claims that "aesthetic production today has become integrated into commodity production generally." By this he appears to mean that the *logic* of aesthetic and cultural production is identical to that of commodity production, or that art practice *is* now fully a capitalist practice, marking the fact that capital has now reached into "hitherto uncommodified areas."[19] Taking postmodern architecture as a prime component of this "new" incursion, Jameson suggests that postmodernism has entailed a change in which both cognitive and social space have been redefined. By dint of late capital's multinational reach and its accompanying forms of representation, our cognitive relation to the "totality" (one of the privileged motifs of the classic Marxist narrative) has been lost. Jameson's point, then, is to champion an alternative "aesthetic of cognitive mapping—a pedagogical culture that seeks to endow the individual subject with some new heightened sense of its place in the global system."[20]

Jameson's argument for a totalizing view of multinational capital, a new cognitive mapping, once again champions the narrative of modes of production (the aptly named "master narrative" or "untranscendable horizon" of all of Jameson's writings). Even while Jameson appears to be attending to such matters as the history of representations themselves, and the analysis of their actual material effects in producing history itself, he demonstrates a certain neglect of them. For example, in calling for a new cognitive mapping, he invokes as a contrast to postmodernist modes the medieval history of cartography with its new instruments and its "whole new coordinate—that of relationship to the totality."[21] Jameson's apparent approval of this "new coordinate" is not balanced by any account of the historical context with which it is implicated; namely, the first waves of European colonial expansion and the elaboration of its technological rationality. Here, in effect, is the blind spot of Jameson's argument, precisely where the old Marxist view of history takes over as template and paradoxically inhibits the urge to historicize.[22]

My claim here, then, is that the analysis of contemporary capitalism must take seriously its own rhetorical injunction to itself—to historicize. That aim is not satisfied by the imposition of historical templates, cyclical forms, and abstract totalities onto material history. So, too, the project of historicizing cannot selectively and eclectically pass through the array of contemporary critical discourse only to emerge with yet another totalizing system, another monolithic view of history and totality. To paraphrase a couple of Barbara Kruger's photocollages: Marxist manias cannot be allowed to stand as science, and Marxist myths cannot be allowed to stand as history.

What seems required is another kind of attention, or attentiveness, which consideration of a text such as Banana Republic might both demand and foster. The attentiveness that both first- and third-world questions and predicaments demand is at least twofold: it necessitates not just a sense of the history of the modes of economic production, but also a willingness to accept that capital's history is aleatory because of its endless ability to overcome particular material conditions and obstacles, extending its reach ever further into all domains of discourse and, indeed, of existence; one of those domains is history itself and the representation of history. The processes of the postmodern figuration of material history produce history as much as they bespeak it, and they are thus crucially part of the overdetermined character of the postmodern condition. The project of historicizing must begin outside the parameters of a master narrative (which ultimately makes of history *one* history or a transhistorical—and thus very nearly *ahistorical*—construct) and insist instead on the *provisionality* of history, spoken through and by representations that alter, submerge, and erase both themselves and other representations. The history of *that* history remains to be addressed.

Postmodernism at Home

Banana Republic is an ongoing dialogue that on any given day starts on the jogging path and ends up in the jacuzzi.

Mel Ziegler

In the 1940s, Joseph Schumpeter coined the phrase *Creative Destruction* to describe the profitable way in which those businesses able to deploy most quickly the latest technological innovations eliminate not only technologically "backward" firms but, one might add, whole industries and styles of business as well.[23] The phrase can easily be applied to the process by which a firm like Banana Republic works at the level of representations. By adopting its own "brand" of postmodernist discourse, Banana Republic has re-placed or restructured a whole history and its discourses—the history of colonialism—and re-presented the current phase of domination in such a way that those discourses cannot properly be called mystifications. Rather, they are *de facto* the active, effective, and real truths of contemporary American culture and need to be treated as such.

The systems of signification that served the ideology of classic imperialist colonialism were clear enough, relying upon the repeated representation of the master/subaltern doublet—a doublet that broke down easily into white/native and so on.[24] The dialectic resolution of such a representation, it might be argued, has by now lost its ability to suggest the stability of the old Pax Britannica, and the doublet has by now had to rerecognize its own negativity and to remark the resentments about and battles over colonial rule. Thus, in the postcolonial situation, to accommodate and enhance the wholesale changes in capital formation, a new system of signification is required.

First of all, the historic end of colonialism brings on the beginning of a repetition: the endless shuffling of roughly equivalent "banana republic" regimes, and this shifting process is certainly represented in one moment of Banana Republic's discourse, as I mentioned earlier. But the major emphasis in the discourse of the catalogs is a revision of both the conflictual view and the comic view of the third world. What replaces these two images is an almost nostalgic one in which the third world is presented as a kind of benign theme park for adults, as well as a place redolent of a certain kind of purity. Banana Republic claims to offer clothes in what they describe as unique authentic colors and patterns, using what are made to sound like precolonial production facilities and 100 percent natural fabrics—hundreds, as they're called. The guiding motif in their publicity, then, is a kind of cult of authenticity. The Zieglers claim that they actually go on safari-type expeditions looking not only for surplus items (ready-made authenticity) but also for the patterns, colors, materials, and styles that are fit to be used for Banana Republic clothes. And ironically, in the trade context of which they consider themselves the vanguard, they suggest that they "visit vanishing cultures ... to celebrate their uniqueness and discourage them from slipping into global homogeneity" (which could be a line from Clifford Geertz!). One of the catalogs, without a hint of irony, proclaims that "in Africa the dawn of the twenty first century casts its shadow on the dawn of man. On this continent there's no mistaking it: You know where you came from."

These kinds of announcement are accompanied in the catalogs by quotations from the travel writings of men such as Sir Richard Burton, Henry Stanley, and Theodore Roosevelt. These in turn are juxtaposed with the writings (very often "reports" on a particular item of clothing) of contemporaries like photographer Carol Beckwith, wildlife biologist Mark Owens, a self-described glacier and bush pilot, and contemporary writers as various as Garry Trudeau, Lawrence Ferlinghetti, Cyra McFadden, and Roy Blount Jr.[25] In most of the seasonal catalogs this peculiar admixture of the historical and the contemporary, along with fairly unabashed references to current affairs or historical events (such as Watergate, Lord Kitchener's subjection of the Sudan, or—in a piece of copy designed to sell "paratrooper briefcases"—the Israeli raid on Entebbe), is accompanied by some thematic motif. In 1986, those motifs consisted in Mel and Patricia's story of a visit to the Soviet Union (full of stereotypical images of the Soviet system and remarks such as "it would be unconscionable to come to Russia without attempting to make contact with dissidents and refuseniks"), a discourse on Africa ("we've opened the pages of this issue to many voices from Africa," few of which turn out to be "native"), and for the Christmas catalog, a series of reflections on receiving gifts (featuring Miss Manners "On Receiving Well").

It is the multivocalism of the catalogs that is their most obvious postmodern feature. The heterogeneity of the discourses contained here produces a kind of swirling texture of differences among which it is hard to discover or define any overarching principle of discursive control. No necessary connection exists between the larger, thematic narratives and the kinds of discourse scattered across the catalog's surface, nor do those motifs necessarily dictate the range of references in the other parts. What does emerge, however, is what I referred to above as the cult of authenticity. To claim "genuineness" for the Banana Republic merchandise, the catalog introduces a variety of references to historical moments in an emulsion of irony and satire, clichés and stereotypes, apocryphal histories and factoids, and so on. Hardly more than a few examples need be given here:

> A menacingly true reproduction of the notorious Red Baron flight helmet. . . . official headgear in our Banana Republic Air Force.
>
> History has been decidedly chilly toward the Seventh Earl of Cardigan for sending 673 British Hussars against 25,000 Russian troops. . . . but Lord Cardigan's sweater . . . has evoked a much warmer response.
>
> In the 1890s Zanzibar was a teeming island marketplace. . . . Among the most prized commodities was unbleached American

calico . . . dubbed "Merikani." Our Merikani shirt is cut from similar cotton . . . and dyed in rich hues the Masai might covet.

Lord Kitchener reconquered the Sudan wearing the four-pocket khaki jacket that evolved into the modern safari jacket . . . [we offer] the authentic bush jacket for adventurers with a low tolerance for the ersatz.

It was 1814. A young British lieutenant, captured by the Nepalese [is represented as having impressed them so much by his bravery that] they said, "We could serve under an officer like you," and thus Britain inherited the famous ghurkas. For them the British developed the classic wide-legged shorts, still without peer in sticky situations.

As with these last two instances, the copy often refers explicitly to some part of colonial history in a way that is nearly always apocryphal and designed either to simply satirize or to evacuate antagonism from the actual history and to install that history as the origin of contemporary and readily available benefits. Even some of the most hated symbols of colonial rule are satirized, but made harmless, by the catalog copy, as in the following picture of the imperial officer's mess at the twilight of colonial rule:

Sir Cedric tamped his pipe and sighed. "Bloody shame, the little blighters going off and becoming self-governing. . . . I'm going to miss some jolly good times." Who could forget the camaraderie of the Congo Cricket Club? The beers and brandies at the Bengal Bridge Club? Or last season's heart-breaking finals of the Botswana Lawn Bowling League?

These brief and almost random examples have to be seen, of course, in the wider context of an attempt to persuade patrons that both current and past histories are in no sense sacrosanct and in every sense negligible. This motif of encouraging the American consumer to reconcile him/herself, this theme of *adaptation* to the third world and its histories, is produced precisely by the multivocalism of a text that self-consciously exploits contradiction and irony (perhaps reaching a climax with Arthur Ashe's little story about shaking hands with Jomo Kenyatta "filled with pride, wonder, and awe that the African tribes had retained their culture through a couple of hundred years of European domination"). The multinational capitalist consumer is made to feel at home in the world: "You'll never overheat or be at a loss for pockets, always look intelligently assembled. . . . You'll feel competent to haggle in the *shuk*, chat up the concierge, sample untranslatable cuisines."

Clearly, this is a stratagem designed both to neutralize and to legitimize the antagonisms of the colonial past and the inequities of the present. But I think it is also something more than that. I have argued elsewhere that one of the distinguishing features of the postmodernist text is its tendency, not simply to rewrite history or to reappropriate and redistribute already available and invested meanings, but to do this in such a way as to "cover over the realization and effects of an historical fall from an original plenitude"; in such a way as to usher in an "era of inflated truth" (multiplied and revisionist versions of reality); and so as to reassert the claims to power of the Author, the Producer.[26]

In its reappropriation of the images and facts of international inequalities, and at the same time arising out of and within contemporary systems of capital domination, Banana Republic's representations aim for just such an inflated truth. Like the kinds of postmodern literary and visual texts to which it is closely germane, the Banana Republic text is not just a series of appropriative moves and gestures. It can also be read as the symptom of an anxious disavowal of its own *moral* dimension. Its concern is to establish the moral veracity of its Author(s)/Producer(s), and the rewriting or restructuring of history is merely a means to that end. What I am suggesting is that at the end of the kaleidoscopic tunnel of the postmodernist text (art-text or commodity-text) there still sits the figure of that most traditional moral authority—the Author/Producer.

If those arguments are at all correct when applied to art-texts or to commodity-texts in postmodernism, they might be taken to suggest an approach to the critique of postmodernism that is different in emphasis from many of the already available ones. One of the more familiar tactics of the left is to claim that the postmodern era and its practices and artifacts are all up for grabs, all ready to be refunctioned or reappropriated for the left as much as for the right. This is the tactic recently advocated by Jameson: "to undo Postmodernism homeopathically by the methods of Postmodernism."[27] It might be equally useful not to forget another, perhaps more old-fashioned, tactic: to attack that covert authority in its den where it sits building an empire on the backs of . . .

NOTES

The author wishes to thank Patrick Hagopian and James Knippling for their comments on earlier drafts of this article.

1. My epigraph is constructed from a phrase in Donald Barthelme's story, "The Rise of Capitalism," in *Sixty Stories* (New York: Putnams, 1981), 207, and a phrase in the Banana Republic catalog for Spring 1986. Further references for catalog quotations will be given in parentheses in the text.

2. Hal Foster, *Recodings* (Port Townsend, Wash.: Bay Press, 1985), 122.

3. Foster, *Recodings*, 124. Compare the use of notions of de- and re-territorialization in Félix Guattari and Gilles Deleuze, *Anti-Oedipus: Capitalism and Schizophrenia* (Minneapolis: University of Minnesota Press, 1983), passim.

4. The "revolutions" in the technological and scientific apparatuses and their political arm, the so-called Reagan Revolution, are now accompanied by notions of revolutions in knowledge itself. See J. J. Servan-Schreiber, *The Knowledge Revolution* (Pittsburgh: Carnegie Mellon Press, 1986), for a particularly bizarre exposition of the technocrat's hopes for the automation and robotization of America's industrial base and the concomitant "manufacture" of new knowledges.

5. Before the inauguration of Banana Republic, Mel Ziegler was a journalist and writer. He was, for instance, credited as editor of Bella Abzug's autobiography, author of a novelization of the movie *Magnum Force* (starring Clint Eastwood) and of *Amen: The Diary of Rabbi Martin Siegel*. Patricia Ziegler was an illustrator and artist. The couple ran for a while an unsuccessful video production company, called Video Verite, making sixty-second spots for television (such as one featuring a convicted burglar talking about home security problems). The first Banana Republic catalogs were collaborations between the two of them, and they are still credited as copywriter and illustrator.

6. Information about Banana Republic (up to date through 1986) and quotations from Mel and Patricia Ziegler are taken from various press reports. Those available contain basically the same information. See, for example, the articles in the following: *Boston Globe*, 4 December 1986; *Daily News*, 21 January 1986; *Direct Marketing*, November 1985; *Metropolitan Home*, January 1985; *New York Times*, 20 August 1985; *San Francisco Sunday Examiner* "California Living Magazine," 11 August 1985.

7. In an equally familiar pattern, the U.S. textile industry is now "fighting back." Many firms are finding it helpful to concentrate on only one or two kinds of clothing or on specific fabric products such as towels or sheets. See "The Comeback Trail," *Business Week*, 8 June 1986. In 1986, some resistance to low-cost imports was, of course, also put up by means of political pressure for trade tariffs and protectionist legislation.

8. Folker Frobel, Jürgen Heinrichs, and Otto Kreye, *The New International Division of Labour* (Cambridge: Cambridge University Press, 1980), 319. This book analyzes the nature and economic effects of the new production and trade practices up to 1975 and, even a decade later, remains the best source.

FPZs and EPZs, which vary greatly in their formal characteristics, are, of course, not confined to economies of the South; indeed, among the first FPZs was the Shannon project in Ireland. Some FPZs began operation in the mid-sixties: those in Kandla, India (1965) and Kao-hsiung, Taiwan (1966), for example.

9. An indication of the turnover rate can be seen in the fact that The Limited and The Gap process about 250 million items of mostly women's clothing per week.

10. Ernest Mandel, *Late Capitalism* (London: New Left Books, 1975), 342.

11. The manufacturing sector has not produced new jobs in the United States since the late seventies. The vast increase in the rates of service and low-management employment comes with a dramatic decrease in per capita income. Between 1979 and 1985 over 40 percent of "new" jobs offered less than $7,400 per annum, and another 45% carried wages between $7,400 and $29,600. See "The Grim Truth About the Job 'Miracle,' " *New York Times*, 1 February 1987, section 3.

12. For a lucid account of the overdetermined causes, processes, and effects of capital flight in the United States, see Barry Bluestone and Bennett Harrison, *The Deindustrialization of America* (New York: Basic Books, 1982).

13. See especially Ernest Mandel, *Long Waves of Capitalist Development* (Cambridge: Cambridge University Press, 1980).

14. Mandel, *Late Capitalism*, 207, 222.

15. This claim is in fact one of the motifs in Volume 3 of *Capital*.

16. Mandel, *Long Waves of Capitalist Development*, viii.

17. Mandel, *Late Capitalism*, 500-522. A telling example is the following: "Mass distribution of Marxist literature—even via the market—ultimately means the mass formation (or heightening) of anti-capitalist consciousness. Ideological production that becomes a commodity in this way threatens to lose its objective function of consolidating the capitalist mode of production, *because of the nature of the use-value sold*" (p. 508; my emphasis).

18. The quotation is from Trinh Minh-ha's movie, *Naked Spaces: Living Is Round* (1985). The filmmaker expresses similar complaints against the "imaginary" function of the third world in Western leftist debate in an interview with Constance Penley and Andrew Ross, *Camera Obscura*, no. 13/14 (1985).

19. Fredric Jameson, "Postmodernism, or The Cultural Logic of Late Capitalism," *New Left Review*, no. 146 (1984), 56. There seems to me a problem in suggesting that this incursion of capital into the aesthetic realm is a postmodern phenomenon, since the commodification of art practice has been a feature of capitalism pretty much from its origins. At any rate, Jameson's general claim that the aesthetic has been wholly commodified is not really arguable. My own emphasis here is different: as I have suggested, in the example of Banana Republic a discourse (that of postmodern aesthetic practice) that had already been commodified *as* "aesthetic" is then taken up again directly into the realm of the "nonaesthetic."

20. Ibid., 92.

21. Ibid., 90.

22. There seem to me to be many other problems, not so much with Jameson's impulse in the article, but with his mode of analysis. For instance, the essay is marred (as are some of Jameson's other writings, such as *The Political Unconscious* [Ithaca: Cornell University Press, 1981], or "Imaginary and Symbolic in Lacan," *Yale French Studies*, nos. 55-56 [1977], 338-95) by an appropriation of Lacan and Althusser, which goes beyond his avowedly eclectic mode into the realm of error. An example of this in "Postmodernism . . ." is the claim (pp. 91-92) that what Althusser's use of Lacan's symbolic-imaginary-real triad "omitted was the dimension of the Lacanian Symbolic itself." Nothing could be further from the truth, as a quick glimpse at Althusser's two essays "Ideology and Ideological State Apparatuses" and "Freud and Lacan" (in *Lenin and Philosophy* [New York and London: Monthly Review Press, 1971]) demonstrates. For instance, Althusser spends several pages of "Freud and Lacan" (pp. 209-16) drawing

out the analogous features of Lacan's symbolic order and what he himself calls "the Law of Culture" or the "Law of Order." Althusser may himself have misappropriated Lacan in many respects, but his sense of the symbolic order was clear (see chapters 1 and 2 of my book, *Discerning the Subject* [Minneapolis: University of Minnesota Press, 1987], for discussion of this).

23. Joseph Schumpeter, *Capitalism, Socialism, and Democracy* (New York: Harper and Row, 1942).

24. See Gayatri Chakravorty Spivak, "The Rani of Sirmur: An Essay in Reading the Archives," *History and Theory* 24, no. 3 (1985), 258.

25. Supposedly each of these writers is rewarded by a $100 honorarium and 35 percent discount on Banana Republic clothing.

26. Paul Smith, "The Will to Allegory in Postmodernism," *The Dalhousie Review*, 62, no. 1 (1982), 105-22.

27. Jameson in an interview with Anders Stephanson, *Flash Art*, no. 131 (December 1986/January 1987), 71-2.

Feminism: The Political Conscience of Postmodernism?
Laura Kipnis

In these, the twilight years of Marxism (so it seems in the industrial-
ized West), a phrase still echoes through the shabby halls of left
theory, halls now bustling with better-dressed post-Marxists scratch-
ing out a story of crisis, decline, and aftermath. Here is the phrase:
"Marxism lacks a theory of the subject." Psychoanalysis, the preemi-
nent theory of the subject, was offered as a provisional remedy:
although initially and officially rejected by a stalwart orthodoxy
wielding such epithets as "bourgeois practice," it was periodically
taken up as a prosthetic device for this politically disabling missing
limb (as feminism has, in its turn, been called upon to supplement
Marxism's missing theory of gender). The unlikely alliance of the
theory of praxis and the talking cure was initially forged in the Frankfurt School, and later came, with Althusser's Lacan connection, to
offer the crucial missing link, a theretofore unwritten theory of ideology. This theoretical renovation would propel the next decade of
Marxist culturalists, while breakaway factions abandoned class altogether for the uncharted waters of sexuality, language, and other signifying practices, the political implications to which psychoanalytic
theory appears to offer access.

The similarly fraught relations between feminism and psychoanalysis can be organized into a comparable narrative. The early repudiation of the psychoanalytic as a prescription for patriarchy (and
Freud as patriarch personified) yielded to what might be called a
homeopathic approach—poison in small doses as a temporary
remedy, one whose curative powers, however, run the risk of producing in the healthy the symptoms of the disease. That this latex-

gloved appropriation of psychoanalysis as a "political weapon" might have ceded, at least in some corner of academic feminist theory, to a transferential relation as interminable as analysis itself is documented by Jane Gallop in her *Reading Lacan*,[1] which is itself both constitutive of and reflexive about the consequent formation of psychoanalytic theory as a professional subspecialty of literary studies. Gallop's book also yields a cautionary narrative about how the political imperative behind the psychoanalytic remedy becomes displaced in the intellectual *frissons* of continental theory. Like tourists seduced, or anthropologists gone native, an initial and tentative foray into the psychoanalytic landscape for accounts of the gendered subject and narrative pleasures seems to have resulted in permanent residence while oppositional elements have, in the meantime, pitched their tents in object relations and set to work constructing the countertheory of the powerful mother. As with Althusser for Marxists, the influence of Lacan within feminist theory seems to have been most definitive on feminist culturalism, particularly literary and film theory.

Despite this brief, tendentious sketch, this essay is not another attempt to effect a rapprochement in what has been described as "the unhappy marriage of Marxism and feminism." I want instead to account for a shared theoretical moment, or conjuncture: the moment in which a political orthodoxy turns heterodox and cohabits with what seemed, initially, the enemy. The narrative of the mésalliance turned true love is, of course, a powerful one in our culture— we have only to look to classics like *It Happened One Night* for an analysis of its structural conditions of possibility, for an account of how the carefully erected exclusion falls. (And it hardly needs pointing out that the tale of the feminist romance with Lacan itself strongly suggests the Harlequin formula: the hero may be, on the surface, rude, sexist, and self-absorbed, but it is he alone who knows the truth of the heroine's desire.)

This recourse to psychoanalysis (which provides no theory of social transformation and historically offers no evidence of political efficacy) in both Marxist and feminist theory seems to take place at a particular theoretical juncture: one marked primarily by the experience of political catastrophe and defeat. The political appropriation of psychoanalysis appears to signal, then, a lack—of a mass movement or of successful counterhegemonic strategies. The disastrous absorption of the European working-class movements into fascism, the decline of the political fortunes of feminism (outside the university) from those boisterous years when it seemed on the verge of becoming a mass movement, these are the events that have preceded the respective detours through the psychoanalytic. Notwithstanding Russell Jacoby's proviso that it is "the mystique of success that generates the fiction of defeat,"[2] the recourse to psychoanalytic theory appears to be implicated in this "dialectic of defeat," in that the appropriation of psychoanalysis invariably alludes to subjective factors recalcitrant to the particular social transformations at issue in the master theory. The political use-value of psychoanalytic theory would thus seem to be its updated account of the organization or etiology of *consent* to patriarchal or capitalist orders, which, as with the formation of the symptom, can now be seen to have its own characteristic form and specificity comparatively independent of its genesis. The emphasis here shifts away from the Gramscian "spontaneous consent" obtained in civil society, a conscious and rational acting-out of interest, and toward a theory of *unconscious* structures of consent negotiated in the suturing effects of various processes of signification, in the specularity of ideology, or in the very construction of gender. Any given assimilation of psychoanalytic theory to a political formulation can also be seen as an index of the chasmal distance between left intellectuals and popular consciousness, in that psychoanalysis here functions to close the gap left by the absence of a historical subject, discursively tying the people into a radical political logic, filling a "space left vacant by a crisis of what . . . should have been a normal historical development."[3]

Where there is a vehement political rejection of psychoanalytic theory—as in American radical feminism, which repudiated psychological explanations of women's behavior, stressing instead that it was "always and only a rational, self-interested response to their immediate material conditions, i.e., their oppression by men,"[4]—it appears to coincide with a denial of consent as a political factor, in favor of an insistence on coercion as the truth of political oppression. And a persistent criticism of cultural feminism,[5] radical feminism's successor, has been its focus on coercion played out in the emphasis on women's status as victim.[6] For a popular feminist theorist like Andrea Dworkin, pornography, rape, and violence against women are the central and absolute determining instances not only in *all* women's lives and psychology but in civilization as a whole. In cognate American academic feminism, we also see the rejection of psychoanalysis, as in, for example, the emotionally charged debate over Freud's repudiation of his seduction theory and the feminist insistence on sociological data of real rape and incest—real victimization—rather than the mere fantasy of seduction posited in the Oedipal theory, with its disturbing corollary, the sexual child.[7]

We can see that a psychoanalytically inflected political theory constructs a particular and specialized theoretical object. A filmic or literary text has to be construed as a symptom-producing entity in order to be an adequate object of psychoanalytic inquiry, whereas it must be, for example, a reflection of an anterior reality (or a disclosure of the real as for Lukács) in order to be held accountable for how it demonstrates that reality. If the theoretical object prescribes a set of theoretical strategies, it simultaneously describes a field of political possibility. Then implicit in the constitution of a theoretical object (i.e., a psychic topography of oppression as opposed to external structures of coercion, as above) is a representation of a political terrain. And as with all representation, there is here a certain appearance of transparency; the textual operations of its own production and organization of meaning are effaced. This is a strategy of containment as well as of possibility. Or, in other words, as would commonly be held in psychoanalytic criticism, this discursive field is structured by its absences and its repressions; it is equally a product of the territory it *cannot* represent. What emerges in the constitution of the theoretical object, then, is a dialectic of the representable and the nonrepresentable, or what is generally called an aesthetics.

The aesthetic topography of a political psychoanalysis lays out something like this. Both Marxist and feminist positions that reject the political appropriation of psychoanalysis seem to favor a realist aesthetics, which is often seen as having direct political effectivity: socialist realism obviously; Lukácsian critical realism (Lukács referred to Freud as a "devastating influence"); images-of-women criticism and the positive-images-of-women campaigns; the feminist appropriation of the realist novel and its project of inventing woman as full-speaking subject; and the politics of the antipornography movement, which relies on an aesthetics of reference to constitute its political object.

The characteristic mark of politico-psychoanalytic theory, however, seems to be the affiliation of politics and aesthetic modernism: strategies of negation, rupture, inwardness. Many theorists of modernism have found it impossible to theorize the twentieth-century avant-garde unless through Freud's theory of dreams and the unconscious. For other writers, only the reverse holds true: for Edward Said, not only is the attitude of modern writers toward the text an essentially Freudian posture, and modernist antinarrational textuality the textual solution of the Oedipal tangle, but Freud's *Interpretation of Dreams* is itself a protomodernist text.[8] And Dominick LaCapra has pointed out that the distinction between high, mass, and popular culture closely resembles and may, in certain respects, have *shaped* Freud's topology of id, ego, and superego, in that, in certain periods, high culture becomes aligned with official state culture in a hegemonic formation that tries to "establish a shared superego . . . extending to other sections of society and culture," an observation that provides an interesting gloss on modernist hegemony in our time.[9] The conjunctions of Marxism and modernism are less mutually constitutive, but equally well known.

The appropriation of psychoanalysis and its thematics of the subject to these various Marxist modernisms is particularly pertinent: initially for the Frankfurt School, and culminating in the Althusserian moment of *Screen*, in which Brecht was adopted as the heir apparent of Lacan and a Barthesian criterion of the writerly text was taken up as an antidote to the regime of phallic vision and the reproduction of the bourgeois subject. However, the current rearticulation of modernism by feminist theorists working at the intersections of deconstruction and psychoanalysis (a well-detailed account of which is given in Alice Jardine's report from the front lines of the French "feminine," *Gynesis*, subtitled *Configurations of Women and Modernity*[10]) suggests a repetitive tendency toward cultural modernism in marginalized vanguard political movements of today. In fact, the appropriation of psychoanalysis in Western Marxism and current feminism could be seen as an epiphenomenon of a regressive tendency toward modernism, problematic inasmuch as it is part of a larger impetus toward the aestheticization of the political, which I will be citing as a dynamic of the crisis of modernity. If psychoanalytic theory can, in this reading, be seen as filling a certain hiatus between politics and aesthetics, the postmodernist critique of modernism would seem to be the starting point in evaluating the consequences of this gesture and pointing a way toward a theory of the absences that constitute first-world radical theory at this juncture.

The problem of aesthetics and politics has been central to an understanding of the shortcomings of existing theories of political transformation. The brunt of Perry Anderson's critique in *Considerations on Western Marxism* is his assessment that Western Marxism devolved into an aesthetic theory dissociated from the political; its central concerns became philosophy and its theorists professional philosophers with little concern or interest in practical politics. Particularly after the war, their orientation was increasingly toward the university, which became both refuge and exile from the brute realities of political struggle outside the university gates. In their work, they maintained a "studied silence" in the areas central to the classic traditions of historical materialism: economics, politics, class struggle. According to Anderson, the very form of the Western Marxist tradition, in fact, takes shape precisely through the displacement of mass practice: theory became "an esoteric discipline whose highly technical idiom measures its distance from politics," a charge that Anderson levels to varying degree against all the denizens of Western Marxism, including, of course, the prescriptive modernism of the Frankfurt School, up to and through Althusser's theory of theoretical autonomy.[11]

The historical alliances of Marxism and modernism help to explain the ensemble of modernism and radical politics today. Indeed, it is perhaps a measure of the late reception of Frankfurt school theory in France that the return to modernism has taken center stage in continental feminism in the work of such writers as Kristeva, Cixous, Irigaray, and Wittig. It also indicates some of the confusions in mapping the affiliations of poststructuralism and postmodernism that these writers have often been classified as *postmodern*, when, in fact, the policies of *écriture féminine* and its practice of displacing revolution and politics to the aesthetic refer us back to that very modernist tradition that these continental theorists are presumed to transcend;[12] and their repudiation of representation, subjectivity, and history clearly set up the same antinomies with the popular that constituted aesthetic modernism from its inception. In this situation, however, rather than merely advocating such a cultural practice, a modernist aesthetic practice seems to be enacted in and through a theoretical-political practice. Political theory has now emerged as aesthetic expression per se, rather than being confined, as for earlier theorists, to the theory of aesthetic expression.

This aestheticization of theory one might see prefigured in Walter Benjamin's well-known warning about the "aestheticization of politics," and his counterprescription that "we" politicize aesthetics. What lurks here is the suggestion that this configuration of politics and aesthetics is not simply a characteristic of fascism, and its reversal not just a prescriptive for left culturalists, but that the configuration of the two is a structural particularity of capital in crisis, signaling the crisis of modernity. The third pole in this configuration would be, as Anderson points out, theory as an autonomous, disconnected activity. In Anderson's critique of a Western Marxist tradition divorced from politics, seeking refuge from political defeat in high culture, we see a theory no longer able to constitute its political object; in the rejection of mass practice, so neatly figured by Adorno's rejection of the New Left, theoretical practice becomes an autonomous moment, a moment later made explicit by Althusser, who saw theoretical practice as its own criterion with no need for verification from external practices. The post-Marxist critique of Marxism as fully implicated in the *grand recits* of modernity, and suffering from the same epistemological crisis, suggests that the crisis of Marxism and the decline of modernism are particularly intertwined. It is disturbing, then, to find the same configuration of politics, aesthetics, and theoretical autonomy that characterizes later Western Marxism operating in current feminist theory.

The earliest feminist appropriations of psychoanalysis for a political aesthetics (work carried out in the same milieu that produced Juliet Mitchell's 1974 defense of Freud, *Psychoanalysis and Feminism*) can be found in Pam Cook and Claire Johnston's writings in *Screen* during the early seventies and, later, Laura Mulvey's influential "Visual Pleasure and Narrative Cinema" (1975), in which psychoanalysis is taken up to demonstrate "the way the unconscious of patriarchal society has structured film form." From its inaugurating moment, this argument was made in the service of a modernist countercinematic practice—Mulvey is herself such a practitioner—and *against* mass culture, which is now repudiated not on the basis of its commodification, as it was for the Frankfurt school, but on the grounds of its phallocentrism, the critique that will be leveled against all forms of realist representation, including language itself. The political contradictions of this kind of left vanguardism seem clear enough. If the analysis of scopophilia in dominant cinema produces remedial cultural practices whose only audience is the traditional audience of high culture, it seems to suggest somehow luring the masses to *Riddles of the Sphinx* as a future political program.

Since the inception of the postmodernist critique of modernism as constituted by its binary opposition to popular culture, it has come to be accepted that the popular, modernism's antinomy, is fully present as a "present absence," in any consideration of modernism; and further, that it is against the "mass" of mass culture that the modernist program directs much of its oppositional energies. This immediately suggests that a politics that devotes itself to refining a modernist poetics is likely to involve an increasing gap between a popular and a marginal political position, and that the consequences of an aestheticism that hinges on increasing self-reference and autonomy from everyday social life might be an increasing distance between radical theory and political practice. Thus, the predilection toward modernism suggests a spiraling dynamic to this aesthetics of defeat: the rejection of and by the popular being compounded by a gravitation toward the hermetic.

What can we say about a feminist appropriation of psychoanalysis that works to reestablish relations of hierarchy in art, reinvesting in high culture while inveighing against a popular audience for its pleasure? Although one contradiction of this position is that, from the standpoint of modernism, mass culture tends to be coded female,[13] it is also conceivable that the "radical political weapon" of psychoanalysis leads into an aestheticizing tendency in feminist theory that is essentially neo-Kantian: a conservative reinvestment in aesthetic autonomy that has provoked, in other quarters, the classification of poststructuralism as "New New Criticism." And with this particular invocation of the aesthetic, one might suspect that the transcendental subject can't be far behind. Interestingly enough, it was Adorno, in his aesthetic writings, who pointed to the similarity in matters aesthetic between the two seemingly antithetical thinkers who form the axis of psychoanalytic modernism, Kant and Freud. For both, Adorno points out, the work of art exists *only* in relation to the subject, but also, by "placing works of art squarely into a realm of psychic immanence . . . [both] lose sight of their antithetical relation to the nonsubjective." Adorno, with his quirky dialectics, explains the mutual blindness like this:

> Perhaps the most important taboo in art is the one that prohibits an animal-like attitude toward the object, say a desire to devour it or otherwise subjugate it to one's body. Now the strength of such a taboo is matched by the strength of the repressed urge. Hence, all art contains in itself a negative moment from which it tries to get away.[14]

This suggests that a political aesthetic that attempts to break with forms of address it characterizes as reaffirming the subject's imaginary coherence does, in fact, hinge on a subjectivity that the aesthetic field is itself constituted by (a universal subjectivity according to Kant). This mutual interdependence of subject and aesthetic is not in any way challenged by a repertoire of modernist techniques now recycled as the break with the scopophilia of visual mass culture and the phallocentrism of language. It is precisely this gap between a radical dismantling of the subject, and the conservative, aestheticist, and antipopulist aesthetic practices that this dismantling puts into circulation and would seem, in fact, to dictate, that I want to explore.

It is clear that the question of subjectivity lies at the epicenter of the current reformulation of modernism. Within what can broadly be called current left theory—Marxism, feminism, left poststructuralism—"the subject" is a rubric that now seems to determine just what political questions we may ask. This "subject" we know by its traits: it is split; it speaks; it is gendered; it is social, or it is a linguistic effect; it is castrated, and it thinks it knows so much. Alternatively, we have its obituary, as narrated by Baudrillard among others: it is occultated, disappears, and dies. Given that discourse is also productive, it is hard not to see this theoretical proliferation of the subject—its production as a site of attention, investigation, and speculation—as symptomatic of some kind of necessity. Its insistent visibility, which provides a certain bolstering of the category itself, provokes the question of what exactly it is that the subject needs bolstering against—its fragmentation in the chop shop of late capitalism, or perhaps some glimmer of self-knowledge that the necessary historical precondition for a critique of the subject is the loss of its legitimating function? What other political determinations can account for such excessive visibility of a category that operated precisely from a blindness to its own determinations, whose greatest desire was to turn itself into an effect of nature? This subject that drops its veils one by one to reveal its naked status as construction, rather than nature, bares everything *except* the answer to its insistent appearance: if everywhere we look the subject is all that is visible, what is it that is hidden?

Inasmuch as the subject is itself an ideological category, the question of its current hypervisibility must be profoundly political; notwithstanding that the field of the visual, as Lacan makes clear, is itself bound up with the constitution of subjectivity. Visibility is a complex system of permission and prohibition, of presence and absence, punctuated alternately by apparitions and hysterical blindness. Let us suppose, initially, that this visibility of the subject, so necessarily tied to the loss of its legitimating function, is another dynamic of the closing off of the political space of modernity, in which consolidation of political power took place under the banner of Enlightenment rationality and reason. In the "centered subject," with its synecdochical relation to the political centrality of the West, lay a mandate to make the rest of the world its object: of conquest, knowledge, surplus-value. Then, in the recent appearance of the category of the "de-centered subject," lurks the synecdoche of the decline of the great imperial powers of modernity, the traumatic loss of hegemony of the West, which here in the psychic economy of the United States, we have continually reflected back to us in compensatory fantasies like *Rambo*, *Red Dawn*, and Ronald Reagan.

What is interesting about this waning modernity is the theoretical crisis it engenders, in which the traditional narratives of liberation fall under suspicion, opening a theoretical void that these various modernisms attempt, but are unable, to fill. What is crucially lacking is a postmodern political discourse. I want to attempt to trace this symptomatic gap as it is manifested in first-world feminist theory, which seems to be suspended between an emergent postmodern political logic and a residual modernism.

It is now common, in feminist theory, to distinguish broadly between Anglo-American feminism on the one hand and continental feminism on the other. This is clearly an inadequate formulation, yet the distinction that emerges in this bifurcation is one I want to momentarily maintain for heuristic purposes: it is a distinction between competing theories of representation, derived from a posture toward the signifier. Terry Eagleton has observed that the history of Marxism itself follows the Saussurean trajectory of the linguistic sign: "First we had a referent, then we had a sign, now we just have a signifier," and according to Eagleton's schema, this final moment, the autonomy of the signifier, is identified with Althusserian Marxism.[15] These successive moments of the sign seem to occur simultaneously within current feminist theory, with the divisions drawn nominally according to *nation* rather than *chronos*, and with the culminating moment of the autonomy of the signifier associated, for feminism, with Lacan, rather than Althusser.

What is generally called American feminism generally relies on a theory of language as transparency. This entails a belief in a recoverable history, in authored productions, in the focus on speech over language, in the conscious over the unconscious, and in the phallus as a biological, rather than a symbolic, entity. In this camp, it is a short trip from a sign to a referent, and this produces, as sites of political engagement, the struggle for the terrain of the realist novel, the demand for access to the discourse of subjectivity, the possibility of an isolated sign or image as a potential site for political action, and in general, a politics of reformism.

Continental, or poststructural, feminism, in contrast to American feminism, follows the Saussurean division of the sign; emphasizes the materiality of the signifier; privileges the synchronic over diachronic, structure over subject, and signification over meaning; and asserts that women have no position from which to speak. Its focus on the priority of system marks the unconscious as the privileged area of exploration and modernist rupture as the privileged aesthetic practice. From this vantage point, the priority of both psychoanalytic theory and modernist aesthetics in poststructural feminism can be seen as a by-product of the Saussurean legacy of the synchronic, which runs through Lévi-Strauss to Lacan.

The contention of poststructural feminists is that naming the political subject of feminism *the female sex* reproduces the biological essentialism and the binary logic that have relegated women to an inferior role. (Kristeva: "The belief that 'one is a woman' is almost as absurd and obscurantist as the belief that 'one is a man.' "[16]) This contention produces, as a site of political attention and engagement, a "space" rather than a sex: the margin, the repressed, the absence, the unconscious, the irrational, the feminine—in all cases the negative or powerless instance. Whereas "American feminism" is a discourse whose political subject is biological women, "continental

feminism" is a political discourse whose subject is a structural position—variously occupied by the feminine, the body, the Other.
From these radical insights of continental feminism we move to
the practice of *écriture féminine*, which in posing a counterlanguage
against the binary patriarchal logic of phallogocentrism, is an attempt
to construct a language that enacts liberation rather than merely theorizing it. For Cixous, it is the imaginary construction of the female
body as the privileged site of writing; for Irigaray, a language of
women's laughter in the face of phallocratic discourse; for both, private, precious languages that rely on imaginary spaces held to be outside the reign of the phallus: the pre-Oedipal, the female body, the
mystical, women's relation to the voice, fluids.[17]

Here we have, once again, the assertion of a political praxis
through essentially modernist textual practices, which relegates the
analysis of the symbolic construction of alterity into an aestheticism
that closes off referentiality like blinders on a horse: in this notion of
literary "productivity," the text itself comes to operate as a transcendental signified, as an ultimate meaning.[18] The attempt to straitjacket
these designated spaces into the text seems an essentially defensive
maneuver, safeguarding against their escape beyond the confines of
écriture into wider social praxis by limiting the dissemination of
these forms of knowledge to the consumers of avant-garde culture.

What would it mean to find these operations now in literary confinement, these procedures held to deconstruct binarisms, dismantle
phallocentrism, and decenter subjects, *outside* writing, to suspend
the current orthodoxy that reality and history are simply texts, while
retaining the radical insights of feminist deconstruction? It is worth
noting that another theoretical discourse, dependency theory in economics (a theory closely linked in time frame to poststructuralism),
in which the object of attention is not textual but is, rather, the connection between economic development and underdevelopment in
the unequal exchange relations of first to third world, tells a story
very similar to that of poststructural feminism, in its account of the
mechanisms by which a dominant term comes to repress a secondary term. And in *this* telling, the deconstruction of these binarisms is
anything but a symbolic practice.[19]

A narrative has emerged in postmodernist theory that reads something like this. Feminism is the paradigmatic political discourse of
postmodernism.[20] Its affirmation of the absence, the periphery, the

Other—spaces in which the position of women is structurally and politically inscribed—has more current political credibility than Marxism, a patriarchal discourse of "mastery/transparency/rationalism," a master code issuing from a transcendent point of view, the path that leads from "totality to totalitarianism, from Hegel to the gulag."

A slightly different narrative can be pieced together from these elements. If Marxism is viewed as the radical political discourse of modernity, and feminism as the radical political discourse of postmodernity, it can be seen that each functions as a dominant articulating principle through which other, disparate political struggles enunciate the possibility of political transformation. According to the crisis-in-Marxism theorists, Marxism's primary and vestigial ambition to unify isolated working-class struggles into a mass movement of the proletariat has hampered its ability today to provide articulations for new and emerging political positions—given transformations in the nature of labor and in the types of world geopolitical struggles of postcolonialism—in addition to its perceived inability to seriously theorize the subalternity of women.

The emergence in feminist theory of the periphery, the absence, and the margin implies a theory of women not as class or caste, but as colony—and this was in fact an analysis made early on in American feminism (and earlier still in Simone de Beauvoir's depiction of woman as Other) by women in SDS casting their controversial break with the male-dominated Left in the political rhetoric of the day:

> As we analyze the position of women in capitalist society and
> especially in the United States we find that women are in a colonial
> relationship to men and we recognize ourselves as part of the Third
> World. (1967)[21]

What this analogy (whose genealogy can be traced back through the New Left, the relation of the New Left to the black-power movement, and the crucial influence on black power by African decolonization movements) suggests is that the theoretical emergence of these political spaces now being described by continental feminists parallels the narrative of the decline of the great imperial powers of modernity, the liquidation of the European empires and the postcolonial rearrangements of the traditional centers on a world scale. It is France, after all, that has produced an influential body of theory based on the centrality of castration in the construction of human subjectivity. Perhaps this is why the American reception of Lacan has been primarily as a literary theory: to confine this disturbing knowledge to the text and recycle it through the recuperative apparatus of literary humanism, rather than allowing the emergence of France as the world capital of theory to perhaps be read as the sequel of its own political decentering and loss of mastery—in the war, in Indochina, in North Africa.

Yet, much of European postwar decolonization took place out of practical and economic necessity more so than out of ideological conviction: the colonial mind persists long after its political and economic structures have been dismantled. Continental feminism offers a radical structural analysis of operations it prefers to call phallogocentrism, but then retreats from the implications of its own analysis into the autonomy of the text, seizing on a modernist refusal of reference to enact its ambivalence. Continental feminism would seem to be the most potentially radical current in contemporary political theory, freeing itself from the essentialism and the liberal tradition of American feminism. Yet, it also seems beset by the same conjunctural elements associated with the depoliticization of Western Marxism, prone to aestheticization, theoretical autonomy, and a deliberate distance from political praxis. It identifies the structural position of a new political subject, inscribing itself into that moment, and is then paralyzed by this knowledge and by its own first-world status, hysterically blind to the geopolitical implications of its own program. And legitimately so, because the knowledge offered here is not benign. It is that real shifts in world power and economic distribution have little to do with *jouissance*, the pre-Oedipal, or fluids, and that the luxury of first-world feminism to dwell on such issues depends on the preservation of first-world abundance guaranteed by systematic underdevelopment elsewhere and by the postponement, by whatever means, of the political decentering that will mean the close of that historical epoch.

This paper was first written during the week of the U.S. bombing of Libya, so euphemistically presented to us by our ruling powers as a "surgical strike." This phrase, along with Reagan's memorable diagnosis of Qaddafi as "flaky," brings to mind another form of surgical strike, the lobotomy, so often performed with ice picks and on women, following the diagnosis of irrationality. Here we have Qaddafi, cast in the role of Frances Farmer, with the U.S. in the role of psychiatric surgeon. (That the colonial is coded female has been clear enough even without the *New York Post*'s artist's rendering of Qaddafi as a woman.) Our network news these days is full of irrational Libyans and irrational Palestinians, needing a little frontal-lobe job, and its own ideological mission is now admitted so freely that CBS's latest slogan for its news is "We keep America on top of the world." The diagnosis of national aspirations that don't coincide with the master plan of the West is "psychopathology," which demands a "cure"—the full array of state-repressive apparatuses: for Libyans, bombs; in the case of women, rape, battery, confinement, and medical and psychiatric abuse—repressive apparatuses in a familial guise.

As is shown in the current hysteria over "international terrorism"—the ultimate conspiracy theory into which our government has managed to fuse the Soviet Union, Islamic fundamentalism, the Sandinistas, and Palestinian nationalism—the reaction to any decentering telos is symptomatic blindness rather than insight: there is an unwillingness and inability to fully comprehend this phenomenon of shifts in power and spheres of influence, and of new forms of political struggle in which civilian tourists are held responsible for the actions of their governments. When retaliation is taken, as has been announced, for "American arrogance," *this* is the postmodern critique of the Enlightenment; it is, in fact, a decentering; it is the margin, the absence, the periphery, rewriting the rules from its own interest.

By associating feminism with these other political struggles and with a particular historical space, I do not mean to efface gendered oppression or actual historical women in the name of some putatively greater oppression. The rise of the current women's movement paralleled (and, according to some more unreconstructed elements, caused) the decline of the black-power movement in the United States, suggesting a metonymy of struggle within this historical space. If feminism *is* read as a decolonizing movement, allied with other decolonizing movements, this is, in a sense, to say that the Right is right when it identifies feminism as a threat to the "American way of life." Yet, this latent knowledge of the political stakes produces the impasse that I think we currently see in feminist theory: after the critique of liberal reformism, after the dismantling of the biologistic, but uplifting, fable that women will, given the chance, construct a nonhierarchical political utopia, the political options are indeed narrower. It is either "out of the mainstream and into the revolution," or out of the revolution and into the text. On the local level, the decline of the narratives of liberation of modernity and the retreat from the political implications of postmodernity have left the field wide open for the Right, which has successfully fought on the terrain of popular interpellation: controlling the terms of popular discourse, arrogating the terrain of nature, family, community, and the fetus; not hesitating to appropriate and rearticulate a traditionally left rhetoric of liberation and empowerment. It is striking that Phyllis Schlafly's antifeminist manifesto, *The Power of the Positive Woman* (1977), opens with the question, "How are women to acquire power in the world?"[22] and in fact, Schlafly modeled herself into one of the most effective political figures outside electoral politics in the United States by using the rhetoric of disenfranchisement to mobilize radical feminism's Other—suburban housewives—into an effective political force. By manipulating the exclusions admittedly operating in feminist discourse of the seventies to marshal fear and *ressentiment* among women who saw feminism as elitist and classist and the ERA (Equal Rights Amendment) as a threat to their tenuous hold on any corner of empowerment in the world, Schlafly created a grass-roots movement that turned the expected ratification of the ERA by liberal feminists into a crashing defeat.

What this suggests is that the insights of a left postmodernism's renegotiation of the popular are relevant to a feminist theory that is increasingly unable to interpellate a popular audience or capture a popular imagination. Instead, avant-gardist strategies of negation— proffered as a counterforce to the technics of a popular culture dedicated to the production of the spuriously self-identified subject— end up producing their own Other: the "mass" of mass culture that resides outside the vanguard elite, outside the intelligentsia, and outside the university. If the popular is seen as an access to hegemony rather than an instrument of domination, what follows is a postmodern strategy of struggle over the terrain of popular interpellation, an acknowledgment that hegemony is won rather than imposed.

But this again presumes that we are only the subject of political transformation, rather than the object. The hypervisibility of the subject, the symptom that introduced this etiology of current theory, parallels its deconstruction on the world stage. The neomodernist desire to locate the space of the margin and the absence within the text—to hold that theory has autonomously arrived at the point at which it achieves recognition of the periphery—is simply to theorize again from first-world interest, to display a hysterical blindness to the fact that the periphery has forced itself upon the attention of the center. To the extent that any deconstructive theory prioritizes the autonomous text, it maintains this blindness; it reinvents and reinvests in the centrality of that center. To the extent that a feminist theory discovers these crucial spaces in textual rather than in political practice, it indicates the resistance of first-world feminists to the dangerous knowledge that in a *world* system of patriarchy, upheld by an international division of labor, unequal exchange and the International Monetary Fund, we first-world feminists are also the beneficiaries.

NOTES

1. Jane Gallop, *Reading Lacan* (Ithaca: Cornell University Press, 1985).

2. Russell Jacoby, *Dialectic of Defeat: Contours of Western Marxism* (New York: Cambridge University Press, 1981).

3. Ernesto Laclau and Chantal Mouffe, *Hegemony and Socialist Strategy: Toward a Radical Democratic Politics* (London: Verso, 1985), 48. Laclau and Mouffe adapt the psychoanalytic theory of suture to theoretical discourse, their discussion of which has influenced the relationship I have made of psychoanalysis and aesthetics.

4. Ellen Willis, "Radical Feminism & Feminist Radicalism," in *The 60s Without Apology*, ed. Sohnya Sayres et al. (Minneapolis: University of Minnesota Press, 1984), 97.

5. The term *cultural feminism* refers to a position within American feminism based on the belief in an immutable male and female sexual essence, or nature, primarily seen as biologically determined rather than culturally constructed. It equates women's liberation with the establishment and practice of a female counterculture based on "female values" such as reciprocity, intimacy, nurturance, and nonviolence. This tendency, probably now the dominant one in mainstream feminism, is the backbone of the feminist antipornography movement, among whose leaders are some of the principal theoreticians of cultural feminism. See Alice Echols, "The New Feminism of Yin and Yang," in *Powers of Desire: The Politics of Sexuality*, ed. Ann Snitow et al. (New York: Monthly Review Press, 1983), 439-59.

6. For an exemplary cultural text in this idiom see Linda Lovelace's *Ordeal* (New York: Citadel/Berkeley, 1980). Catherine MacKinnon, the antipornography activist, has argued that women cannot be considered capable of informed consent within the context of patriarchy (in debate with Ellen Willis, Champaign-Urbana, July 1983), and it is this disavowal that women can be anything but complete victims that authorizes Lovelace's narrative (of being held hostage for over five years and forced to make porn movies) as a feminist parable.

7. See, for example, Christine Froula, "The Daughter's Seduction: Sexual Violence and Literary History," *Signs* (Summer 1986), 621-44.

8. Edward Said, *Beginnings* (New York: Columbia University Press, 1985), 169-73.

9. Dominick LaCapra, "History and Psychoanalysis," *Critical Inquiry* (Winter 1987), 245.

10. Alice Jardine, *Gynesis: Configurations of Woman and Modernity* (Ithaca: Cornell University Press, 1985). Jardine tends to use the term *modernity* rather than modernism, and those writers she classifies as postmodernist I would see as modernist — Jardine's analysis doesn't theorize modernism through its antinomy to the popular, enabling the correlation of poststructuralism and postmodernism.

11. Perry Anderson, *Considerations on Western Marxism* (London: Verso, 1976), see chapter 3, "Formal Shifts."

12. Andreas Huyssen, "Mapping the Postmodern" *New German Critique* 33 (Fall 1984), 38. Huyssen is referring to theories of textuality in general.

13. This point is raised by both Tania Modleski in "The Terror of Pleasure: The Contemporary Horror Film and Postmodern Theory," and Andreas Huyssen in "Mass Culture as Woman: Modernism's Other," both in *Studies in Entertainment: Critical Approaches to Mass Culture*, ed. Tania Modleski (Bloomington: Indiana University Press, 1986).

14. Theodor Adorno, *Aesthetic Theory* (New York: Routledge & Kegan Paul, 1984), 16-17.

15. Terry Eagleton, "The End of English" (Paper delivered at the School of the Art Institute of Chicago, April 1986).

16. Julia Kristeva, "Women Can Never Be Defined," in *New French Feminisms*, ed. Elaine Marks and Isabelle de Courtivron (New York: Shocken Books, 1981), 137.

17. See Toril Moi's *Sexual/Textual Politics* (New York: Methuen, 1985) for a comparison of the Anglo-American and continental traditions and a critique of the politics of *écriture féminine*.

18. Fredric Jameson, *The Prison House of Language* (Princeton: Princeton University Press, 1972), 182. Jameson is writing about *Tel Quel* here (including Kristeva), and about Derrida, who has invented a new transcendental signified, "namely that of script itself."

19. On dependency theory see André Gunder Frank, *Capitalism and Underdevelopment in Latin America* (New York: Monthly Review Press, 1969).

20. Two recent examples in aesthetic theory are Craig Owens's "The Discourse of Others: Feminists and Postmodernism," in *The Anti-Aesthetic: Essays on Postmodern Culture*, ed. Hal Foster (Port Townsend, Wash.: Bay Press, 1983), and Huyssen's "Mass Culture as Woman."

21. Quoted in Alice Echols, *The Radical Feminist Movement in the United States, 1967-75* (unpublished doctoral dissertation, University of Michigan, 1986), 32.

22. Phyllis Schlafly, *The Power of the Positive Woman* (New York: Jove, 1977).

Putting the Pop Back into Postmodernism
Lawrence Grossberg

Discussions of postmodernism increasingly dominate writings in cultural theory and criticism, and they are already entering into more popular discourses of and about popular culture. But the term *postmodernism* is beguiling, not only because it appears to place us outside history, or, at least, already within the future, but also because it is such a "readerly" term; it leaves so much to the imagination of the reader. Although everyone seems to agree that significant changes have occurred in almost all the domains of our lives, and that new cultural, social, and historical elements and configurations are active in the contemporary world, there is little agreement about how to interpret these changes, or even where to begin the "diagnosis" of the "postmodern." As with other terms of periodization, the issue is not its origins but its resonances and the particular ways in which it has slid from one discourse into another. Its embrace of multiple codings and rejection of hierarchies have defined a radical antiessentialism that has rapidly spread into the arts and art criticism, popular culture, and finally, in the inevitable return of the repressed, to a description of new forms of historical existence and social experience.

Within each of the domains in which postmodernism has appeared, there have been debates about the various emergent practices, about the extent of their dominance of the terrain, and about whether they are actually new practices or merely inflections and configurations of already existing ones. But the real locus of debate has been the question of the relations between the domains. The most powerful claim of the discourses of postmodernism is to have defined a significant register or plane of contemporary life that cuts across the various domains of existence. Like so many other terms of cultural theory, *postmodernism* moves, perhaps too quickly and easily, between cultural and sociohistorical questions. There is little agreement about the nature and structure of the relations that cut across the domains, about the connections between economic and political structures, social relations and historical developments, cultural practices and lived experiences. Here we find that the postmodernist debates have often merely repeated many of the assumptions of previous controversies in cultural politics, by assuming that the connections between various elements are self-revealing.[1]

Even more disturbing is the assumption that the very "postmodernity" of particular practices or events can be read directly off their surfaces, especially since a founding insight of postmodernism is that it has become increasingly difficult to confidently assume the identity or significance of particular events. Some would claim that this is a result of a crisis in theory and criticism in which the text has become a babel of voices and the audience a fragmented mob wildly appropriating what they can into their own lives. Others have argued that it is a result of real changes that have taken place and are now coded, however obliquely, into the various social and cultural practices that define contemporary life in late capitalism. The problem of interpreting any cultural text, social practice, or historical event must always involve constructing a context around it, mapping out its lines of connection with other practices, texts, relations, and so on. Such contexts are not merely a matter for empirical investigation, although such investigations are necessary if the contexts are not to become the imaginary projections of particular empowered communities, e.g., the intertextual fantasies of critics. In the case of cultural practices, these contexts include, but are not exhausted by, topographies of consumption and taste that determine which of the vast intertextual possibilities are effective. But contexts are not entirely empirically available because they are not already completed, stable configurations, passively waiting to receive another element. They are not guaranteed in advance but are rather the site of contradictions, conflicts, and struggles.

In Gramscian terms, any interpretation (for that matter, any historical practice) is an articulation, an active insertion of a practice into a set of contextual relations that determines the identity and effects of both the text and the context. Articulation is the continuous deconstruction and reconstruction of contexts. These articulated connections are sometimes fought over, consciously or unconsciously, but in any case, an articulation is always accomplished (a victory can be won without a battle) and will always have political consequences. The notion of articulation abandons critical theories built upon models of communication, of the difference between encoding (production) and decoding (consumption), a difference that divides interpretation into the search for intended or preferred meanings and received or effective meanings. Articulation rejects the assumption that the two moments are, even analytically, separable, as if each were completed or completable. Instead, it describes the ongoing struggle to produce the text by inserting it into a network of "naturalized" relations. Encoding is a continuous force (e.g., producers continue to make statements), and decoding is already active in the efforts to encode. One cannot separate the materiality of a text from its appropriation, nor can one separate structures from practices.

The theory of articulation has important implications for our understanding of the relations between domination, subordination, resistance, and opposition. Its disdain for any assumed historical necessity and its emphasis on the reality of struggle direct the critic toward the complex and contradictory relations of power that intersect and organize an audience's relation to particular cultural texts. It does not say that people always struggle, or that when they do, they do so in ways we condone. But it does say, both theoretically and politically, that people are never merely passively subordinated, never totally manipulated, never entirely incorporated. People are engaged in struggles with, within, and sometimes against real tendential forces and determinations in their efforts to appropriate what they are given. Consequently, their relations to particular practices and texts are complex and contradictory: they may win something in the struggle against sexism and lose something in the struggle against economic exploitation; they may both gain and lose something economically; and although they lose ideological ground, they may win some emotional strength. If peoples' lives are never merely determined by the dominant position, and if their subordination is always complex and active, understanding culture requires us to look at how practices are actively inserted at particular sites of everyday life and at how particular articulations empower and disempower their audiences.

In this respect, we need to recognize that empowerment can take a variety of forms; in particular, there is a difference between positive and negative empowerment.[2] Most cultural criticism focuses on culture's critical relation (negativity) to the dominant positions and ideologies. Politics becomes defined as resistance to or emancipation from an assumed reality; politics is measured by difference. But empowerment can also be positive; celebration, however much it ignores relations of domination, can be enabling. Opposition may be constituted by living, even momentarily, within alternative practices, structures, and spaces, even though they may take no notice of their relationship to existing systems of power. In fact, when one wins some space within the social formation, it has to be filled with something, presumably something one cares for passionately. The "functionalism" of the identity that is constructed here opens the possibilities of positive empowerment. And it is here that questions of desire and pleasure must be raised as more than secondary epiphenomena. Critical theory too often sees pleasure as, at best, a momentary disruption of structures of power that is inevitably recuperated; it never explores the actual functioning of pleasure itself. Moreover, it tends to locate pleasure within romantic traditions of opposition (e.g., urban pleasures are valorized more often than suburban).[3] Although such moments of passion and positivity are never necessarily politicized, they do constitute a part of the terrain of everyday life that we must enter into to open up its contradictions, thereby "renovating and making 'critical' an already existing activity."[4] In fact, the debates about postmodernism define an important site of articulation and struggle in the contemporary world. If we accept that new practices and events have appeared on the cultural and historical terrain (the postmodern), their significance and politics are never guaranteed in advance.[5] How they are articulated—interpreted, appropriated, located within larger configurations of social and cultural practices— will determine their meanings and effects for new forms of popular political struggle. Consequently, we must challenge the very terms within which the postmodernist debates have structured the terrain, refusing to accept that their assumptions about these emergent cultural configurations merely describe a taken-for-granted reality, a new common sense. Nietzsche warns us that when we study monsters, we must take care to avoid becoming monsters. Yet the post-modernists have often constructed the world, and the people in it, in their own images of monstrosity. They have expunged the functional positivity from the culture of everyday life; they have ignored the complexity of the articulation of such practices in everyday life and failed to examine the extent to which and the ways in which these practices are empowering.

The Postmodernist Debates

It is crucial to remind ourselves that postmodernism is only one way of demarcating the intellectual and political terrain and could be contrasted with the broader difference that has been more recently suggested by notions of "post-Enlightenment" culture.[6] This has important consequences for the way in which the field has been historically and structurally constituted. For example, postmodernism makes aesthetic difference the measure, if not the agent, of historical difference. Consequently, the antiessentialism of postmodern practices—their celebration of the local, the contextual, the fragment— can only function as the negation of modernist practices. To accept this, however, is to assume that this antiessentialism is inherent within and self-evidently available upon the surface of postmodern practices. Thus, the debates begin by assuming that practices speak their own truth, a truth that is not constructed but merely reported. Further, its privileging of the aesthetic often leads to a particular reading of essentialism that privileges identity over difference and, hence, to a reading of antiessentialism as the celebration of difference. This conflation of the postmodern with poststructuralism ignores the more radical vision that rejects the very logic of identity and difference. The European theorists—often cited as the sources of postmodern critical work, including Baudrillard, Foucault, Deleuze, and Guattari—have all argued for a theory of otherness rather than difference. For example, Baudrillard has argued, against Marx and Saussure, that the erasure of the privileged term of identity (e.g., the signified, or use-value) cannot be taken to suggest the primacy of productive difference captured in the second term (e.g., the signifier, or exchange-value). Difference itself collapses into ineffectivity. If there is no signified, there is no signifier; to say that everything has become exchange-value is to render the very concept of exchange value useless. There is no reality waiting behind the surfaces that increasingly replace them; the very difference between surface and reality is ineffective.[7]

There are, I would argue, three interrelated but independent sites of debate within postmodernist discourses: ideology, power, and historical ontology. Again, the primacy of the aesthetic in structuring the field makes it almost inevitable that the dominant concern of the postmodernist debates is ideological and textual. Postmodern practices are usually described by constructing a set of features that are necessarily constitutive, features that express or embody the contemporary ineffectivity of the difference between signifier and signified, image and reality, original and copy, identity and difference, part and whole, surface and depth, truth and politics. In various combinations, postmodern practices are described — negatively — as denying totality, coherence, closure, expression, origin, representation, meaning, teleology, freedom, creativity and hierarchy; and — positively — as celebrating discontinuity, fragmentation, rupture, surfaces, diversity, chance, contextuality, egalitarianism, pastiche, heterogeneity, quotations, and parodies. Yet this description of a practice of reflexive fragmentation renders it available only in its purely negative aspect — as antiessentialism — since these practices are all present in, if not significantly constitutive of, the modernist project. This is often responded to with a second condition: namely, that the particular postmodernity of a specific practice can only be understood as a negation of a narrowly constructed tradition of modernism. This avoids the more complex question of the relations between modern and postmodern practices.

There are two major positions within the postmodernist debates over the ideological status of particular practices: the first, rooted in art criticism, is concerned with the commodity status of the work of art and its relationship to the larger context of commodification and the politics of representation; the second, rooted in literary criticism, reads texts as signs of history. The former, most clearly presented in the work of Hal Foster, Craig Owens, Rosalind Krauss, and Andreas Huyssen,[8] is predicated on the assumption that "in cultural politics today, a basic opposition exists between a postmodernism which seeks to deconstruct modernism and resist the status quo and a postmodernism which repudiates the former to celebrate the latter: a postmodernism of resistance and a postmodernism of reaction."[9] This distinction replaces and displaces the older (and admittedly exhausted) distinctions between high and mass art and between the avant-garde and mainstream culture, but, at the same time, it structurally reproduces, within the aesthetic field itself, an intrinsic ideological difference between "authentic" works—which necessarily resist the commodification of art and life—and "coopted" works— which allow and even celebrate their own commodification. Insofar as the distinction does not correspond to different points of origin (modes of production) or reception (audiences), the elitism of the old mass culture debates has disappeared. But insofar as the distinction is located within "the text itself," in how the text determines its own consumption (often transposed back to the intentions of the artist), old forms of elitism have merely been superseded by new forms. Even if we accept the premise that the distinction exists as it has been described, and that it can be read off of textual differences, such an aesthetics of postmodernism fails to question the place of such practices—even the celebration of the commodity—within the everyday lives of people. It is simply assumed that such practices, whether in relations of production or consumption, can have no positive function. Pleasure, for example, can only be politically correct as the pleasure—however temporary—of resistance; only when positivity is derived from negativity can it be politically justified.

The work of Fredric Jameson[10] is the clearest example of a position within the postmodernist debates that reads cultural practices as the ideological sign of contemporary history. Jameson sees the "truth" of postmodern cultural practices, not on their surfaces (although their status as postmodern is given on their surfaces), but in their relationship to a deep structure (a metanarrative) of real historical processes: the transformation from monopoly to late capitalism, multinationalism, and the saturation of everyday life by the commodity form. For Jameson, postmodern texts are the displaced signs of the new political-economic context, a displacement that is accomplished by the mediation of experience. Textual practices are not merely the reflections of economic structures; they are the expressions of how we experience such structures, experiences already contaminated by ideology. Culture expresses and determines experience, which, in turn, reflects and is determined by political-economic reality. Textual fragmentation is a sign of the real fragmentation of our subjectivity, which is itself a sign of the intentional (both ideological and material) fragmentation of space in multinational capitalism. Once again, in Jameson's account, there is little space for the pleasures of such texts, for the ways they are used as the sites of celebration and empowerment by people in their everyday lives. Michele Barrett[11] has pointed to the appallingly negative image of pleasure operating in this theory. This is evident, for example, in Jameson's inability to acknowledge the new forms of social activities and relations that have emerged, especially among youth, in the spaces of the postmodern architecture that he describes.

For both Foster and Jameson, it is the critic's taken-for-granted understanding of political and economic structures, and of the historical narrative, that defines the ideology and politics of postmodern practices. There is no space for contradictions within either the text or its relationship to political struggle. For Jameson, for example, we need new "maps" to enable us to understand the organization of space in late capitalism. The masses, on the other hand, remain mute and passive, cultural dopes who are deceived by the dominant ideologies, and who respond to the leadership of the critic as the only one capable of understanding ideology and constituting the proper site and form of resistance. At best, the masses succeed in representing their inability to respond. But without the critic, they are unable even to hear their own cries of hopelessness. Hopeless they are and shall remain, presumably until someone else provides them with the necessary maps of intelligibility and critical models of resistance.

If Jameson makes postmodern texts the sign of history, and Foster makes them the site of an already-defined struggle against that history, Jean Baudrillard[12] presents a more radical vision of the postmodern as the very form and substance of historical reality. Postmodern practices are the very fabric of reality, the historical site of the collapse of any gap between ideology and history, between appearance and reality, between meaning and representation. For Baudrillard, difference is no longer effective; every difference has imploded, rendering all the binary constructions of a meaningful reality useless and inoperative. Baudrillard is not merely claiming that all relations of difference from which identity is constructed have become problematic. It is not merely that the primacy of the signifier has replaced the power of the signified, but that the very realm of meaning and signs has disappeared; similarly, the fact that the difference between reality and appearance and between reality and representation has collapsed (the former in the nineteenth century, the latter as a result of the media's negation of their own mediation) means that appearance, meaning, and reality have disappeared. Reality as the site of the origin of effects, desires, and powers has drifted away, leaving us in a "hyperreality" that is always and only a simulacrum. In the simulacrum, nothing exists outside "the compulsive repetition of the codes"; it is merely that which can be modeled, that which already fits the model, that is positioned as the "hyperreal." We live in "the age of events without consequences"[13] in which the real is only a formal category. Interestingly, Baudrillard is rarely used in the radical form that his own theory suggests; he is more typically appropriated back into a situationist critique of commodification and the simulation of an authentic reality (which is still apparently hiding behind the scene but being pushed farther back by capitalist strategies), as if it were simply a matter of the image having become more real than reality. For Baudrillard, the difference has become irrelevant; it no longer matters or makes a difference.

Of all the positions within postmodernist debates, Baudrillard's is the one most willing to celebrate the practices and situations it describes. Yet, the celebration takes a particular form: it is celebration in the face of inevitability, an embracing of nihilism without empowerment, since there is no real possibility of struggle. It is, in fact, celebration as resignation, since the only response to the collapse of difference is the celebration of an indifference "at least as great."[14] The elitism of this negativity (masquerading as something else) is obvious in the assumed privileged position from which Baudrillard is able to confidently describe contemporary existence, outside of the everyday lives of its actors. Further, that description allows for no contradictions and no possibility of struggle, in either the present or the future. The masses already live the indifference Baudrillard proposes; they refuse to struggle, to speak, or to be spoken for. Although this appears to place the masses at the leading edge of history, since only they already live within the simulacrum, embracing the disappearance of agency and activity, it is in reality the critic — Baudrillard — who speaks and even denies the masses the right or the desire to speak. The critic becomes the only voice — the voice of the ventriloquist — in history.

The negativity of Baudrillard's celebration of the postmodern depends in part on his theory of power, and it is this third site of debate that has marked the most visible contribution of the French to the postmodernist debates: structure has become the very locus of power. For Baudrillard, power exists in the binary codes that continue to construct differences (e.g., between subject and object, appearance and reality, activity and passivity, power and resistance) as if they were still effective. But the only effect of such codes is to occlude the fact that these differences are no longer constitutive of the (hyper)real, that the simulacrum needs them only as an "alibi." Power is no longer in reality but in the continuing appearance of the real. Power has disappeared, collapsed into its simulation. For Foucault, Deleuze, and Guattari, any hierarchy—and consequently, any code, structure, or unity—entails the operation of power.[15] Hence, reality must be treated exclusively as local fragments within which power operates merely as the microphysical constitution of otherness. Thus, political struggle can be defined solely by its fundamental opposition to any structure. There can be no vision of alternative structures or of the oppressiveness of the local context. There is only an ongoing battle between the forces of structuration, which organize identities and differences, and the forces of radical negativity. Local opposition to any structure—deterritorialization—is the only form of political struggle.

In this postmodernist theory of power, the celebration of specific possibilities gives way to the celebration of the empty possibility of otherness, without continuity and without any possible purchase on the larger structures that organize everyday existence. This suggests something that resembles a politics of terrorism, of pure negativity, built upon an absolute and abstract principle of "resistance" as the other of "power." But the ability to draw this distinction depends upon the particular elitist relationship that the critic establishes to those who are struggling.[16] Although the position seems to acknowledge the reality of peoples' struggles, such struggles are allowed only insofar as they speak their radical negativity and refuse to offer themselves as reterritorializations. But, in fact, such real struggles are never truly allowed to speak, for that would require us to recognize their contradictions and the forms of positivity that they claim for themselves.

Postmodernism and the Popular Sensibility

My claim, then, is that the various postmodernist debates and positions have failed to account for the power and place of the emergent
social and cultural practices precisely because they ignore their articulation into everyday life. Remaining within the discursive terrain of
the dominant ideological apparatuses, the debates have ignored the
celebratory empowerment (as well as the particular forms of disempowerment) that such practices may enable. In fact, these debates
continue to privilege aesthetic practices that have appropriated those
strategies (minus the enormous passion often invested in them) that
have become the norm of popular culture in the age of mass media.
(It is, for example, this return to the terrain of the popular—as the
vernacular—that is at the heart of postmodern architectural practices.)

The failure of the postmodernist debates results in part from their
surprising lack of attention to popular culture and everyday life, even
in spite of their acknowledgment of the importance of the collapse of
the difference between high and popular culture. When it is at all
considered, popular culture is treated as if it were either high art—
amenable to the same kinds of critical concerns and practices as the
more institutionally sanctioned forms of culture—or documentary
evidence—as if its status as popular were insignificant to its active
insertion into the lives of people. As a result, the postmodernist
debates have failed to consider the relations between postmodern
practices and hegemonic (or popular) political formations. They
have ignored what Gramsci, Benjamin, and Lefebvre have all recognized, that power increasingly enters into and struggles over the
domain of everyday life and common sense.

Popular culture is not simply the incorporation of high-cultural
practices into less powerful, and certainly less political, forms. Popular culture is not merely the appropriation of strategies and structures developed elsewhere, an appropriation that inevitably weakens
the power of these "higher" aesthetic-signifying forms. Such a view
ignores the complex forms of incorporation and transformation that
occur as specific cultural practices move between different configurations and domains of our lives. In fact, specific postmodern practices are often most powerfully present precisely within forms of
popular culture, while many of the strategies of contemporary art

increasingly draw upon more common forms of mass communication. Ultimately, we ought to ask whether the postmodern can be understood in purely textual terms or whether, in fact, it depends upon what Pierre Bourdieu calls a difference in "aesthetic sensibilities."[17]

Bourdieu asks us to *begin* with socially distributed and historically determined practices of appropriation, of consumption, and of the active insertion of specific forms into peoples' everyday lives. He distinguishes between two sensibilities. The dominant sensibility subordinates function to form, life to art. It treats everything—whether works of art, profane cultural objects, social events, and even natural objects—"in and for themselves, as form rather than function."[18] It is indifferent to questions of how we invest ourselves in the world through the objects in our environment. Because it takes culture too seriously, it refuses to take life seriously. By articulating everything as form, it frees itself from any consideration of needs, functions, or passions. The popular sensibility, on the other hand, affirms the "continuity between art and life, which implies the subordination of form to function."[19] It articulates everything into the richly textured and contradictory world of everyday life. The dominant—legitimated—sensibility neutralizes any affective relations to cultural objects, reducing life to its formal conception of art; the popular sensibility incorporates legitimated art objects and questions of form into life, into the ideological, material, and affective structures of everyday concerns.

The specificity of popular culture depends precisely on its close relation to affective economies. After all, any practice is articulated into a situation or context that not only is meaningful but also has a particular "coloration," a particular feel or mood; it is marked by different forms and quantities of energy (i.e., the same object, with the same meaning, is very different in different affective contexts). Life is mapped out intelligibly and also by definitions of what matters; there are not only maps of meaning but maps that both describe and prescribe how we invest our energies, our desires, our passion, and even our "selves" in the world, maps that tell us how to generate energy, how to navigate our way into and through various moods, and how to live within emotional histories. This is not to say that popular culture is not engaged in ideological structures or that there are no relations between ideological and affective structures and politics.

It is only if we begin to recognize the complex relations between affect and ideology that we can make sense of people's emotional life, their desiring life, and their struggles to find the energy to survive, let alone struggle. It is only in the terms of these relations that we can understand people's need and ability to maintain a "faith" in something beyond their immediate existence. Such faith, which is at least part of what is involved in political struggle, depends upon affective investments that are articulated into but not constituted by structures of meaning.

The significance and politics of postmodern practices are too important to be left to debates about postmodernism. Nor can these questions be addressed merely by postulating a relationship between such isolated practices, whether individually or as a movement, and the social formation. Such practices can be understood only in relation to a particular historical formation constructed at the intersection of the range of interacting cultural practices, and the configurations of popular sensibility with which people appropriate such practices and articulate them into their everyday lives. This formation is never simple or noncontradictory. Both the field of cultural practices and the domain of popular sensibilities extend across a broad range of differences. And different cultural practices, as well as different popular sensibilities, are constantly opposing, undercutting, and reinflecting each other within the unstable formation of everyday life. Thus, the practices that have become the focus of the postmodernist debates have to be located within this broader context, within which their significance, importance, power, and effectivity are constituted and fought over. We cannot simply assume that they define the dominant moment of our popular existence simply because they are emergent, or because they are the most interesting practices on the cultural horizon. This is, at least in part, what is being struggled over in the current debates about postmodernism. Navigating the space between utopianism and nihilism, we must understand how the apparent loss of a certain set of critical positions and differences may yet be empowering. Postmodern practices point to the articulation of certain modernist practices and concepts into a popular sensibility, which exists only in the larger structure of the formation of everyday life. This incorporation involves selections, redistributions, the construction of particular connections and an affective investment in particular sites, i.e., the construction of forms of positivity and celebration. By shifting the terrain, from form to sensibility, and from culture to everyday life, we can begin to recognize that anything can be postmodern, but that the postmodern does not exhaust the popular.

Finally, this articulation operates at a particular historical and experiential juncture, which is marked by what Jameson has called "the waning of affect" but which is more accurately seen as the collapse of the relation (the difference) between affect and meaning. It is the historical event of an absent relation between these two registers (forms of effectivity) that frames and inflects the forms of fragmentation and indifference to which the postmodernist debates point. It is not that we do not continue to have an affective relation to the world but that such relations are not anchored in and do not correspond to other available social maps. Contemporary ideological structures seem incapable of making sense of certain affective experiences. The latter cannot be represented because they have apparently been determined elsewhere, in a different scene. These affective moments are "free-floating" and autonomous, rather than being stitched into the structures of meaning and subjectivity that make our lives intelligible. But this does not mean that we do not continue to live within and experience ourselves in terms of particular ideological meanings and values; simply that these are increasingly unrelated to our affective moods, that they cannot speak to them.[20] Thus, we are unable to organize our affective lives so as to invest ourselves into them in significant ways, unable to make their apparent inevitability matter. It is not that nothing matters, but that it does not matter what does, as long as something does. As Pat Aufderheide has recently written, "This is the generation that inherited the cry, 'I can't get no satisfaction.' And they live its contradictions, grabbing at satisfactions while rejecting the possibility itself. It's a punk ethos, nihilism constructed punishingly with the tools of consumer passion."[21] Thus happiness becomes an impossible (ideological) but necessary (affective) reality, or rather, its affective relevance collapses into its extreme ideological images. Our ideological and affective maps are unable to intersect, to articulate one another. And while we continue to necessarily assume their historically constructed unity, we find ourselves increasingly living within their autonomous spaces.

We appropriate events and practices into this space, using them not as representations or interpretations but simply as empowering signposts—billboards—that mark, perhaps even celebrate, the gap itself. (Another image that offers itself is the meaningless and apparently useless bric-a-brac that our grandparents used to collect.) Billboards are not signs of a displaced meaning or reality; they are not signifiers within larger economies of intelligibility. We drive past billboards without paying attention, because we already know what they say, or because we know it doesn't matter. We are usually driving too quickly anyway, and we have seen them all before. But they do tell us what road we are on, what direction we are following; they reaffirm that we are in fact moving, even if we are going nowhere: "[it is as if] the motive of this scavenging is *to go on*; not to progress, because we no longer believe in progress . . . [it is] the desperate determination to go on at any cost."[22] But billboards do more than mark the mere fact of our affective existence; they enable it as well. They are, in that sense, like the "tags" of hip-hop culture, marking sites of investment and empowerment. The postmodern sensibility appropriates practices as boasts that announce their own—and consequently our own—existence, like a rap song boasting of the imaginary (or real— it makes no difference) accomplishments of the rapper. They offer forms of empowerment not only in the face of nihilism but precisely through the forms of nihilism itself: an empowering nihilism, a moment of positivity through the production and structuring of affective relations.

Postmodern billboards are empowering precisely because they enable us to continue to struggle to make a difference, despite the fact that we take it for granted that such struggles are impossible. The postmodern sensibility reconnects the two distanced economies through a specific articulation: it appropriates ideological signs into affective boasts. Within its sensibility, everything is located within the maps of the differential investment of energy. The postmodern reduces reality and ideology to a question of affect: whether and how particular ideological elements matter is not determined by their meanings but by how they can be incorporated into particular mattering maps, particular affective structures. Consequently, affect is stitched into reality without the mediation of ideology, although the ideological surfaces always provide the sites of reality, the raw material for its affective economies, or its maps of what matters. In ideological terms, it no longer matters what matters, but in affective terms, it is the only thing that matters; it is the only possible difference. The postmodern becomes the paradoxical strategy by which we live an impossible relation to the future. For example, by shifting from the ideological to the affective, the terror of the absence of the future (for which one must seek an ideological answer that is simply not available) is transformed into the impossibility or irrelevance of any framework that could make sense of the absence. Similarly, it is the everydayness of the apocalypse that is boring and banal. Postmodern celebrations of violence and destruction are predicated upon their meaninglessness, a meaninglessness that frees them to be relocated and identified affectively.

From Post-modernism to Pop-modernism

In 1967, one event seemed to symbolically and practically mark the emergence of a national, if not international, self-conscious formation of youth culture. The event was the release of the Beatles' *Sgt. Pepper's Lonely Hearts Club Band*. Langdon Winner described the week following its release as "the closest Western Civilization has come to unity since the Congress of Vienna in 1815," and the usually more cynical Greil Marcus gleefully cites his observation that "for a brief while the irreparably fragmented consciousness of the West was unified, at least in the minds of the young."[23] Seven years later, rock critic Jon Landau attended a Bruce Springsteen concert in which he saw "the rock and roll future," and in 1976, his vision became reality. Nineteen years after Sgt. Pepper marked the release of another album that, in many ways, seems to have unified the population of youth again: *Bruce Springsteen Live*. But everything has changed: the body of youth, the form of its temporary unity, the means by which that unification has been accomplished, and the political import of the moment. Springsteen's success cannot be explained away simply by the commercial "hype" that has obviously accompanied and perhaps, to some extent, orchestrated his rise to stardom. After all, the Beatles—and Sgt. Pepper—were also hyped and supported by large advertising campaigns. Nor can the difference between the two moments be explained away by pointing to the existence of a politicized community of youth in the sixties and its absence in the eighties. For it is the particular form of that absence and its relation to Springsteen's success that need to be interpreted. Only by acknowledging its predictability, even if in retrospect, and our own ambiguity in the face of it, can we begin to come to terms with it. To quote Winner again, "The whole of his musical persona is haunted by an unsettling sense of *déjà vu*. Rock and roll heroes of the 1950s appeared where we least expected them. . . . Springsteen appeared exactly where he was expected."[24]

How do we account for Springsteen's popularity and the specific forms it has taken? How do we understand its political possibilities? Obviously, an adequate response would require a complex, multidimensional analysis that would locate Springsteen in a variety of historical registers: his relation to rock and roll, to other forms of popular culture, and to historical events and his appeal to different social fractions, and so forth. We might begin with a number of rather obvious observations. First, Springsteen's success has been neither gradual nor sudden; in fact, it is difficult to know precisely how to describe its qualitative trajectory. Second, there is a wide range of interpretations, among critics as well as fans, of both his music and his success. Third, his audience is extraordinarily heterogeneous. His images of youth and adulthood seem not to impose any limits on its potential audience. His images of working-class experience and aspirations are somehow able to speak to middle-class adolescents. His male expressions of loneliness and sexual desire are somehow able to speak to women across a wide range of ages and classes. And his Americanist imagery is capable of striking responsive chords across not only political but national boundaries as well.

Although critics often try to read his songs as if they communicated something about the shared experiences and beliefs of his audiences, it is obvious—one need only attend his concerts, speak to his fans, or attend to the ways they listen to and punctuate their singing along with particular songs—that the power of his songs depends upon concrete images, and images of Springsteen as well, and is affective: as Marshall Berman writes, "It is extraordinary how Bruce Springsteen has worked his way into so many people's lives. Ask them to think of their peak experiences over the past decade: alongside intimate private moments with their lovers, spouses, and kids, in deepest privacy, they'll remember moments in immense public spaces with Bruce and 20,000 others. And the fact that the feeling is shared and multiplied—indeed promoted and orchestrated—doesn't diminish the ecstasy and communion. I remember my moment . . . I had to see the people around me, and see myself, with new eyes. I felt at that moment that I would trust this man with my life."[25] Although this enormous affective power is often noted, its implications are rarely embraced.

How do we understand this passionate identification with Springsteen and his music? What is its relation to his current level of popularity, if the strength and the form of that passionate investment have always defined his relations to his fans? If his current success depends upon something entirely different, we need to ask why that affective structure has suddenly become widely available, or conversely, why it has suddenly been appropriated by a widely heterogeneous audience. The answer, I believe, depends upon two significant developments within his musical presence. The first is rather simple: if it was the affectivity of the songs that initially made them so powerful for his fans, his recent albums have explicitly focused upon the particular affective structures and contradictions of postmodernity. Springsteen, especially since *The River*, sings about the contradiction between faith or dreams and reality. Springsteen's songs are billboards of being trapped simultaneously inside one's own dreams and inside someone else's reality. He sings about the necessity and the impossibility of meaning; he celebrates the very prisons that such meanings prepare for us ("Glory Days," "Growing Up," and so on). Springsteen constantly announces that he wants it all, and even if he is willing to pay the price, he doesn't quite know what "all" is.

The context of rock and roll gives this affective contradiction a specific form and his music a specific power. I have elsewhere described rock and roll as marking the historically emergent indifference of terror and boredom.[26] This describes the dominant affective experience of youth in postwar America. Not only have these two poles become pervasive in everyday life, but they have lost any historically constructed guarantees of where they are to be located, of how they are connected to specific events. Similarly, they have lost any historically constructed position in an economy of meaning that could define their difference. The result is that our affective existence is increasingly defined by the collapse of the difference between the extremism of terror and the nullity of boredom, between the terror of boredom and the boredom of terror, between the uncontrollability of affect and its absence. There are, of course, a variety of ways in which this position could be remarked and responded to: for example, one could choose to empower terror without reservation (with or without actual risk) and, hence, constantly seek to live life on the edge, as uncontrollable. Alternatively, rock and roll appropriates the condoned irresponsibility of the social position of youth and constructs an economy of fun. Rock and roll empowers its fans simply by privileging, not only the very celebration of fun, but also the particular forms of fun appropriated by particular groups of fans. It constructs maps that mark the sites of investment from the various billboards of its own cultural surfaces—music, dance, style, language, sex, and so forth. It transforms the very signs of its affective contradiction into the billboards of its affective empowerment (noise, violence, repetition, and so on).

But this has always been visible in Springsteen's music and accounts, in part, for the success of *Born to Run*. More recently, a second—historically older—affective structure has emerged in his music: the indifference of subjectification and commodification. This contradiction does not mean that there is no difference between subjectivity and commodity, but rather, that they no longer seem to bear any relation to each other as demands upon our own identities; instead they slide past and across one another. We are forced to live in both, unable to position them within a larger context that places us within their difference. In the end, their difference doesn't matter. That is, according to Benjamin, the condition of the masses: a failure to live what Foucault has called the "epistemological doublet."[27] The result is that everyday life is simultaneously constituted as unpredictable and totally predictable, uncontrollable and totally controlled, full of meaning and meaningless. I have argued elsewhere that this affective structure is increasingly dominant in postmodern appropriations of televisual culture.[28] Thus, it makes sense that Springsteen's success has arisen at the moment when, in fact, there is a broad attempt to articulate rock and roll to televisual forms—whether through music videos (which have obviously contributed significantly to Springsteen's popularity), the increasing use of popular music on television series, various lip-synching programs, the current Monkees revival, and so on. In this context, it is important to note that Springsteen has successfully used a wide range of video styles.

Springsteen's ability to offer a response to this particular affective contradiction suggests three additional features of his popularity:

first, it is his own image as a rock-and-roll performer, so powerfully appropriated by his fans, that seems to offer some way out of the dilemmas his songs propose. Second, this image is that of an ordinary person, exactly like us. (This is in part the function of his famous stories, his rather nondescript rock-and-roll style of dress, and the legends about his interactions with his fans.) And finally, his image of "authenticity" is (and this is widely recognized by his fans) constructed, artificial. We know that the "spontaneity" of each show, each gesture, each story is an illusion, but it is an illusion that many fans like to see repeatedly performed. This is, in fact, precisely the empowering form of television: the construction of what one can call the "mundane exotic." Springsteen simultaneously celebrates his fans' ordinariness and asserts their fantastic (even if phantasmic) difference. The ordinary becomes extraordinary. Springsteen empowers the fans' identity within the mainstream, giving them an identity in their very lack of a difference, or in the artificiality of a temporarily constructed difference in their affective lives. This becomes more real, and more important, than their social differences and experiences. Reality and image slide into one another within the postmodern sensibility. Springsteen has literally found a way to redefine authenticity onto the television screen. And this may explain his extraordinary ability to appear before audiences of one hundred thousand people without losing the power of his presence or his relationship with, and his control of, the audience.

In conclusion, then, I am suggesting that Springsteen's success is, at least in part, the result of his ability to successfully operate in the two affective economies that have become the differentiated domains of rock and television. In fact, the two structures—and especially the empowering responses to them—are contradictory. Rock and roll's economy of fun is elitist and totalizing; it works by the imaged demarcation of difference. It constructs a variety of configurations of billboards, each of which serves only to construct an imaginary difference, without necessarily postulating an identity, between those within its spaces and those remaining outside. The affective economy of television is democratic and always incomplete, and works by the imaginary assertion of identity. This distinction can be seen not only in the social practices within which each is consumed but also in the sources and forms of pleasure that each generates. The rock economy marks a boundary around the fan, a boundary of privileged access to the appropriation of the music and consequently to fun. Rock-and-roll fans are elitist: they are the only ones who understand what constitutes rock and roll. And, in the moment of fun, there is the affective experience of "having it all," even if only temporarily. On the other hand, television empowers its fans by celebrating the ordinariness of the exotic and the exoticism of the ordinary; it makes everything equal. Everything becomes an image to be appropriated onto the screen. Operating at the intersection of these two economies, Springsteen is both celebrating identity and difference, democratic equality and elitist hierarchy. Whether Springsteen will be able to maintain this precarious position, or whether the position itself will be generalized and become more widely available, will determine his continued popularity. But the significance of his popularity—in the past, present, and future—depends upon the very possibility of constructing affective systems that organize the various contradictions of postmodern existence. These are the cultural and historical conditions, conditions "not of our own making," within which, as critics, we must struggle to find new ideological and political positions.

NOTES

1. For example: "Television, just because it's an emblematic expression of Sartre's 'serial culture' in electronic form, is also a perfect model of the processed world of postmodern technology. And why not? TV exists, in fact, just at that rupture-point in human history between the decline of the now-passe age of sociology and the upsurge of the new world of communications (just between the eclipse of normalized society and the emergence of radical semiurgy as the language of the 'structural' society). TV is at the border-line of a great paradigm-shift between the 'death of society' (modernism with its representational logic) and the 'triumph of an empty, signifying culture' (the 'structural paradigm' of postmodernism). In the Real World of television . . ." Arthur Kroker and David Cook, *The Postmodern Scene: Excremental Culture and Hyper-Aesthetics* (New York: St. Martin's Press, 1986), 272.

2. Despite Tania Modleski's efforts in her introduction to *Studies in Entertainment: Critical Approaches to Mass Culture,* ed. Tania Modleski (Bloomington: University of Indiana Press, 1986) to construct such notions of empowerment as noncontradictory celebrations of the popular, recent work in cultural studies, including my own, is clearly intended to argue that critics must avoid reducing the politics of popular cultural practices to any single dimension or measure. Empowerment need not deny the possibility of disempowerment, or of forms of empowerment that are oppressive. It does, however, register the fact that people must find something positive in the forms of popular culture that they celebrate. A brilliant example of such an analysis is Janice Winship, " 'A girl needs to get streetwise': Magazines for the 1980s," *Feminist Review* 21 (1985), 25-46. She writes:

It is time that as feminists we thought carefully about the political implications of . . . an image [that] too easily produces a knee-jerk response in feminists . . . although superficially the image may resemble classic porno pics, the representations of gender is being actively tampered with.

What we also need to bear in mind is that for the 1980s New Young Women (middle-class, educated young women) that image simply does not and cannot mean the same thing as similar images did five to ten years ago for us "older" feminists . . . it is partly because, however indirectly, feminism has given these young women a knowledge and a strength to act in the world which also allows them to laugh at and enjoy those images in a way many of us could not, and cannot. The question now is, are *we* strong enough to acknowledge that our politics have to shift in order to take account of these changes? (pp. 45-46)

3. See, for example, Iain Chambers, *Popular Culture: The Metropolitan Experience* (London: Methuen, 1986).

4. Antonio Gramsci, *Selections from the Prison Notebooks*, trans. Quintin Hoare and Geoffrey Nowell Smith (New York: International Publishers, 1971), 331. For a range of Marxist-Gramscian perspectives on the questions of postmodernism, see the inteview with Stuart Hall, and the responses by Lawrence Grossberg, Dick Hebdige, Iain Chambers, John Fiske and Jon Watts, and Angela McRobbie in the special issue, devoted to the work on Stuart Hall, of *Journal of Communication Inquiry* 10 (Summer 1986).

5. For example, Todd Gitlin assumes not only that the "recombinant" form of televisual texts are obvious but that it is equally obvious that this is nothing but a sign of cultural exhaustion. Thus, he effectively merely recreates one of the positions of the mass-culture debates. Todd Gitlin, *Inside Prime Time* (New York, Pantheon, 1983), especially chap. 5.

6. Consequently, Félix Guattari, who is often positioned as a leading "postmodern theorist," can attack postmodernism in "The Postmodern Dead End," *FlashArt*, no. 128 (1986), 40-41.

7. Jean Baudrillard, *For a Critique of the Political Economy of the Sign*, trans. Charles Levin (St. Louis: Telos Press, 1981) and *Simulations*, trans. Paul Foss, Paul Patton, and Philip Beitchman (New York: Semiotext(e), 1983).

8. See Hal Foster, ed. *The Anti-Aesthetic: Essays on Postmodern Culture* (Port Townsend, Wash.: Bay Press, 1983); Brian Willis, ed. *Art After Modernism: Rethinking Representation* (New York: The New Museum of Contemporary Art, 1984); Hal Foster, *Recodings: Art, Spectacle, Cultural Politics* (Port Townsend, Wash.: Bay Press, 1985); Rosalind E. Krauss, *The Originality of the Avant-Garde and Other Modernist Myths* (Cambridge, Mass.: M.I.T. Press, 1985); and Andreas Huyssen, *After the Great Divide: Modernism, Mass Culture, Postmodernism* (Bloomington: Indiana University Press, 1986).

9. Hal Foster, "Postmodernism: A Preface," in Foster, *The Anti-Aesthetic*, xi-xii.

10. Fredric Jameson, "Postmodernism, or the Cultural Logic of Late Capitalism," *New Left Review*, no. 146 (1984), 53-92; and Anders Stephanson, "An Interview with Fredric Jameson," *FlashArt*, no. 131 (1986-87), 69-73.

11. Michele Barrett, "The Place of Aesthetics in Marxist Criticism," in *Marxism and the Interpretation of Culture*, ed. Cary Nelson and Lawrence Grossberg (Urbana: University of Illinois Press, 1988).

12. See Baudrillard, *Simulations*, and Jean Baudrillard, *In the Shadow of the Silent Majorities . . . or The End of the Social and other Essays*, trans. Paul Foss, Paul Patton, and John Johnston (New York: Semiotext(e), 1983).

13. Jean Baudrillard, "On Nihilism," *On the Beach*, n.d.

14. Jean Baudrillard, "Interview," *FlashArt*, no. 130 (1986).

15. See Michel Foucault, *Power/Knowledge: Selected Interviews & Other Writings 1972-1977*, ed. Colin Gordon (New York: Pantheon, 1980); Gilles Deleuze and Félix Guattari, *Anti-Oedipus: Capitalism and Schizophrenia*, trans. Robert Hurley, Mark Seem, and Helen R. Lane (Minneapolis: University of Minnesota Press, 1983). For an interesting and useful appropriation of these ideas for a reconsideration of feminism in a postmodern context, see Donna Haraway, "A Manifesto for Cyborgs: Science, Technology, and Socialist Feminism in the 1980s," *Socialist Review*, no. 80 (1985), 65-107.

16. Gayatri Chakravorty Spivak, "Can the Subaltern Speak," in Nelson and Grossberg, eds., *Marxism and the Interpretation of Culture*, 697-713.

17. Pierre Bourdieu, *Distinction: A Social Critique of the Judgement of Taste*, trans. Richard Nice (Cambridge, Mass.: Harvard University Press, 1984).

18. Ibid., 3.

19. Ibid., 4.

20. This rupture is, I believe, the overdetermined product of a number of historical events in the postwar years, events that seriously challenged our ability to make sense of our feelings about the world, ourselves, normalcy, and the future (e.g., the incorporation of apocalyptic images into the mass media and popular culture). While history seemed to demand a different structure of affective investments, there seemed to be no way of making sense of the emerging relations. What resulted was a crisis in the relationship between common sense and faith. This is not to suggest that there was a historical moment in which there was a perfect correspondence between them but simply that there is a historical difference in how these two economies are and can be articulated to each other. The change is quantitative and partial, but its effects are real and increasingly visible.

21. Pat Aufderheide, "Sid and Nancy: Just Say No," *In These Times*, 11 (19-25 November 1986), 14.

22. Peter Schjeldahl, "Irony and Agony," *In These Times*, 10 (20 August-2 September, 1986).

23. Cited in Greil Marcus, "The Beatles," in *The Rolling Stone Illustrated History of Rock and Roll*, ed. Jim Miller (New York, Random House, 1980), 183.

24. Langdon Winner, "Bruce Springsteen," in Miller, *History of Rock and Roll*, 466.

25. Marshall Berman, "Bruce Springsteen: Blowin' Away the Lies," *Village Voice*, 9 December 1986, 87.

26. Lawrence Grossberg, " 'I'd rather feel bad than not feel anything at all': Rock and Roll, Pleasure and Power," *Enclitic* 8 (1984), 94-111; and "Rock and Roll in Search of an Audience or, Taking Fun (Too?) Seriously," in *Popular Music and Human Communication: Social and Cultural Perspectives*, ed. James Lull (Beverly Hills: Sage, 1987), 175-97.

27. Walter Benjamin, "The Work of Art in the Age of Mechanical Reproduction," in *Illuminations*, ed. Hannah Arendt (New York: Harcourt, Brace and World, 1986); Michel Foucault, *The Order of Things: An Archaeology of the Human Sciences* (New York: Pantheon, 1970).

28. Lawrence Grossberg, "The In-difference of Television or, Mapping TV's Popular Economy," *Screen*, 28-2 (Spring 1987), 28-45.

Living with Contradictions: Critical Practices in the Age of Supply-Side Aesthetics

Abigail Solomon-Godeau

It should have become abundantly clear in recent years that the function of criticism, for the most part, is to serve as a more or less sophisticated public relations or promotional apparatus. This is less a function of the critic's active partisanship (Diderot and Baudelaire, for example, are historically associated with the artists Greuze and Guys, whom they championed as exemplars) than a consequence of the fact that most contemporary art criticism is innocent of its own politics, its own interests, and its own ideology. In fact, the promotional aspect of most art criticism derives from the larger institutional and discursive structures of art. In this respect, the scholarly monograph, the temporary exhibition, the discipline of art history, and last but not least, the museum itself, are essentially celebratory entities. Further—and at the risk of stating the obvious—the institutions and discourses that collectively function to construct the object "art" are allied to the material determinations of the marketplace, which themselves establish and confirm the commodity status of the work of art.

Within this system, the art critic normally functions as a kind of intermediary between the delirious pluralism of the marketplace and the sacralized judgment seat that is the museum. Recently, however, even this mediating process has been bypassed; artists such as Julian Schnabel, to take one particularly egregious example, have been propelled from obscurity to the pantheon without a single serious critical text ever having been produced in support of their work.

The quantum increase in the scale of the international art market, the unprecedented importance of dealers in creating (or "managing") reputations and manipulating supply and demand, the emergence of a new class of "art consultants," and the large-scale entry of corporations into the contemporary art market have all contributed to the effective redundancy of art criticism. Art stars and even "movements," with waiting lists of eager purchasers in their train, stepped into the spotlight before many art critics knew of their existence.[1] This redundancy of criticism, however, can hardly be understood as a consequence of these developments alone. Rather, the current state of most art criticism represents the final dissolution of what was, in any case, only a fragile bulwark between market forces and their institutional ratification, a highly permeable membrane separating venture capital, so to speak, from blue-chip investment. As a result, art criticism has been forced to cede its illusory belief in the separateness or disinterestedness of critical discourse.

In this essay I am primarily concerned with the condition—and position—of critical practices within art criticism and artmaking in the age of Reagan. In contradistinction to business-as-usual art promotion and the atavistic, cynical, and mindless art production exemplified by pseudoexpressionism, critical practices, by definition, must occupy an oppositional place. But what, we must ask, is that place today? Within the map of the New York art world, where is that place of opposition and what is it in opposition to? Second—and integrally linked to the first set of questions—we must ask what defines a critical practice and permits it to be recognized as such. What, if anything, constitutes the difference between a critical practice and a recognizably political one? If artists as dramatically distinct as, for example, David Salle and Sherrie Levine, can both say that their work contributes to a critique of the painterly sign, what common political meanings, if any, ought we attribute to the notion of critical practice? Last—and here is where I am most directly implicated—what is the nature, the terms, even the possibility, of a critical practice in art criticism? Is such a practice not inevitably and inescapably a part of the cultural apparatus it seeks to challenge and contest?

Postmodernist Photography: The Third Time Around, a Case History

When I think of it now, I don't think what Julian Schnabel was doing was all that different from what I was trying to do.

Sherrie Levine, "Art in the (Re)Making," interview with Gerald Marzorati, *Artnews* (May 1986)

By way of exploring these questions, and in the interest of providing some specificity to the discussion, I want to concentrate primarily on the evolution and development of postmodernist photographic work from the late 1970s to the present, using it as a case history in which to explore the salient issues. This corpus of work, identified with its now fully familiar strategies of appropriation and pastiche; its systematic assault on modernist orthodoxies of immanence, autonomy, presence, originality, and authorship; its engagement with the simulacral; and its interrogation of the problematics of photographic mass media representation may be taken as paradigmatic of the concerns of a critical postmodernism or what Hal Foster has designated as "oppositional postmodernism."[2] The qualifier "critical" is important here, inasmuch as the conceptualization and description of postmodernism in architecture—chronologically anterior—was inflected rather differently.[3] There, it signaled, among other things, a new historicism and/or repudiation of modernist architecture's social and utopian aspirations, and a concomitant theatricalization of architectural form and meaning. In literary studies, the term *postmodernism* had yet another valency and made its appearance in literary criticism at an even earlier date.[4] Within the visual arts, however, postmodernist photography was identified with a specifically critical stance. Critics such as Benjamin Buchloh, Douglas Crimp, Rosalind Krauss, *et al.*, theorized this aspect of postmodernist photographic work as principally residing in its dismantling of reified, idealist conceptions enshrined in modernist aesthetics—issues devolving on presence, subjectivity, and aura. To the extent that this work was supported and valorized for its subversive potential (particularly with respect to its apparent fulfillment of the Barthesian and Foucauldian prescriptions for the death of the author and, by extension, its subversion of the commodity status of the art object), Sherrie Levine and Richard Prince were perhaps *the* emblematic figures. For myself, as a photography critic writing in opposition to the academicized mausoleum of late-modernist art photography, part of the interest in the work of Vicky Alexander, Victor Burgin, Sarah Charlesworth, Silvia Kolbowski, Barbara Kruger, Sherrie Levine, Richard Prince, Cindy Sherman, Laurie Simmons, and Jim Welling (to cite only those I have written about) lay in the way their work directly challenged the pieties and proprieties with which art photography had carved a space for itself precisely as a modernist art form.[5] Further, the feminist import of this work—particularly in the case of Kruger and Levine—represented a theoretically more sophisticated and necessary departure from the essentialism and literalism prevalent in many of the feminist art practices that emerged in the seventies.[6]

In retrospect, Levine's production of the late seventies to the present reveals both the strength and weakness of this variant of critical postmodernism as a counterstrategy to the regnant forms of art production and discourse. The changes in her practice, and the shifts in the way her work has been discursively positioned and received, are themselves testimony to the difficulty and contradiction that attend critical practices that operate squarely within the framework of high-art production.

Levine's work first drew critical notice in the late 1970s, a period in which the triumph of the right was as much manifest in the cultural sphere as in the political one. As one might well have predicted for a time of intense political reaction, these symptoms of morbidity included the wholesale resurrection of easel painting exemplified by German, Italian, and American pseudoexpressionism, a wholesale retrenchment against the modest gains of minority and feminist artists, a repression (or distortion) of the radical art practices of the preceding decade, a ghastly revival of the mythology of the heroicized (white male) artist, and last, the institutional consolidation and triumphant legitimation of photography as a fully "auratic," subjectivized, autonomous, fine art.[7]

Against this backdrop, one aspect of Levine's work consisted of directly rephotographing from existing reproductions a series of photographs by several canonized masters of photographic modernism (Edward Weston's nude studies of his son Neil, Eliot Porter's technicolor landscapes, Walker Evans's FSA pictures) and presenting the work as her own. With a dazzling economy of means, Levine's pictures deftly upset the foundation stones (authorship, originality, subjective expression) on which the integrity and supposed autonomy of the work of art is presumed to rest. Moreover, her selection of stolen images was anything but arbitrary; always the work of canonized male photographers, the contents and codes of these purloined images were chosen for their ideological density (the classical nude, the beauty of nature, the poor of the Great Depression) and then subjected to a demystifying scrutiny enabled and mobilized by the very act of (re)placing them within quotation marks. Finally, the strategy of fine-art-photography appropriations had a tactical dimension. For these works were produced in the wake of the so-called photography boom—meaning not simply the cresting of the market for photographic vintage prints, but the wholesale reclassification of all kinds of photography to conform with Kunstwissenschaft-derived notions of individual style and authorial presence.

It goes without saying that Levine's work of this period, considered *as* a critical practice (feminist, deconstructive, and literally transgressive—the Weston and Porter works prompted ominous letters from their estate lawyers) could make its critique visible only within the compass of the art world; the space of exhibition, the market framework, art (or photography) theory and criticism. Outside of this specialized site, a Sherrie Levine could just as well be a "genuine" Edward Weston or a "genuine" Walker Evans. This, in fact, was one of the arguments made from the left with the intention of countering the claims for the critical function of work such as Levine's and Prince's (Prince at that period was rephotographing advertising images, excising only the text). The force of this criticism hinged on the work's insularity, its adherence to, or lack of contestation of, the artworld frame, and—more pointedly—its failure to articulate an alternative politics, an alternative vision.

In l982, for example, Martha Rosler wrote an article entitled "Notes on Quotes" focusing on the inadequacies of appropriation and quotation as a properly *political* strategy: "What alternative vision is suggested by such work? [She is referring here specifically to Levine.] We are not provided the space within the work to understand how things might be different. We can imagine only a respite outside social life—the alternative is merely Edenic or Utopic. There *is* no social life, no personal relations, no groups, classes, nationalities; there is no production other than the production of images. Yet a critique of ideology necessitates some materialistic grounding if it is to rise above the theological."[8] Rosler's use of the term *theological* in this context points to one of the central debates in and around the definition—or evaluation—of critical practice. For Rosler, failure to ground the artwork in "direct social analysis" reduces its critical gesture to one of "highlighting" rather than "engaging with political questions that challenge . . . power relations in society." Moreover, to the extent that the artwork "remains locked within the relations of production of its own cultural field," and limited to the terms of a generic rather than specific interrogation of forms of domination, it cannot fulfill an educative, much less transformatory, function.

But "theological" in its opprobrious sense can cut both ways. It is, in fact, a "theological" notion of the political—or perhaps one should say a scriptural notion—that has until quite recently effectively occluded issues of gender and subjectivity from the purview of the political. Rosler's objections are to some degree moored in a relatively traditional conception of what constitutes the political in art ("materialistic grounding," "direct social analysis"). Thus, Rosler's characterization of a purely internal critique of art as ineffective because theological can, from a somewhat different vantage point, be interpreted as a theologized notion of the political. It is, moreover, important to point out that while unambiguously political artists (unambiguous because of their choice of content) are rarely found wanting for their total exclusion of considerations of gender, feminist artists are frequently chastised by left critics for the inadequacy of *their* political content. Nevertheless, the echoing cry of the women's movement—the personal is political—is but one of the remappings of political terrain that have engendered new ways of thinking the political and new ways of inscribing it in cultural production.

But perhaps even more important, to the extent that art is itself a discursive and institutional site, it surely entails its own critical practices. This has in fact been recently argued as the significance and legacy of the historical avant-garde.[9] For Peter Bürger, the Kantian conception of self-criticism is understood not in Greenberg's sense of a *telos* of purity and essence, but rather as a critical operation performed within and upon the *institution* of art itself. Thus, art movements like dadaism and constructivism and art practices such as collage, photomontage, and the Duchampian readymade are understood to be performing a specifically political function to the extent that they work to actively break down the notion of aesthetic autonomy and to rejoin art and life. Bürger's rigorous account of art *as* an institution in bourgeois culture provides a further justification for considering internal critiques such as Levine's as a genuinely critical practice. Cultural sites and discourses are in theory no less immune to contestation, no less able to furnish an arena for struggle and transformation than any other.[10] This "in theory" needs to be acknowledged here because the subsequent "success" of postmodernist photography as a *style* harkens back, as I shall argue, to problems of function, of critical complicity, and the extreme difficulty of maintaining a critical edge within the unstable spaces of internal critique.

In the spring of 1982, I curated an exhibition entitled "The Stolen Image and Its Uses" for an alternative space in upstate New York. Of the five artists included (Alexander, Kolbowski, Kruger, Levine, and Prince), Levine was by far the most controversial and sparked the most hostility. It was, in fact, the very intensity of the outrage her work provoked (nowhere greater than among the ranks of art photographers) that appeared, at the time, to confirm the subversive effects of her particular strategies. But even while such exhibitions or lectures on Levine's works were received outside New York with indignation, a different kind of appropriation of existing imagery, drawn principally from the mass media, was beginning to be accorded theoretical recognition across a broad range of cultural production. It was less easy to see this kind of appropriation as critically motivated. Fredric Jameson, for example, could in part identify his conception of postmodernism with the strategies of appropriation, quotation, and pastiche.[11] That these strategies could then be said to unify within a single field of discourse the work of Jean-Luc Godard and the work of Brian DePalma constitutes a problem for critical practice. Not only did such an undifferentiated model suppress a crucial consideration of (political and aesthetic) difference, it also implied the impossibility of cultural opposition within a totalizing system, a position accorded growing intellectual prestige within the art world through the later writings of Jean Baudrillard. Rooted in such a framework, an appropriative strategy such as Levine's (although Jameson does not mention the specific practice of appropriation) could only figure as a synecdochal symptom within a master narrative on postmodernism.[12]

By 1983, plundering the pages of glossy magazines, shooting advertisements from the television set, or "simulating" photographic
tableaux that might have come from either of these media had
become as routine an activity in the more sophisticated art schools as
slopping paint on canvas. In January of that year the Institute of Contemporary Art in Philadelphia mounted an exhibition entitled
"Image Scavengers." Included in the exhibition were representatives
of the first wave of appropriators and pasticheurs (Kruger, Levine,
Prince, Cindy Sherman) and several other artists whose work could
be allied to the former only by virtue of their formal devices. Invited
to contribute a catalog essay, Douglas Crimp was clearly disturbed at
the domestication of what he had himself theorized as the critical
potential of photographic appropriation. Under the title "Appropriating Appropriation," his essay initiated a reconsideration of the adequacy of appropriation as a critical mode. "If all aspects of the culture
use this new operational mode," he wrote, "then the mode itself
cannot articulate a specific reflection upon that culture."[13] Thus,
although appropriative and quotational strategies had now become
readily identifiable as a descriptive hallmark of postmodern culture,
the terms by which it might once have been understood to be performing a critical function had become increasingly obfuscated and
difficult to justify.

By this time, Levine's practice had itself undergone various alterations. In 1982, she had largely abandoned photographic appropriations and was confiscating German expressionist works, either by
rephotographing them from book reproductions, or by framing the
reproductions themselves. In 1983 and 1984, however, she began
making handmade watercolor and pencil copies after artbook illus-
trations, extending her *oeuvre*, so to speak, to include non-expres-
sionist modern masters such as Malevich and El Lissitsky. Her copies
after expressionist drawings, such as Egon Schiele's contorted and
angst-ridden nudes, were particularly trenchant comments on the
pseudoexpressionist revival; master drawings are, after all, especially
privileged for their status as intimate and revealing traces of the artist's unique subjectivity. In 1985, Levine made what might, or might
not, be considered a radical departure from her earlier work and
began to produce quite beautiful small-scale paintings on wood
panels. These were geometrical abstractions—mostly stripes—
which, Janus-like, looked backward to late-modernist works or mini-

malism and forward to the most recently minted new wave in the art world—neo-geo. Additionally, she accompanied her first exhibition of this new work with unpainted panels of wood in which one or two of the knots had been neatly gilded.

Mutatis mutandis, Levine had become a painter, although I would argue, still a somewhat singular one. Her work, moreover, had passed from the relatively marginalized purview of the *succès d'estime* to a new visibility (and respectability), signaled, for example, by her cover article in the May 1986 *Artnews*. In several of the comments she made to her interviewer, Levine explained her need to distance herself from the kind of critical partisanship that not only had helped establish her reputation, but—more important—had, to a great degree, developed its position and analysis in relation to her work. Levine's professed discomfort with a body of critical writing that positioned her as a critical, indeed an adversarial, presence hinged on two factors. In championing Levine's work as either a post-structuralist exemplum, or a demolition derby on the property relations that subtend the integrity of the art object, the (mostly male) critics who had written about her had overlooked, or repressed, the distinctly feminist import of her work.[14] But Levine also took issue with the interpretation of her work that stressed its materialist critique. In this regard, Levine insisted that hers was an aesthetic practice that implied no particular quarrel with the economic determinations of cultural production. Consequently, insofar as her critical supporters had emphasized those aspects of her work that subverted the commodity status of the artwork and demolished those values Walter Benjamin designated as the "theology of art," Levine began to believe that her activity *as* an artist was itself being repressed: "I never thought I wasn't making art and I never thought of the art I was making as not a commodity. I never thought that what I was doing was in strict opposition to what else was going on—I believed I was distilling things, bringing out what was being repressed. I did collaborate in a radical reading of my work. And the politics were congenial. But I was tired of no one looking at the work, getting inside the frame. And I was getting tired of being represented by men."[15]

The repositioning of Levine's work, with respect to both its meaning (now presented as a form of troubled obsequy mourning "the uneasy death of modernism") and the nature of her activity (commodity making), is disturbing from a number of perspectives. First, it involves its own forms of historical repression. Thus, nowhere in the article was any reference made to Levine's two-year collaboration with the artist Louise Lawler, enacted under the title "A Picture Is No Substitute for Anything."[16] What is troubling about such an omission is that it parallels—no doubt wholly unintentionally—the institutional and discursive repressions that construct partial and falsified histories of art in the first place and in which the exclusion of women and radical practices are particularly conspicuous.[17] Second, it repressed the active support of women critics, such as myself and Rosalind Krauss. But, more ominously, it traced a move from a position of perceptible cultural resistance to one of accommodation with existing modes of production and an apparent capitulation to the very desires the early work put in question. Whether this move is to be understood strategically (the need to be visible, the need to survive) or developmentally (an internal evolution in the artist's work) is not in itself a useful question. Far more important to consider here are the material and discursive forces that both exceed and bind the individual artist. Whether artists choose to publicly define their positions in opposition to, or in strategic alliance with, dominant modes of cultural production is important only insofar as such definitions may contribute to a collective space of opposition. But, in the absence of a clearly defined oppositional sphere and the extreme rarity of collaborative practice, attempts to clarify the nature of critical practice must focus on the artwork's ability to question, to contest, or to denaturalize the very terms in which it is produced, received, and circulated. What is at stake is thus not an ethics or a moral position but the very possibility of a critical practice within the terms of art discourse. And, as a fundamental condition of possibility, critical practices must constantly address those economic and discursive forces that perpetually threaten to eradicate their critical difference.

Some notion of the juggernaut of these forces can be obtained from a consideration of the parallel fortunes of Levine's earlier photographic appropriations and, indeed, postmodernist photography as a whole. In 1985, for example, three large group exhibitions featuring postmodernist photography were mounted: "Signs of the Real" at White Columns, "The Edge of Illusion" at the Burden Gallery, and most grotesque of all, "In the Tradition of: Photography" at Light Gallery. Not the least of the ironies attendant upon the incorporation of postmodernist photography into the now expanded emporium of photography was the nature of the venues themselves: the Burden Gallery was established in January 1985 to function as the display window of *Aperture*, the photographic publication founded by Minor White and customarily consecrated to modernist art photography; the Light Gallery, a veritable cathedral of official art photography, represents the stable of officially canonized modernist masters, living and dead. The appearance of postmodernist photography within the institutional precincts of art photography signaled that whatever difference, much less critique, had been attributed to the work of Levine, *et al.*, it had now been fully and seamlessly recuperated under the sign of art photography, an operation that might be characterized as deconstruction in reverse.

How had this happened? The Light Gallery exhibition title—"In the Tradition of: Photography"—provides one clue, elaborated in an essay that accompanied the show. Postmodernist photography is here understood to be that which follows modernist photography in the same fashion that postimpressionism is thought to follow impressionism. The first of the two epigraphs that introduced the essay was taken from Beaumont Newhall's *History of Photography*—a sentence describing the conservatism of pictorial, i.e., premodernist, art photography (that which preceded the Light Gallery regulars). The second epigraph consisted of two sentences from one of my essays, "Photography after Art Photography," asserting that the stakes that differentiate the two modes are a function of their position in relation to their institutional spaces. In much the same way that the modernist hagiographer Beaumont Newhall and I were equally useful in framing the thesis that postmodernist photography is part of an evolutionary *telos* having to do only with the internal development of art photography, so, too, did the gallery space both frame and render equivalent the two practices. This reduction of difference to sameness (a shorthand description for the eventual fate of most, if not all, initially transgressive cultural practices) was emblematically represented by the pairing—side by side—of a Sherrie Levine rephotograph of a Walker Evans and—what else?—a "real" Walker Evans beneath the exhibition title. That postmodernist photographic work and art photography came to inhabit the same physical site (although with the exception of the Levine/Evans coupling, the two were physically separated in the installation) is of course integrally linked with the nature of commercial space in the first place. In the final analysis, as well as a Marxist analysis, the market is the ultimate legitimizer and leveler. Thus, among the postmodernist work, one could also find excerpts from Martha Rosler's 1977 book project *The Bowery in Two Inadequate Descriptive Systems* (originally published by the Press of the Nova Scotia College of Art and Design). Variously an uncompromising critique of conventional humanist muckraking documentary photography, a text/image artwork, and an examination of the structuring absences and ideological freight of representational systems, *The Bowery* ... was exhibited at the Light Gallery amid the range of postmodernist photographs and bore a purchase price of $3,500 (purchase of the entire set was required). But what was finally even odder than the effect of going from the part of the gallery in which the Aaron Siskinds, Cartier-Bressons, and Paul Strands hung to the part devoted to the postmodernists was the revelation that postmodernist photography, once conceived as a critical practice, had become a "look," an attitude, a *style.*

Within this newly constructed stylistic unity, the critical specificity of a Rosler, a Prince, a Levine could be reconstituted only with difficulty (and only with prior knowledge). In large part, and in this particular instance, this was a consequence of the inclusion of a "second generation" of postmodernist photographers—Frank Majore, Alan Belcher, Stephen Frailey, and so forth—whose relation to the sources and significance of their appropriative strategies (primarily advertising) seemed to be predominantly a function of fascination. Insofar as stupefied or celebratory fascination produces an identification with the image world of commodity culture no different from the mesmerization of any other consumer, the possibility of critique is effectively precluded. Frank Majore's simulations of advertising tableaux employing props such as trimline telephones, champagne glasses, pearls, and busts of Nefertiti all congealed in a lurid bath of fiftieslike photographic color are cases in point. By reproducing the standard devices of color advertising (with which Majore, as a professional art director, is intimately familiar) and providing enough modification to accentuate their kitschiness and eroticism, Majore succeeds in doing nothing more than reinstating the schlocky glamor of certain kinds of advertising imagery within the institutional space of art. But unlike the strategies of artists such as Duchamp, or Warhol, or Levine, what is precisely *not* called into question is the institutional frame itself.[18]

The alacrity with which this now wholly academicized practice was institutionally embraced by 1985 (in that year Majore had one-person shows at the International Center of Photography, the 303 Gallery, and the Nature Morte gallery) was possible precisely because so little was called into question.

Although this more recent crop of postmodernist artists could only become visible—or saleable—in the wake of the success of their predecessors, the shift from margin to center had multiple determinations. "Center," however, must be understood in relative terms. The market was and is dominated by painting, and the prices for photographic work, despite the prevalence of strictly limiting editions and employing heroic scale, are intrinsically lower. Nonetheless, the fact remains that in 1980, the work of Levine or Prince was largely unsalable and quite literally incomprehensible to all but a handful of critics and a not much larger group of other artists. When this situation changed substantially, it was not *primarily* because of the influence of critics or the efforts of dealers. Rather, it was a result of three factors: the self-created cul-de-sac of art photography that foreclosed the ability to produce anything new for a market that had been constituted in the previous decade; a vastly expanded market with new types of purchasers; and the assimilation of postmodernist strategies back into the mass culture that had in part engendered them. This last development may be said to characterize postmodernist photography the third time around, rendering it both comprehensible and desirable and simultaneously signaling its near-total assimilation into those very discourses (advertising, fashion, media) it professed to critique. The current spate of Dior advertisements, for example, featuring a black-and-white photograph from the fifties on which a contemporary model (photographed in color) has been montaged bears at least a family resemblance to the recent work of Laurie Simmons. But where Simmons's pictures derived their mildly unsettling effects from a calculated attempt to denaturalize an advertising convention, the reappearance of the same montage tactic in the new Dior campaign marks the completion of a circuit that begins and ends in the boundless creativity of modern advertising.

The cultural loop that can be traced here is itself part of the problematic of critical practice. The more or less rapid domestication and commodification of art practices initially conceived as critical has been recognized as a central issue at least since the time of the Frankfurt School. This means that irrespective of artistic intention or initial effect, critical practices not specifically calibrated to resist recuperation as aesthetic commodities almost immediately succumb to this process. In this respect, the only difference between the fate of postmodernist photography and previous practices is the rapidity of the process and the ease, if not enthusiasm, with which so many of the artists accommodated themselves to it.

As was the case with its pop-art predecessors, the first wave of postmodernist photography pillaged the mass media and advertising for its "subject," by which I include its thematics, its codes, its emblems. These were then variously repositioned in ways that sought to denaturalize the conventions that encode the ideological and, in so doing, to make those very ideological contents available to scrutiny and contestation. Thus, Cindy Sherman's black-and-white movie stills — always her and never her — aped the look of various film genres to underscore their conventionality, whereas her infinite tabulation of the "images of women" they generate revealed their status as equally conventionalized signs producing a category (woman) and not a subject. Additionally, the cherished notion of the artist's presence *in* the work was challenged by the act of literally inscribing the author herself and revealing her to be both fictional and absent.[19] Similarly, Richard Prince's rephotographs of the "Marlboro Man" advertisements, which he began to produce in the early years of the Reagan administration, pointedly addressed the new conservative agenda and its ritual invocations of a heroic past. Here, too, the jettisoning of authorial presence was a component of a larger project. By focusing on the image of the cowboy — the individualistic and masculine icon of American mythology — Prince made visible the connections among cultural nostalgia, the mythos of the masculine, and political reaction. Recropping, rephotographing, and recontextualizing the Marlboro men permitted Prince to unpack the menace, aggression, and atavism of such representations and reveal their analogical link to current political rhetoric.

In contrast to practices such as these, work such as Majore's abjures critique, analysis, and intervention on either its purported object — the seductiveness of commodity culture, the hypnotic lure of simulacra — or the material, discursive, and institutional determinations of art practice itself. Not surprisingly, the disappearance of a critical agenda, however construed, has resulted in an apparent collapse of any hard-and-fast distinction between art and advertising. In pop art, this willed collapse of the aesthetic into the commercial function carried, at least briefly, a distinctly subversive charge. The erasure of boundaries between high and low culture, high art and commodity, operated as an astringent bath in which to dissolve the transcendentalist legacy of abstract expressionism. Moreover, the strategic repositioning of the images and objects of mass culture within the gallery and museum reinstated the investigation and analysis of the aesthetic as an ideological function of the institutional structures of art. Postmodernism as style, on the other hand, eliminates any possibility of analysis insofar as it complacently affirms the interchangeability, if not the coidentity, of art production and advertising, accepting this as a given instead of a problem.

Perhaps one of the clearest examples of this celebratory collapse was an exhibition mounted in the fall of 1986 at the International Center of Photography entitled *Art & Advertising: Commercial Photography by Artists*.[20] Of the nine artists represented, four came from the ranks of art photography (Sandi Fellman, Barbara Kasten, Robert Mapplethorpe, Victor Schrager), two from the first wave of postmodernist photography (Cindy Sherman and Laurie Simmons) and two from the second (Stephen Frailey and Frank Majore), and William Wegman, whose work, which has encompassed both video and conceptualism, falls clearly into none of these camps. As in the numerous gallery and museum exhibitions organized in the preceding years, the new ecumenicism that assembles modernist art photography and postmodernist photography functions to establish a familial harmony, an elision of difference to the profit of all.

Addressing the work of Frailey, Majore, Simmons, and Sherman, the curator Willis Hartshorn had this to say:

> The art of Stephen Frailey, Frank Majore, Laurie Simmons and Cindy Sherman shares a concern for the operations of mass media representation. For these artists to work commercially is to come full circle, from art that appropriates the mass media image, to commercial images that reappropriate the style of their art. However, for the viewer to appreciate this transformation implies a conscious relationship to the material. The viewer must understand the functions that are being compared through these self-referential devices. Otherwise, the juxtapositions that parody the conventions of the mass media will be lost.[21]

Now firmly secured within the precincts of style, postmodernist photography's marriage to commerce seems better likened to a love match than a wedding of convenience. Deconstruction has metamorphosed into appreciation of transformation, whereas the exposure of ideological codes has mellowed into self-referential devices. And insofar as the museum, in the age of Reagan, can institutionally embrace and legitimize both enterprises—art and commerce—Hartshorn is quite right in noting that a full circle has been described. For those for whom this is hardly cause for rejoicing, the history of postmodernist photography is cautionary rather than exemplary.

Working with Contradictions

The notion of a critical practice, whether in art production or criticism, is notoriously hard to define. And insofar as critical practices do not exist in a vacuum, but derive their forms and meanings in relation to their changing historical conditions, the problem of definition must always be articulated in terms of the present. Gauging the *effectiveness* of critical practices is perhaps even more difficult. By any positivist reckoning, John Heartfield's covers for AIZ (Arbeiter Illustriete Zeitung) had no discernible effect on the rise of fascism, although he was able to draw upon two important historic conditions unavailable to contemporary artists (a mass audience and a definable left culture). Still, the work of Heartfield retains its crucial importance in any consideration of critical practice insofar as it fulfills the still valid purpose of making the invisible visible and integrally meshing the representation of politics with the politics of representation. In other words, its critical function is both externally and internally inflected.

Although Heartfield is clearly a political artist, few contemporary artists concerned with critical practice are comfortable with the appellation *political*: first, because to be thus defined is almost inevitably to be ghettoized within a (tiny) art world preserve; second, because the use of the term as a label implies that all other art is *not* political; and third, because the term tends to suggest a politics of content and to minimalize, if not efface, the politics of form. It is for all these reasons that throughout this essay I have chosen to employ the term *critical practice* in lieu of *political practice*. That said, the immediate difficulty of definition must still be addressed, and it is made no easier by the fact that a spate of recent practices—so-called simulationism, neo-geo, postmodernist photography in all its avatars—lays claim to the mantle of critical practice. Whether one is to take such claims at face value is another matter. But if we assume that critical practices conceptually assume both an activity and a position, the emphasis needs be placed on discursive and institutional function. In this regard, Walter Benjamin's rhetorical question of 1938 is still germane: "Rather than ask, 'What is the *attitude* of a work to the relations of production of its time?' I should like to ask, 'What is its *position* in them?' "[22] The relevance of this question is that it underscores the need for critical practices to establish a contestatory space in which the *form* of utterance or address speaks to otherwise unrecognized, or passively accepted, meanings, values, and beliefs that cultural production normally reproduces and legitimizes. Insofar as contemporary critical practices operate within a society in which, as Victor Burgin observes, "the market is 'behind' nothing, it is *in* everything,"[23] the notion of an "outside" of the commodity system becomes increasingly untenable. This would suggest that the definition or evaluation of a critical practice must be predicated on its ability to sustain critique from within the heart of the system it seeks to put in question.

If we are to grant that a range of postmodernist photographic work that emerged at the end of the 1970s did in fact initially function as a critical practice, it did so very much within these terms. First of all, unlike other contemporaneous critical practices that positioned themselves outside the art world and sought different audiences (for example, Fred Lonidier's *Health and Safety Game*, Jenny Holzer's *Truisms, Inflammatory Essays*, and *Survival* series, the London Docklands project, Mary Kelly's *Post-Partum Document*, and D. Art's *Form Follows Finance*, to mention only a few),[24] postmodernist photography for the most part operated wholly within the parameters of high-art institutions. As the photographic work of Sherrie Levine clearly demonstrates, the critical specificity of such practice is only operative, can only be mobilized, within a particular context. Its instrumentality, in other words, is a consequence of its engagement with dominant (aesthetic) discourses whose constituent terms (and hidden agendas) are then made visible as prerequisites for analysis and critique. As circumstances change (for example, with the assimilation of appropriation into the culture at large), so too does the position of the artwork alter.

But within the overarching category of immanent critique, it is important to distinguish between those practices that elucidate, engage with, or even contest their institutional frame, and those that suspend or defer their institutional critique in the belief that such critique is already implied within the terms of their focus on the politics of representation. Representation is, after all, itself contextually determined, and the meanings thereby produced and disseminated are inseparable from the discursive structures that contain and enfold them. Consistent with the terms of Peter Bürger's formulation, there is by now a lengthy history of art practices of the former type, ranging from those of the historical avant-garde through more recent production exemplified by Michael Asher, Daniel Buren, Marcel Broodthaers (d. 1976), Hans Haacke, Louise Lawler, and Christopher Williams. It is, I think, of some significance that the work of these artists has more or less successfully resisted the reduction to stylistics to which postmodernist photography so rapidly succumbed. This is in part due to the fact that, with the exception of Buren, these are all *protean* practices, whose changing forms are determined by the issues the work addresses, its venue, its occasion, the historical moment of its making. This formal flexibility not only militates against the fixity of a signature style but emphasizes the tactical and contingent aspect of critical practice that defines and redefines itself in response to particular circumstances. Working with contradictions entails not only a strategy of position as such but a degree of maneuverability as well.

This in turn suggests that art practices predicated on the production of signature styles rather than constantly modified interventions may be especially vulnerable to neutralization of their purported critique. The history of postmodernist photography overall would appear to confirm this analysis. As various theorists have argued, a position of resistance can never be established once and for all, but must be perpetually refashioned and renewed to address adequately those shifting conditions and circumstances that are its ground.[25]

It is one thing, however, for a critic to map out what she believes to be the necessary conditions for a critical practice and quite another to actively deal with, assess, or articulate a position in relation to the work she actually confronts. Here, both critic and artist, situated within the restricted realm of high culture, are from the very outset enmeshed within a particularly dense matrix of contradiction. Once the decision is made to operate within the institutional space of art rather than outside it, critical writing and critical art are alike caught up in and subject to the very conditions such work attempts to contest. This is particularly the case with critical advocacy. Critical practice, if it is not to reduce itself to the tedium (and moralism) of the jeremiad, must be equally concerned with advocacy and partisanship. My own critique of the triviality and conservatism of official art photography was integrally related to my support of alternative photographic practices. This support, in turn, inevitably became part (a small part) of a cultural apparatus of undifferentiated promotion in the service of supply-side aesthetics. Critical advocacy, irrespective of the terms in which it is couched, is either from the outset part of the commodity system (for example, in the format of the museum or gallery exhibition catalog, or the commercial art magazine essay or review) or secondarily appropriated to it (as in the assimilation of critical writing into art journalism or the gallery press release). This means that critical writing, regardless of the writer's politics, can in no way consider itself as independent of the cultural apparatus it seeks to contest. This is not, however, to claim that there are no differences. Nor is this to suggest that critical writing is to be reduced to the opposite poles of partisanship or attack. On the contrary, ideally the work of the critic and the work of the artist—to the degree that they both conceive their practices critically—are theoretical, if not actual, collaborations. As is true of those art practices with which such criticism collaborates, learns from, and shares its agenda, working with contradictions necessitates a practical sense of what those contradictions imply—what they enable and what they preclude.

Thus, although the prevailing conditions of cultural production are hardly cause for optimism, neither are they cause for unrelieved despair; it is, after all, the very existence of discernible contradictions that allows for the possibility of critical practices in the first place. That said, perhaps the most daunting of all the contradictions that critical practices must negotiate is the direct consequence of problematizing the concept of the political in art. In this regard, the writing of Brecht, the practice of Heartfield, and the prescriptions of Benjamin can no longer be looked to as the *vade mecum* of critical practice. For if we accept the importance of specificity as a condition of critical practice, we are thrown into the specifics of our *own* political conditions and circumstances in the sphere of culture. To the extent that these include a refusal of inside/outside dichotomies, ("the market is *in* everything"), an interrogation of the notion of prescription itself (authoritative modes, practices, models), a recognition of the contingency and indeterminacy of meaning, and a general acknowledgment of the inescapable complicity of all practices within cultural production, it becomes increasingly difficult to say with any assurance what critical practices should actually or ideally seek to do. Needless to say, the putting in question of traditional conceptions of political correctness, of determinate and fixed positions of address, of exhortative or didactic modes of critique, has been exclusively the project of feminism and a part of the left. The regnant right knows no such uncertainty as it consolidates its position with increasing authoritarianism, repressiveness, and certainty. To have thus problematized the conditions of political enunciation within cultural production at a moment of extreme political reaction is perhaps the most daunting contradiction of all.

NOTES

I would like to gratefully acknowledge the advice, suggestions, good counsel, and unstinting support of Rosalyn Deutsche in the writing of this essay.

1. "Neo-geo," also referred to as "simulationism," the latest art package to blaze across the art-world firmament, is a good case in point. The artists involved (Ashley Bickerton, Peter Halley, Jeff Koons, Haim Steinbach, Meyer Vaisman—to name only the most prominent) were the subject of massive media promotion from the very outset. See, for example, Paul Taylor, "The Hot Four: Get Ready for the Next Art Stars," *New York Magazine*, 27 Oct. 1986, 50-56; Eleanor Heartney, "Simulationism: The Hot New Cool Art," *Artnews* (Jan. 1987), 130-137; Douglas C. McGill, "The Lower East Side's New Artists, A Garment Center of Culture Makes Stars of Unknowns," *The New York Times*, 3 June 1986. The media blitz was subsequently ratified by a group exhibition at the Sonnabend Gallery and, on the museological front, by an exhibition at the Institute for Contemporary Art, Boston ("Endgame: Reference and Simulation in Recent Painting and Sculpture," 25 Sept.-30 Nov., 1986) with an accompanying catalog featuring essays by prominent art historians and critics such as Yves-Alain Bois, Thomas Crow, Hal Foster. For a less exalted and intellectualized view of this phenomenon, see "Mythologies: Art and the Market," an interview with Jeffrey Deitch, art adviser to Citibank, in *Artscribe International*, (April/May 1986), 22-26. The interest of this interview lies in the way it clearly indicates the determinations and mechanisms in the fabrication and marketing of a new art commodity.

2. See Hal Foster, "Postmodernism: A Preface," in *The Anti-Aesthetic: Essays in Postmodern Culture*, ed. Hal Foster (Port Townsend, Wash.: Bay Press, 1983), ix-xvi. The conception of postmodernism in the visual arts as a critical practice was established in

the following essays: Douglas Crimp, "Pictures," in *Art after Modernism: Rethinking Representation*, ed. Brian Wallis (Boston: David R. Godine, 1984), 175-87; "On the Museum's Ruins," in Foster, *The Anti-Aesthetic*, 43-56; "The Photographic Activity of Postmodernism," *October* 15 (Winter 1980), 91-101; "The End of Painting," *October* 16 (Spring 1981), 69-86; "The Museum's Old, the Library's New Subject," *Parachute* 22 (Spring 1981), 32-37. For a theorization of postmodernism as an allegorical procedure see Craig Owens, "The Allegorical Impulse: Toward a Theory of Postmodernism," parts I and II, *October* 12 (Spring 1980), 66-86 and *October* 13 (Summer 1980), 59-80; and Benjamin H. D. Buchloh, "Allegorical Procedures: Appropriation and Montage in Contemporary Art," *Artforum* (September 1982), 43-56. See, further, Rosalind Krauss's important essays "Sculpture in the Expanded Field" in Foster, *The Anti-Aesthetic*, 31-42 and "The Originality of the Avant-Garde," in Krauss, *The Originality of the Avant-garde and Other Modernist Myths* (Cambridge, Mass.: MIT Press, 1985), 151-70. For a synopsis of the above essays see Hal Foster, "Re: Post" in Wallis, *Art after Modernism*, 189-201. See also my essay "Playing in the Fields of the Image," *Afterimage* (Summer 1982), 10-13.

3. See Robert Venturi, Denise Scott Brown, Steven Izenor, *Learning from Las Vegas* (Cambridge, Mass.: MIT Press, 1972), and Charles Jencks, *The Language of Postmodern Architecture* (New York: Rizzoli, 1977).

4. Irving Howe and Harry Levin were using the term in the late fifties.

5. See my "Winning the Game When the Rules Have Been Changed: Art Photography and Postmodernism," *Screen* 25, no. 6 (Nov./Dec. 1984), 88-102 and "Photography after Art Photography," in Wallis, *Art after Modernism*, 75-85.

6. The occlusion of feminism from the postmodernist debate, remarked upon by Andreas Huyssen, among others, is significant. It is by no means incidental that many, if not most, of the central figures within oppositional postmodernism in the visual arts, film, and video, have been women, and much of the work they have produced has been directly concerned with feminist issues as they intersect with the problematics of representation. See note 15.

7. On the implications and ideology of the revival of pseudoexpressionism, see Benjamin H. D. Buchloh "Figures of Authority, Ciphers of Repression," in Wallis, *Art after Modernism*, 107-36, and "Documenta 77: A Dictionary of Received Ideas," *October* 22 (Fall 1982), 105-26; Rosalyn Deutsche "Representing the Big City," in *German Art in the Twentieth Century*, ed. Irit Rogoff and MaryAnne Stevens (Cambridge: Cambridge University Press, forthcoming), and with Cara Gendel Ryan, "The Fine Art of Gentrification," *October* 31 (Winter 1984), 91-111; Craig Owens, "Honor, Power, and the Love of Women," in *Art in America* (Jan. 1982), 12-15. On the construction of photography as an "auratic" art, see Crimp, "The Photographic Activity of Postmodernism" and "The Museum's Old, the Library's New Subject," and Abigail Solomon-Godeau, "Winning the Game When the Rules Have Been Changed."

8. Martha Rosler, "Notes on Quotes," *Wedge* 3 (1982), 72.

9. Peter Bürger, *The Theory of the Avant-Garde*, trans. Michael Shaw (Minneapolis: University of Minnesota Press, 1984).

10. The theorization of a localized "site specificity" for contestatory and oppositional practices is one of the legacies of Louis Althusser and, with a somewhat different inflection, Michel Foucault. See Michel Foucault, "The Political Function of the Intellectual," *Radical Philosophy* 12 (Summer 1977), 12-15, and "Revolutionary Action:

'Until Now,'" in *Language, Counter-Memory, Practice; Selected Essays and Interviews by Michel Foucault*, ed. Donald F. Bouchard (Ithaca, N.Y.: Cornell University Press, 1977), 218-33.

11. See Fredric Jameson, "Postmodernism, or The Cultural Logic of Late Capitalism," *New Left Review* 146 (July-August 1984), 53-92. An earlier, less developed version of this essay, entitled "Post-Modernism and Consumer Society" is reprinted in Foster, *The Anti-Aesthetic*, 111-25.

12. For various critiques of Jameson's arguments, see Mike Davis, "Urban Renaissance and the Spirit of Postmodernism," *New Left Review* 151 (May-June 1985), 107-18; Terry Eagleton, "Capitalism, Modernism and Postmodernism," *New Left Review* 152 (July 1985), 60-73; and Douglas Crimp, "The Postmodern Museum," *Parachute*, forthcoming.

13. Douglas Crimp, "Appropriating Appropriation," in *Image Scavengers*, exhibition catalog, University of Pennsylvania, Institute of Contemporary Art, 8 December 1982-30 January 1983, 27.

14. Craig Owens, "The Discourse of Others: Feminists and Postmodernism," in Foster, *The Anti-Aesthetic*, 57-82 is an important exception.

15. Quoted in Gerald Marzorati, "Art in the (Re)Making," *Artnews* 85, no. 5 (May 1986), 97.

16. The activities, events, and objects produced under the rubric of "A Picture Is No Substitute for Anything" collectively and individually functioned to foreground the mechanisms of cultural production, exhibition and reception. While the working title implicitly points to—by denying—the fetish status of paintings, the practices themselves (for example, inviting an art public to the studio of Dmitri Merinoff, a recently deceased expressionist painter, the mailing [and exhibition] of gallery announcements, one-night only exhibitions in which Levine and Lawler exhibited and arranged each other's work, the production of embossed matchbooks bearing the legend "A Picture Is No Substitute for Anything") were constituted as tactical interventions within the structures of art. Inscribing themselves in the mechanisms of publicity, display, and curatorship served to focus attention on the framing conditions of art production which are thereby revealed to be structurally integral, rather than supplemental to the field as a whole. See, for example, Andrea Fraser, "In and Out of Place," *Art in America* (June 1985), 122-28; Kate Linker, "Rites of Exchange," *Artforum* (Nov. 1986), 99-100; Craig Owens, review of Levine/Lawler exhibition, *Art in America* (Summer 1982), 148; Guy Bellavance, "Dessaissiment Re-appropriation," *Parachute* (Jan.-Feb. 1982-83), 14-19; Benjamin H. D. Buchloh, "Allegorical Procedures"; Louise Lawler and Sherrie Levine, "A Picture Is No Substitute for Anything," *Wedge* 2 (Fall 1982), 58-67.

17. That the official museum version of modernism we inherit is in every sense partial and, more important, *founded* on these exclusions and repressions is a recurring theme in Benjamin H. D. Buchloh's essays. See also Rosalyn Deutsche, "Representing the Big City," and Douglas Crimp, "The Art of Exhibition" and "The Postmodern Museum." In the last-named essay, certain problems in Fredric Jameson's theorization of postmodernist culture are seen to derive from his acceptance of the official, museological, and *auteurist* version of modernism.

18. My use of the term *institutional frame* is intended in its broadest, most inclusive sense. Thus, what is at issue is not simply the physical space that the artwork inhabits,

but the network of interrelated discourses (art criticism, art history), and the sphere of cultural production itself as a site of ideological reproduction within the social formation.

19. This aspect of Sherman's work was of particular importance to critics such as Douglas Crimp. For an interpretation of Sherman's photographs that stresses their feminist critique, see Judith Williamson, "Images of 'Woman,'" *Screen* 24, no. 6 (Nov./Dec. 1983), 102-16.

20. "Art & Advertising: Commercial Photography by Artists," International Center of Photography, 14 September—9 November, 1986.

21. Willis Hartshorn, gallery handout.

22. Walter Benjamin, "The Author as Producer," in *Reflections*, ed. Peter Demetz (New York: Harcourt, Brace, Jovanovich, 1938), 222.

23. "In contemporary capitalism, in the society of the simulacrum, the market is 'behind' nothing, it is *in* everything. It is thus that in a society where the commodification of art has progressed apace with the aestheticisation of the commodity, there has evolved a universal rhetoric of the aesthetic in which commerce and inspiration, profit and poetry, may rapturously entwine." Victor Burgin, "The End of Art Theory" in Victor Burgin, *The End of Art Theory: Criticism and Postmodernity* (London: Macmillan, 1986), 174.

24. On Fred Lonidier's work and the London Docklands Project, see *Cultures in Contention*, ed. Diane Neumaier and Douglas Kahn (Seattle: The Real Comet Press, 1985). On Jenny Holzer, see Bruce Ferguson, "Wordsmith: An Interview with Jenny Holzer," *Art in America* (December 1986), 108-15. On Mary Kelly, see Mary Kelly, *Post-Partum Document* (London: Routledge & Kegan Paul, 1983). On "Form Follows Finance" see Connie Hatch, "Form Follows Finance," introduction by Jim Pomeroy, in *Obscura* 2, no. 5, 26-34.

25. For an excellent discussion of these issues, see Victor Burgin, *The End of Art Theory*.

Marginality and the Ethics of Survival
George Yúdice

On a trop souvent parlé de marginalité à propos (des expériences des étudiants, des jeunes, des femmes, des mouvements pour la défense et la reconquête de la nature, pour la revendication des diversités culturelles, raciales, sexuelles, des tentatives de rénovation des conceptions traditionelles de la lutte sociale, à commencer par celles des travailleurs). Il est très vrai que la marginalité à vite été tirée vers le centre et que les revendications minoritaires sont difficilement parvenues à se détacher de celles du "marais." Et, cependant, chacune d'elles, tout en suivant son propre discours, représente potentiellement les besoins de la plus grand majorité.*

Félix Guattari and Toni Negri[1]

There was a time when to be "marginal" meant to be excluded, forgotten, overlooked. Gradually, throughout this century, first in the discourses of anthropology, sociology, and psychoanalysis, "marginality" became a focus of interest through which "we" (Western culture) discovered otherness and our own ethnocentric perspectives. Today, it is declared, the "marginal" is no longer peripheral but central to all thought. Contemporary poststructuralist thought has apotheistically reclaimed "marginality" as a liberating force.[2] By demonstrating that the "marginal" constitutes *the* condition of possibility of all social, scientific, and cultural entities, a new "ethics of marginality" has emerged that is necessarily decentered and plural,[3] and that constitutes the basis for a new, neo-Nietzschean "freedom" from moral injunctions.[4]

"Marginality" is a concept that straddles modernity and postmodernity; it is operative in pluralist utopias and radical heterotopias, following a logic of exclusion in the former and a tactics of singularity in the latter. Now, because it is central to both modes of thought, its relevance to action—i.e., politics, which operates according to different, even contradictory logics—may become confused. On the one hand, liberal pluralism calls for the incorporation of the "marginal" into a framework that necessarily co-opts it (see the commentary below on Wayne Booth); the postmodern tactician, on the other, often *uses* the "marginal" to make a case for his or her own subversive potential (see the commentary later on Michel de Certeau). And, furthermore, in both examples the concept is inflated to such proportions that it loses its critical edge, its contribution to concrete struggles against oppression and domination. For if it becomes a matter of a recompensatory "I'm OK, you're OK" inclusion or a leveling attribution of subversive "marginality" to all,[5] the strategy of struggle is reduced to the hierarchy of a queue in which the "marginal" waits to enter the paradise of equal rights or it is blasted into a Brownian motion of liberated flows to which the new forms of domination under postmodernity (no longer only the domination of an easily identifiable repressive state) may be quite impervious.

Wayne Booth's attempt to engage in the "becoming-marginal" or "becoming-woman" of postmodernity is exemplary inasmuch as it reveals liberal pluralism's incapacity to maintain the difference of the "marginal."[6] Booth adopts the "marginal" voice of the feminist critic to correct an injustice and, like the protagonist of *Black Like Me*, to share the pathos of a redemptive position.[7] But because Booth is *not really* a woman (i.e., does not have the distinctive features sociosemiotically ascribed to woman inscribed in his own body and psyche), he can take his dose of "marginality" and go on to other issues. In any event, "marginality" does not last; it seems to move ineluctably toward the mainstream in his pluralist utopia: "But it is not the marginality that troubles me; what was extremely daring fifteen years ago is now only slightly marginal and tomorrow may be mainstream" (FI, 169).

It seems to me that Booth can move from one type of criticism to another because he gives them all equal weight in some hypothetical critical pantheon. In his contribution to *Critical Inquiry*'s special issue on "Pluralism," he reproduces just such a pantheon in which all gods have separate but equal status:

> In my criticism courses, incidentally, it is here that Plato or the Marxists or Kenneth Burke or the feminists—ideological critics in general—come into their own. Played against each other, and against my "congenital" formalism, they *demonstrate* pluralism.[8]

We see, then, that Booth's notion of pluralism is of the "I'm OK, you're OK" type, in which everything is allowed in its proper place and so long as it engages in a congenial, if not "congenital," "shared conversation," one that, of course, utterly changes the tenor of Bakhtin's notion of a conflictive "dialogue," which Booth invokes *sans* struggle: "We should always be trying, in genuine dialogue with each other about the texts we are questioning, to determine what meanings and experiences make sense—a plurality of senses—in this shared conversation, here in this room together" (PC, 479). Of course, what vitiates Booth's attempt to share the pathos of "marginality" is that he has no social analysis or critique to offer. "Marginality" is only temporary and partial; presently gendered, it is nevertheless classless and raceless. The pluralist can focus on one feature of "marginality," integrate it into his or her experience, and get over its awesomeness when it has entered the familiar mainstream.

For the postmodernist, on the contrary, "marginality" must keep its particularity, must remain minoritarian: "the problem is one of a becoming-minority: not to act like, not to do like or imitate the infant, fool, woman, animal, stutterer, or foreigner, but to become all that, in order to invent new forces or new weapons."[9] In a sense, the postmodernist has taken the old "myths of marginality" and turned them on their heads, endowing them with a "positive," "subversive" sense. The "laziness," "shiftlessness," and "cynicism" attributed to the "marginal" by liberal sociologists and anthropologists of the fifties and sixties are transformed here into "radical" and "subversive" tactics of resistance and advantage.

Michel de Certeau,[5] for example, argues that through *la perruque* ("the worker's own work disguised as work for his employer": 25) workers subvert the established order's injunctions for division of labor, competition, profitability, and so forth. It must be pointed out, however, that such "tactics" are wielded not only by workers but by the very same managers (and other elites) who enforce the established order. Recent scandals involving brokers who *use* "inside information" against the "rules" of the Securities Exchange Commission demonstrate that elites also practice these "popular tactics" to their own ends, ripping off the "system" much more profitably than any worker or "marginal" person. Given this characterization of the "subversiveness" of "everyday practices," how can we distinguish among the various modes of "bucking the system": the "getting over" in school by a black teenager from the South Bronx, the *perruque* of the secretary who "filches" company time to write love letters, and the use of inside information to make hundreds of millions in the stock market?

The answer is to *distinguish* among the practitioners of such tactics in terms of how the tactics enable them to survive and challenge their oppressibility. Otherwise, these generalized "diversionary tactics" obliterate the specificity of the motives for which they are employed. De Certeau, like Deleuze and Guattari, conceives "subversion" affirmatively, that is, as an "other" economy (*potlach*, deterritorialized flows) always constrained by a system—capitalism sublates, but always by transformation into another mode of oppression—that allows subversion only along the "fault lines" (providing "lines of escape") of the system.

> This individualistic axiom [of market economies] is, of course, now surfacing as the question that disturbs the free market system as a whole. The *a priori* assumption of an historical Western option is becoming its point of implosion. However that may be, the *potlach* seems to persist within it as the mark of another type of economy. It survives in our economy, though on the margins or in its interstices. It is even developing, although held to within modern market economy. Because of this, the politics of the "gift" *also* becomes a diversionary tactic. In the same way, the loss that was voluntary in a gift economy is transformed into a transgression in a profit economy: it appears as an excess (a waste), a challenge (a rejection of profit), or a crime (an attack on property). (de Certeau: 27)

There was a time when only certain individuals were considered guilty (or worthy) of transgression. Here, however, we get a universalization of the "tactics of the weak against the strong" (but where the "strong" also use the same "tactics," i.e., the broker's crime), which becomes crucial for postmodern intellectuals like de Certeau and others who need to theorize the possibility of their own subversiveness. If the only possibility of subversion were constituted by the oppressed as "privileged" agents of revolution, these intellectuals would have no means (forgetting Gramsci's "organic intellectuals," of course) to wage a viable struggle "against the system." In a world in which "one does not expect a revolution to transform the laws of history" (de Certeau: 25), subversion consists of taking the "lines of flight" provided by the system itself and outrunning it into ever greater entropic "deterritorializations," stretching capitalism's limits until it yields to a pure flow of positivity in which "escape" is no longer allative (toward) or elative (from). Translated into everyday practices, this utopian heterotopia is no longer populated by the madmen and revolutionaries of modernity but rather by the ordinary, including, or, perhaps, even privileging, those who subvert through the "*perruque* of writing itself":

> We can make textual objects that signify an art and solidarities; we can play the game of free exchange, even if it is penalized by bosses and colleagues when they are not willing to "turn a blind eye" on it; we can create networks of connivances and sleights of hand; we can exchange gifts; and in these ways we can subvert the law that, in the scientific factory, puts work at the service of the machine and, by a similar logic, progressively destroys the requirement of creation and the "obligation to give." I know of investigators experienced in this art of diversion, which is a return of the ethical, of pleasure (profit is produced by work done for the factory), and often at a loss, they take something from the order of knowledge in order to inscribe "artistic achievements" on it and to carve on it the graffiti of their debts of honor. To deal with everyday tactics in this way would be to practice an "ordinary" art, to find oneself in the common situation, and to make a kind of *perruque* of writing itself. (de Certeau: 28)

The Ethics of Écriture

In proposing a "*perruque* of writing," de Certeau is only extending a certain (European) modernist aesthetic-ethic to everyday practices and thus rethinking the vivification of art that the surrealists had proposed. There may be no "revolution" possible in the (traditional) "political" sense, but one postmodernist take on the modernist concept of "revolution" is to remove it from the privileged place of "art" and extend it to the everyday. Such a "revolution," however, no longer entails *Aufhebung* but an unceasing dissolution of the (Western) subject. This is how Kristeva defines the "ethical imperative" of art:

> "Ethics" should be understood here to mean the negativizing of narcissism within a *practice*; in other words, a practice is ethical when it dissolves those narcisstic fixations (ones that are narrowly confined to the subject) to which the signifying process succumbs in its sociosymbolic realization. . . . The text, in its signifying disposition and its signification, is a practice assuming all positivity in order to

negativize it and thereby make visible the *process* underlying it. It can thus be considered, precisely, as that which carries out the ethical imperative.[10]

Although Kristeva does not use modernist women writers as examples, women do enunciate the *demand* for a new ethics, for they are participating in the rapid dismantling that our age is experiencing."[11] In her latest writings, Kristeva has reconciled this demand for an ethics of dissolution with the demand for love embodied in the transference process of psychoanalysis, which makes possible *jouissance*. Psychoanalytic practice, like art, achieves for Kristeva the ethical imperative of dissolving the impossible desire with which modernity has constructed identity, especially sexual identity.

For Kristeva, as for Lacan, psychoanalysis is one privileged practice—privileged insofar as it works with the constitutive signifiers of the self—which responds to the ethical imperative of Foucault's call for an "aesthetics of existence": "From the idea that the self is not given to us, I think that there is only one practical consequence: we have to create ourselves as a work of art."[12] Whether or not Foucault took the *rapport à soi* of the Greek free*man* of classical antiquity as a model for our current ethical conduct is beside the point; what is important is that he sought to ground a new ethics in forms of self-activity relatively autonomous of moral and political codes.[13] The choice to explore such an ethics is particularly postmodern in that it becomes the only reason for action in a world whose heterogeneity continually dissolves the subject, and with it any universal grounding for knowledge and action.

This aesthetics of self-formation is a "postmodern condition" in the Lyotardian sense of contemporary discourse's "propensity for self-citation ... for reexamin[ing] its own internal communication and in the process question[ing] the nature of the legitimacy of the decisions made in its name."[14] It is this lack of legitimizing foundations that enables Foucault to draw the parallel between our period and that of the Greeks:

> Well, I wonder if our problem nowadays is not, in a way, similar to this one, since most of us no longer believe that ethics is founded in religion, nor do we want a legal system to intervene in our moral, personal, private life. Recent liberation movements suffer from the fact that they cannot find any principle on which to base the

elaboration of a new ethics. They need an ethics, but they cannot find any other ethics than an ethics founded on so-called scientific knowledge of what the self is, what desire is, what the unconscious is, and so on. (Foucault, "On the Genealogy of Ethics," 343)

Foucault may be too hasty here; he may not find any principles — except for those in modernist art—for ethical conduct among the movements of the so-called first world,[15] but they can be found among the dominated and oppressed peoples of "peripheral" or "underdeveloped" countries and in that very same first world. Certainly the Christian Base Community movement, as I shall argue below, practices a self-oriented ethics. The problem with Foucault's analysis, as I see it, is that the examples are drawn from the aesthetic practice of the Greek freeman and, more important, from modernist art. In both cases only elites engage in these particular types of self-analysis and self-formation. This does not mean, however, that Foucault's framework prohibits a priori other types of self-formation related to different social groups. On the contrary, insofar as knowledge, politics (power), and ethics mutually condition each other,[16] despite their relative autonomy, the particularities of the group that engages in ethical practices (its knowledges, its politics) must be taken into consideration. If Foucault could trace the genealogy of ethics for the dominant groups, it should be equally possible to trace that of dominated and oppressed peoples.

This realization should lead us to question the very construal of the "postmodern" according to a predominantly elitist perspective (modernist art for Franco-European poststructuralist intellectuals, the implosion or leveling of meaning and community among the North American middle classes) and to ask what role is played by oppressed minorities in the United States and Europe, as well as by oppressed peoples in Africa, Asia, and Latin America. My objective here is not to impugn or revile an "ethics of (modernist) self-formation" but to recognize that there are other ethical practices alongside it and that, perhaps, ethical practices may not exist in a state of purity or be easily categorized within such rubrics as the "modern" or the "postmodern." In the hands of a different group, certain practices take on different values; and this difference may be experienced in terms of rapprochement or conflict. Action (including discursive action), I would argue, operates more in keeping with a Bakhtinian interpenetration of orientations, such that any given orientation has neither exclusive propriety over itself nor any *final* significance.[17]

Until recently the "postmodern" has neglected "marginals"—defined in relation to oppression—either because their experience is not "modern" in the elitist sense of the European avant-garde or because vis-à-vis the "decentering" experience of the North American middle classes (especially the emergent high-tech "yuppies") their identity is, it is argued, "fixed" in resistance to the power of domination.[18] It would be equally problematic, however, to claim the "postmodernity" of the oppressed and subaltern, for that maneuver might serve to theorize the futility of a politics of empowerment. The attacks by certain poststructuralist intellectuals on a feminist empowerment respond to this double bind of the "marginal," who, despite being the vehicle of the valorized "marginalization" of the "decentered" enlightened elites, is chastised for seeking the material conditions (equal rights, equal pay, institutional recognition, etc.) that the elites already enjoy.[19] The very attack on the notion of identity is problematic in this respect, for identity is a major weapon in the struggles of the oppressed.

I would also like to argue that the current buzz notion of a "politics of desire" or a "politics of the signifier"—used to characterize the political repercussions of contesting representations—need not exclude the representational practices of oppressed "marginal" groups, for they are already inscribed with a contestatory signification. That is precisely why the mainstream media have launched a campaign to demarginalize, decolor, degender with such propaganda as the emergence of a "postfeminist" generation, as well as a black and Latino capitalist class "independent" of group ethos. (Gays and lesbians, much harder to demarginalize, are either stigmatized as the "sinful" AIDS-ridden Other or are left unrepresented in the media.)

Writing of(f) the Marginal

I should like to turn now to some examples of writing in relation to the "marginal" that problematize the idea that there is a postmodern ethics centered on the aesthetics of self-formation with a "politics of the signifier" that is *effectively* contestatory. I draw my examples not

from mass culture but from autobiographical or quasi-autobiograph-
ical confrontations with an ethnically based identity.[20]

Richard Rodriguez's *Hunger of Memory* can be understood as an
écriture that questions how the self is constituted. Its arguments
against affirmative action and bilingual education, because these policies construct a certain minority identity, are a significant indictment
of liberal morality (or hypocrisy, to be more exact). Against the
ethnic refuge that liberalism holds out to the "marginalized," Rodriguez proposes to write his ticket into a materialist(ic) middle class,
very much identified with the "California cult of the self," which Foucault found odious.[21]

Rodriguez's basic argument is that anyone who is reflective
enough to attempt to re-create the past, identity or ancestry, does so
only by means of a romantic illusion: "The child who learns to read
about his nonliterate ancestors necessarily separates himself from
their way of life."[22] Writing is the "natural" result of those who become aware of this separation, and it is the very structure of
écriture — its *spacing*, in a Derridean sense — that Rodriguez takes advantage of in his apotheosis of the Symbolic: not the Symbolic of the
Law of the (genealogical) Father (whom Rodriguez rejects) but, rather, the Law of the Anglo. English displaces Spanish just as his teachers
replace his parents as role models, as the public replaces (and ban-
ishes) the private, and as the middle class erases the lower class:

> I was not proud of my mother and father. I was embarrassed by
> their lack of education . . . they were not like my teachers. (52)

> But I do not give voice to my parents by writing about their lives. I
> distinguish myself from them by writing about the life we once
> shared. (186)

> Only when I was able to think of myself as an American, no longer
> an alien in *gringo* society, could I seek the rights and opportunities
> necessary for full public individuality. The social and political
> advantages I enjoy as a man result from the day that I came to
> believe that my name, indeed, is *Rich-heard Road-ree-guess*. (27)

> I write today for a reader who exists in my mind only
> phantasmagorically. Someone with a face erased; someone of no
> particular race or sex or age or weather. A gray presence. Unknown,
> unfamiliar. All that I know about him is that he has had a long
> education and that his society, like mine, is often public (*un gringo*).
> (182)

Rodriguez "escapes" his own "marginality" by essentializing difference in the abstract transferential Other that a modernist writerly practice makes available. This is the "irreducible" otherness that stands between his self and that of concrete Others with whom he might establish some form of solidarity. It is this writerly Other that enables him to close the door on intimacy and the "truth" of community: "Intimacy is not trapped within words. It passes through words. It passes. The truth is that intimates leave the room. Doors close" (39). "The loss," however, "implies the gain" (27) of entry into the material world of the middle class. Through writing he condemns the multiplicity of voices of the oppressed (including his own family) to silence and a reified alienness. After working one summer with migrant laborers, to attempt some sort of reconciliation with his desire for identification, he further corroborates his difference from them by rendering them silent:

> Their silence stays with me now. The wages those Mexicans received for their labor were only a measure of their disadvantaged condition. Their silence is more telling. They lack a public identity. They remain profoundly alien . . . I had finally come face to face with *los pobres.* (138-39)

At the end of the book, Rodriguez has fully managed to silence the "marginality" of his family and ethnic belonging. Silence for him is a way of "repress[ing] them" (185).

If we feel repelled by Rodriguez's repression of marginality, how do we launch a viable counterattack? Pluralism—the "I'm OK, you're OK"—acceptance of marginality, is successfully defeated, in my opinion, by Rodriguez's justifiable refusal to be essentialized by white, bourgeois, liberal pieties (notwithstanding his eager acceptance of the economic and social rewards of that same white bourgeoisie):

> A dainty white lady at the women's club luncheon approaches the podium after my speech to say, after all, wasn't it a shame that I wasn't able to "use" my Spanish in school. What a shame. But how dare her lady-fingered pieties extend to my life!
>
> There are those in White America who would anoint me to play out for them some drama of ancestral reconciliation. . . . But I reject the role. (4-5)

The "ethical substance" ("the prime material of [one's] moral conduct")[23] of Rodriguez's *rapport à soi* is his "marginality," and his writing is the "self-forming activity" by which he "manages" that substance and as such it is a practice with political repercussions. *Écriture* is not an unproblematic liberatory practice as Kristeva might have it or desire it. On the contrary, it is riddled with ambiguity, contradiction, even bad faith. That Rodriguez's writing has contributed to the passing of Proposition 63 (whereby Spanish is banished as a public language and English is made monologically official) is not the worst of his bad faith. It is the very desire to control the formation of the self, to claim proprietary rights on a form of language precisely by wreaking violence on it that boomerangs in Rodriguez's self-annihilation. Is there *jouissance* in the writerly enactment of the fantasy of cutting off his dark skin (mark of subalternity) as a symbolic means of cutting the tie to the group? In the end, his self(?)-formed, middle-class anonymity is wrested, stolen, extorted from the heteroglossia of sociality at the expense of the "marginalized."

The loss of affect that Frederic Jameson includes in his survey of postmodern characteristics is part and parcel of an aesthetic that explores the "marginal" and yet is incapable of any form of solidarity with it. This is brought out more clearly than even Rodriguez's erasure of "*los pobres*" in Joan Didion's *Salvador*. Didion's postmodern experience is evident in her capacity to immerse herself in the abject, this cadaverous and obscenely anonymous Other without registering any affect whatsoever: "These bodies . . . are often broken into unnatural positions, and the faces to which the bodies are attached (when they are attached) are equally unnatural, sometimes unrecognizable as human faces, obliterated by acid or beaten to a mash of misplaced ears and teeth or slashed ear to ear and invaded by insects."[24] On the contrary, in a parody of touristic advertising language, which may not be ironic (for then she would concede it some meaningfulness and human relevance), she describes body dumps as "visitors' must-do, difficult but worth the detour" (20). Indeed, she comments on her own alienation by rejecting the irony of the existence of a futuristic shopping mall in the midst of this "place [which] brings everything into question," and has a "local vocation for terror":

> I wrote it down dutifully, this being the kind of "color" I knew how to interpret, the kind of inductive irony, the detail that was supposed to illuminate the story. As I wrote it down I realized that I was no longer much interested in this kind of irony, that this was a story that would not be illuminated by such details, that this was a story that

would perhaps not be illuminated at all, that this was perhaps even less a "story" than a true *noche obscura*. (36)

This uninterpretable "story"—it is, in fact, a form of the sublime, an abject mystical *noche obscura*—is a prelude to Didion's attempts to describe the unrepresentability of Salvadoran reality. It cannot be represented because language has ceased to refer. Hence the displacement of language to meaningless numbers as an attempt to capture the "ineffable" (61). Reality is abolished and replaced with an obscene simulation by the proliferation of meaningless trumped-up documents and the adoption of solutions "crafted" in the language of advertising in Washington or Panama or Mexico. (65)

If the "texture of life in such a situation is essentially untranslatable" (103), it is because Didion has refused to become involved in what is all around her: "As I waited to cross back over the Boulevard de los Heroes to the Camino Real I noticed soldiers herding a young civilian into a van, their guns at the boy's back, and I walked straight ahead, not wanting to see anything at all" (p. 36). Indeed, the very reference to mutilated bodies and to the simulated character of life in El Salvador has a critical edge to it; and she is also quick to see "cultural impotence." But nowhere does she witness even one counterhegemonic expression. No doubt its human relevance—and its ex-centricity to the postmodernist lens that does not register meaningfulness—precludes interviews with mass organizations of peasants, workers, students, and women or a visit to the guerrilla zones of control. In other words, the aesthicoideological underpinnings of her putative "testimonial" reportage transform her testimony into a self-reflection on her own alienated vision. She cannot "see" the subjects of the counterhegemonic project because her vision registers only the surface of her postmodern hallucination. These subjects have not so much "dissolved" as "disappeared."[25] Didion's book has been touted as a "consummate political artwork,"[26] but its "politics of the signifier" achieve only the thrill of the postmodern sublime, not the *compassion* of the reader. The blurb on the cover bears witness to the appeal of such a vicarious thrill; the mutilation of Salvadorans contaminates our own flesh with a *jouissance* that is not just a *petite mort*: "Joan Didion brings this insanely violent world to life so that it ends up invading *our flesh*."

This particular "politics of the signifier" is contradictory, for in its exploration of self-constitutivity it does not question the nature of the alterity from which it enunciates. If such a politics is the "self-forming activity" of ethics, as Foucault defines the practice, and if the self-as-art is the *telos* or mode of being to which it aspires, what is its "mode of subjection," the "call" to recognize its moral obligation? If it is the "freedom" of "self-disengagement and self-invention,"[27] it is flawed by its uncritical use of "marginality" to achieve its *telos*.

The Experience of Oppression and the Ethics of Survival

In contrast to Didion's book, *I . . . Rigoberta Menchú. An Indian Woman In Guatemala*, as the subtitle in Spanish avows—"My name is Rigoberta Menchú and that is how my *conciencia* was born"—is about the formation of consciousness-conscience, that is, of the subjective and moral dimensions of identity, in an utterly marginalized Indian woman who has to struggle for survival at every step of her life. I should say that, lest this account be condemned for its essentialism, Menchú's notion of identity formation does not rely on a romanticized "ancestral reconciliation," Rodriguez's bugbear, but rather on a cultural and political practice necessary for survival (her ethical "mode of subjection"). Elisabeth Burgos-Debray, her transcriber/editor, acknowledges how Menchú's practice, simultaneously political and cultural, makes Rodriguez's problem irrelevant in her situation: "unlike the Indian rebels of the past, who wanted to go back to precolumbian times, Rigoberta Menchú is not fighting in the name of an idealized or mythical past. On the contrary, she obviously wants to play an active part in history and it is that which makes her thought so modern."[28]

Menchú describes the abject contempt and rejection that Indians experience and describes the practices by which they attempt to overcome these evils, not by separation, but by the acceptance of otherness. It is this otherness that opens them to the world; to survive, their very definition of identity must *incorporate* new elements:

> My dreams came true when we started organising. . . . We women had to play our part as women in the community, together with our parents, our brothers, our neighbors. We all had to unite, all of us together. We held meetings. We began by asking for a community

school. We didn't have a school. We collected signatures. I was
involved in this. I played a key role because I was learning Spanish.
(120)

The learning of Spanish, unlike Rodriguez's learning of English and
concomitant abandonment of Spanish, does not lead Menchú and
other Indians to disavow their native tongues. Instead, Spanish opens
them to an expanded identity. Menchú sees herself participating in
the regeneration of her culture, "as an Indian first, and then as a
woman, a peasant, a Christian" (120). She also identifies with the
poor *ladinos*. The *ladino* who taught her Spanish helped her understand that there were many areas in which the two ethnicities could
ally in a struggle against oppression and exploitation:

> That *compañero* taught me many things, one of which was to love
> *ladinos* a lot. He taught me to think more clearly about some of my
> ideas which were wrong, like saying all *ladinos* are bad. He didn't
> teach me through ideas, he showed me by his actions, by the way he
> behaved towards me ... the example of my *compañero* made me
> really understand the barrier which has been put up between the
> Indian and the *ladino*, and that because of this same system which
> tries to divide us, we haven't understood that *ladinos* also live in
> terrible conditions, the same as we do. (165)

In contrast with Didion's text, which aestheticizes the abject,[29]
Rigoberta Menchú's text is, rather, a *testimonial* of *incorporation* and
embodiment made possible by the struggle for survival. Religion,
like other cultural practices, is a form of social reproduction. Thus,
when Rigoberta Menchú argues that the objective of Christianity is to
create God's kingdom here on earth, she means that it "will exist
only when we all have enough to eat" (160). Although Didion's text
evokes an anorectic experience, Menchú's emerges from the experience of undernourishment. And it is the practical use of Catholicism
for the purpose of nourishment and survival that makes it reconcil-
able with traditional Indian practices. The significance of all Indian
expression is to embody the image of the earth (107). Indian religi-
osity emanates from Indian culture, which in turn is considered to be
a product of a dialogical relationship with the earth and nature. Land,
and nature in general, which not only provide material sustenance
but also embody *Dios Mundo* (earth god), cannot be owned or
exploited instrumentally. The child's hands are ritually purified so
that he or she may never rob (i.e., take from the community, the

social body) nor "abuse nature" (i.e., the natural body) (32). The Indian analysis of existential and social strife, then, begins with the condemnation of private or state ownership of the land (142).

Indians turn to Christianity (in its "primitive" mode) as a means to express their desire to maintain an integrated social harmony (106). When their view of this harmony is upset by instrumental reason and economic exploitation of land and labor, they convoke religious meetings in which they appeal to both God and nature and use Catholicism's sacred texts as "popular weapons" for vindication. They "hear" the possibility for the redemption of the oppressed in their readings of these texts:

> We began to study the Bible as a principal document. The Bible has many stories like ours regarding our ancestors ... The important thing is that we have begun to integrate that reality as our own reality ... Let's take "Exodus" as an example, which is a text we have studied, which we have analyzed. It deals with Moses, who tried to free his people from oppression, who did his utmost so that his people could be liberated. We compared the Moses of those times with us, the "Moses" of today. (156-57)

Seeking texts that can *enact* their struggle, they turn to the examples of Judith, David, and most significantly, Christ, who died for the survival of others. In other words, their suffering and collective survival is embodied in Christ's passion (158). In embracing Christ as the symbol of revolutionary consciousness-conscience, Rigoberta Menchú's community also embraces him as the most important of a panoply of "popular weapons" (160), which include both Christianity and Marxism:

> I don't own my life, I've decided to offer it to a cause. ... The world in which we live is so criminal, so bloodthirsty, that I might lose it at any moment. That's why, as the only alternative, I turn to the struggle, just violence, as I have learned in the Bible. That's what I tried to make a marxist *compañera* understand who asked me how I could make revolution and be a Christian. I told her that not all the truth was in the Bible but that it wasn't in marxism either. ... In the revolutionary process we have to defend ourselves against the enemy but we also have to defend our faith as Christians, and we also have to think ahead to after victory when we'll have many great tasks before us as Christians to bring about change. ... Together we can build a popular Church, a real church, not a hierarchy nor a building, but a change for us as persons. I have taken that option as a

contribution to the popular war of the people. And I know and I am
confident that the people are the only ones capable . . . of
transforming society. And that's not a theory. (270)

Religion and identity are, of course, problematic terrains for "self-
forming activity," but not universally so, for under certain circumstances, as in the case of the Christian Base Community movement in
Latin America, they provide the point of departure for a radical questioning of the oppressed self and its oppressors. Liberation theologians have explored the ethical imperative of this questioning. For
Enrique Dussel, for example, the "metaphysical transcendence"
opened up by the "praxis of liberation" is not an essence but "the
plenary critique of the established, fixed, normalized, crystallized,
dead" in which others are oppressed.[30]

The mode of subjection is "hearing the voice of the other" and
coming into a relation with its exteriority, which is "located beyond
the foundation of totality" (158). The very nature of the struggle for
survival among the oppressed creates a situation of unfixity and
open-enededness that makes possible new unfoldings. Dussel calls
this the "analectic moment": "The analectical refers to the real
human fact by which every person, every group or people, is always
situated 'beyond' (ano-) the horizon of totality. Negative dialectic is
no longer enough. The analectical moment is the support of new
unfoldings" (158). Where Foucault privileges the "aesthetics of existence," liberation theologians put "politics [at] the center of ethics,"
although the analectical is conditioned by the "poietic." (170). We
might say that a "pratical poetics" is the ethical "self-forming activity,"
in which the "self" is "practiced" in solidarity with others struggling
for survival. Menchú, in fact, has turned her very identity into a
"poetics of defense." Her oppression and that of her people have
opened them to an unfixity delimited by the unboundedness of
struggle. And yet she has made an ethico-poetic decision to keep her
identity a "secret," an indeterminate foundation for her own experience of freedom. Her words describe the ethics of the specific intellectual:

> That is my cause. As I've already said, it wasn't born out of something
> good, it was born out of wretchedness and bitterness. It has been
> radicalized by the poverty in which my people live. It has been
> radicalized by the malnutrition which I, as an Indian, have seen and
> experienced. And by the exploitation and discrimination which I've

felt in the flesh. And by the oppression which prevents us from performing our ceremonies,and shows no respect for our way of life, the way we are. At the same time, they've killed the people dearest to me, and here I include my neighbors from my village among my loved ones. Therefore, my commitment to our struggle knows no boundaries nor limits. This is why I've traveled to many places where I've had the opportunity to talk about my people, because it's not easy to understand just like that. And I think I've given some idea of that in my account. Nevertheless, I'm still keeping my Indian identity a secret. I'm still keeping secret what I think no-one should know. Not even anthropologists or intellectuals, no matter how many books they have, can find out all our secrets. (246-47)

If we are to take Foucault at his word that the "specific intellectual" of our day is "no longer the rhapsodist of the eternal, but the strategist of life and death,"[31] such struggles as the one Didion "covers" in her testimonial have to be confronted by those of us in the "regimes of truth" of the metropolitan countries that are engaged in producing death among the oppressed and subaltern. We need not speak for others, but we are responsible for a "self-forming activity" that can in no way be ethical if we do not act against the "disappearance" of oppressed subjects. This is the stance Foucault advocated with regard to the Soviet gulag and the "problem of Poland":

we have to raise the problem of Poland in the form of a nonacceptance of what is happening there, and a nonacceptance of the passivity of our own governments. I think this attitude is an ethical one, but it is also political; it does not consist in saying merely, "I protest," but in making of that attitude a political phenomenon that is as substantial as possible, and one which those who govern, here or there, will sooner or later be obliged to take into account.[32]

This very argument has to be applied not only with respect to the struggles within Western countries (be they capitalist or socialist) but also in struggles throughout Asia, Africa, and Latin America. Gayatri Spivak has remarked that Foucault's uncovering of the power regimes centered on the clinic, the asylum, the prison, and the university (let's add the USSR and Poland) are "screen-allegories that foreclose a reading of the border narratives of imperialism" (let's add, among people of color).[33] The Christian Base Communities use the biblical scriptures as the vehicles for *hearing* the voices of the oppressed; we must also avail ourselves of such vehicles that are possible within our secular culture and that do not run counter to our own struggles among racial, ethnic, sexual, and class minorities. There are no guarantees, of course, that articulations across our own social movements, on the one hand, and with oppressed groups abroad, will be possible and/or successful.[34] Our ethical practice, then, is the political art of seeking articulations among all the "marginalized" and oppressed, in the interests of our own survival.[35]

NOTES

1. Félix Guattari and Toni Negri, *Les Nouveaux Espaces de Liberté* (Paris: Dominique Bedou, "Collection Reliefs," 1985), 27.

2. I say "reclaimed" because "marginality" was an operative notion in the thought of classical sociology. Georg Simmel, for example, in "The Stranger," raises it to the status of an "objective freedom" akin to Freud's notion of the "uncanny," i.e., a combination of strangeness and familiarity, distance and nearness, indifference and involvement, which makes possible creativity and/or apprehension of truth. See *The Sociology of Georg Simmel*, ed. and trans. Kurt H. Wolff (New York: The Free Press, 1950), 402-08. Simmel's attribution of greater cognitive and ethical freedom to the "stranger" (or marginal person) continues to be operative in the arguments of post-structuralists and theorists of contemporary social movements. Sidonie Smith, for example, argues that ". . . woman speaks to her culture from the margins. While margins have their limitations, they also have their advantages of vision. They are polyvocal, more distant from the centers of power and conventions of selfhood. They are heretical." (*A Poetics of Women's Autobiography. Marginality and the Fictions of Self-Representation* [Bloomington: Indiana University Press, 1987], 176.)

The study of marginal populations in political science, sociology, and anthropology produced a vast literature, whose "blame-the-victim" myths—the marginalized are apathetic, lazy, cynical, unskilled, unwilling to integrate into the larger social system, etc., characteristics that are built into the marginal personality according to Oscar Lewis's proposal of a "culture of poverty"—Janice Perlman and others have exposed. See Janice E. Perlman, *The Myth of Marginality. Urban Poverty and Politics in Rio de Janeiro* (Berkeley: University of California Press, 1976) and Carlos G. Vélez-Ibáñez, *Rituals of Marginality. Politics, Process, and Cultural Change in Urban Central Mexico, 1969-1974* (Berkeley: University of California Press, 1983).

3. When Lacan declares "the subject . . . ex-centric to himself [such that] consciousness is not the center of his being," everyone becomes ex-centric or marginal; with Deleuze and Guattari, we even become potential "schizorevolutionaries" setting loose, "deterritorializing" the authoritarian (Oedipal) subjections of sociality. For Foucault, this "liberation" of the "marginal" is evinced by "difference over uniformity, flows over unities, mobile arrangements over systems." See Jacques Lacan, *The Language of the Self*, ed. Anthony Wilden (Baltimore: Johns Hopkins University Press, 1968), 181; Michel Foucault, "Preface," in Gilles Deleuze and Félix Guattari, *Anti-Oedipus: Capitalism and Schizophrenia*, trans. Robert Hurley, Mark Seem, and Helen R. Lane (Minneapolis: University of Minnesota Press, 1983).

4. John Rajchman has explored this "ethics" in Foucault and Lacan. See *Michel Foucault: The Freedom of Philosophy* (New York: Columbia University Press, 1985);

"Ethics after Foucault," *Social Text* 13/14 (Winter/Spring 1986), 165-83; "Lacan and the Ethics of Modernity," *Representations* 15 (Summer 1986), 42-56.

5. "Marginality is today no longer limited to minority groups, but is rather massive and pervasive; this cultural activity of the nonproducers of culture, an activity that is unsigned, unreadable, and unsymbolized, remains the only one possible for all those who nevertheless buy and pay for the showy products through which a productivist economy articulates itself. Marginality is becoming universal. A marginal group has become the silent majority." (Michel de Certeau, *The Practice of Everyday Life*, trans. Steven F. Rendall [Berkeley: University of California Press, 1984], xvii.)

6. Well known among the many deconstructive or disruptive tactics which privilege "becoming-woman" are: Derrida's "writing is woman," that is, the unfixable nonessence of woman's dissimulation of the Law (castration) is the "untruth of truth" of "Man's" inscriptions; textuality is a "hymen" which "inscribes castration's effect within itself" and as such it is a "margin where the control over meaning or code is without recourse, poses the limit to the relevance of the hermeneutic or systematic question." (*Spurs; Nietzsche's Styles/Eperons: Les Styles de Nietzsche* [Chicago: University of Chicago Press, 1978], 51, 101, *et passim.*) For Deleuze and Guattari, all subversive "becomings begin and pass through the becoming-woman. It's the key to the other becomings." (*A Thousand Plateaux. Capitalism and Schizophrenia*, trans. Brian Massumi [Minneapolis: University of Minnesota Press, 1987], 277.) "Woman," then, is not so much an identity but the practice of the "ruin of representation" (as in Sarah Kofman's phrase) of Western "Man" and "his" rationality. For a critique of this speaking or writing as "woman" by male theoreticians, see Alice Jardine, *Gynesis. Configurations of Woman and Modernity* (Ithaca, N.Y.: Cornell University Press, 1985). Like the feminists who seek to change their status and are "dismissed as anachronistic along with Man and History" (35), so too the "marginal" must confront the postmodern imperative to *remain marginal.* This is precisely the problem which I address here.

7. "Any critic, male or female, who tries to break through the hegemony of male voices is going to sound, as I have no doubt sounded here at least to some readers, a bit marginal, perhaps greatly so. Everyone who has attempted feminist criticism can tell you stories of how that kind of marginality feels." (Wayne C. Booth, "Freedom of Interpretation: Bakhtin and the Challenge of Feminist Criticism," *Critical Inquiry* 9 [September 1982], 45-76; reprinted in *Bakhtin. Essays and Dialogues on His Work*, ed. Gary Saul Morson [Chicago: University of Chicago Press, 1986], p. 169.) Subsequent references to "Freedom of Interpretation" are cited in the text as FI, with page number(s) following.

8. Wayne C. Booth, "Pluralism in the Classroom," *Critical Inquiry* 12, no. 3 (Spring 1986), 478. Subsequent references to "Pluralism in the Classroom" are cited in the text as PC, with page number(s) following.

9. Gilles Deleuze and Claire Parnet, *Dialogues* (Paris: Flammarion, 1977), 11; quoted in Jardine, *Gynesis*, 215.

10. Julia Kristeva, *Revolution in Poetic Language* (New York: Columbia University Press, 1984), 233.

11. Julia Kristeva, "Women's Time," in *Feminist Theory: A Critique of Ideology*, ed. Nannerl O. Keohane, *et al.* (Chicago: University of Chicago Press, 1982), 38.

12. Michel Foucault, "On the Genealogy of Ethics: An Overview of Work in Progress," in *The Foucault Reader*, ed. Paul Rabinow (New York: Pantheon Books, 1984), 343, 348, 351.

13. "I think we have to get rid of this idea of analytical or necessary link between ethics and other social or political structures." (Foucault, "On the Genealogy of Ethics," 350.)

14. Jean-François Lyotard, *The Postmodern Condition: A Report on Knowledge* (Minneapolis: University of Minnesota Press, 1984), p. 62.

15. The "Californian cult of the self" does not qualify for Foucault as a practice of self-formation as opposed to a true essence discoverable through the rule-governed procedures of "psychological or psychoanalytical science, which is supposed to tell you what your true self is." ("On the Genealogy of Ethics," 362.)

16. See "Politics and Ethics: An Interview" and "Polemics, Politics, and Problematizations: An Interview with Michel Foucault," in *The Foucault Reader*, 377 and 384.

17. "Prior to this moment of appropriation, the word does not exist in a neutral and impersonal language . . . but rather it exists in other people's mouths, in other people's contexts, serving other people's intentions: it is from there that one must take the word, and make it one's own. And not all words for just anyone submit equally easily to this appropriation, to this seizure and transformation into private property." ('Discourse in the Novel," in *The Dialogic Imagination*, ed. Michael Holquist, trans. Caryl Emerson and Michael Holquist [Austin: University of Texas Press, 1981], 293.)

18. "In the countries of the Third World, imperialist exploitation and the predominance of brutal and centralized forms of domination tend from the beginning to endow the popular struggle with a centre, with a single and clearly defined enemy. Here the division of the political space into two fields is present from the outset, but the diversity of democratic struggles is more reduced." (Ernesto Laclau and Chantal Mouffe, *Hegemony and Socialist Strategy. Towards a Radical Democratic Politics* [London: Verso, 1985], p. 131.)

19. Elizabeth Fox-Genovese makes a similar critique of those deconstructive intellectuals who discard the identity-based experiences of oppressed others in the construction of canons in the academy: "From the perspective of those previously excluded from the cultural elite, the death of the subject or the death of the author seems somewhat premature. Surely it is no coincidence that the Western white male elite proclaimed the death of the subject at precisely the moment at which it might have had to share that status with the women and peoples of other races and classes who were beginning to challenge its supremacy." ('The Claims of a Common Culture: Gender, Race, Class and the Canon," *Salmagundi* 72 (Fall 1986), 134.)

20. "It seems to me, that all the so-called literature of the self—private diaries, narratives of the self, etc.—cannot be understood unless it is put into the general and very rich framework of these [ethical] practices of the self." (Foucault, "On the Genealogy of Ethics," 369.)

21. See note 15.

22. Richard Rodriguez, *Hunger of Memory: The Education of Richard Rodriguez* (Boston: Godine, 1982), 161.

23. For Foucault, "ethics" comprises four dimensions: 1) the "ethical substance" which delimits what moral action will apply to (e.g., the pleasures among the Greeks, the flesh among the early Christians, sexuality in Western modernity); 2) the "mode of subjection" or the "way in which the individual establishes his relation to [moral obligations] and puts [them] into practice" (e.g., by divine law, by reason, by convention, by the pursuit of beauty as among the Greeks); 3) the "ethical work" of self-formation or asceticism (e.g., moderation of the pleasures through dietetics, economics and ero-

tics among the Greeks, self-decipherment among the Christians, self-help procedures in the "California cult of self"); 4) the "telos" or "place [an action] occupies in a pattern of conduct" such as that of salvation, immortality, freedom, or self-mastery. Michel Foucault, *The Use of Pleasure* (New York: Vintage, 1986), 26-28.

It should be pointed out that this "genealogy of ethics" traces only the practices of certain groups (usually the elites) in the historical periods Foucault studies. Evidently, slaves, women, and children are excluded for classical antiquity; barbarians under Christianity; colonized peoples and slaves in modernity; the oppressed of contemporaneity. The questioning of the ethical practices of these elites necessarily has political consequences that cannot be—*are not*—bracketed in actual practice. The freedoms of self-formation of the Greek citizen or the French theorist are underwritten by the constraints that the systems they live in foist upon oppressed peoples. My access to the computer on which I am writing this piece, for example, is dependent upon the conditions for technological development that the military-industrial complex has made possible, the very same conditions that involve research in informatics for the purposes of domination here and abroad.

24. Joan Didion, *Salvador* (New York: Washington Square Press, 1983), 16-17.

25. See Jean Franco, "Death Camp Confessions and Resistance to Violence in Latin America," *Socialism and Democracy* 2 (Spring/Summer, 1986), 5-17, for one of the most eloquent treatments of mutilation, disappearance and other repressive measures in relation to postmodernity and the "emergent ethics of survival" as practices that, although emanating from the experiences of given groups such as the Mothers Movements, cannot be essentialized.

26. The blurbs that meet the reader's eye on turning the cover connect the "politics" of such *écriture* with a (Baudrillardian) simulational horror: "a surrealist docudrama," "a poetic exploration in fear," "Joan Didion writes with a muted outrage that appalls the mind and stiffens the spine," "Bodies are found everywhere—in vacant lots, in garbage, in rest rooms, in bus stations . . . bodies, bodies—and vultures to feed on them wherever they lie . . . A CHILLING ACCOUNT," "HORRIFYING . . . the daily appearance of unexplained corpses, the constant presence of weapons in the hands of unidentifiable men . . . EL SALVADOR HAS TRULY BECOME THE HEART OF DARKNESS."

One has to trust the "wisdom" of the marketing industry to understand the prurient taste for horror that links desire to read this book with the desire to see the *Texas Chainsaw Massacre*, *The Terminator*, *Angel Heart*, and other displays of mutilation. Stories of solidarity overcoming oppression do not sell in our market. Like pornographic representations of violence against women, works such as *Salvador* draw much of their fascination from the violation of "marginal" Others, the oppressed.

27. Rajchman argues that the freedom of Foucault's new ethic "lies neither in self-discovery or authenticity nor in the 'free-' play of language, but in a constant attempt at self-disengagement and self-invention." (*Michel Foucault: The Freedom of Philosophy*, 38.)

28. Rigoberta Menchú, *I, Rigoberta Menchú. An Indian Woman in Guatemala*, ed. and introd. Elisabeth Burgos-Debray, trans. Ann Wright (London: Verso, 1984), xiii. Subsequent references may have slight alterations of translation.

29. Kristeva gives the most compelling account of this abject "self-forming activity," in which the "I," transformed along with the body into vomit, is expelled, and separated from nature (mother and father), thus making dialogue (and solidarity) impos-

sible: "Along with sight-clouding dizziness, *nausea* makes me balk at that milk-cream, separates me from the mother and father who proffer it. 'I' want none of that element, sign of their desire; 'I' do not want to listen, 'I' do not assimilate it. 'I' expel it. But since food is not an 'other' for 'me,' who am only their desire, I expel *myself*. I spit *myself* out, I abject *myself* within the same motion through which 'I' claim to establish myself." (Julia Kristeva, *Powers of Horror. An Essay on Abjection* [New York: Columbia University Press, 1982], p. 34.)

30. Enrique Dussel, *Philosophy of Liberation* (Maryknoll, N.Y.: Orbis, 1985), 58-59.

31. Michel Foucault, "Truth and Power," in *Power/Knowledge: Selected Interviews and Other Writings, 1972-1977* (New York: Pantheon, 1980), 129.

32. Michel Foucault, "Politics and Ethics: An Interview," 377. For the "Gulag question," see "Powers and Strategies," in *Power/Knowledge*, 135-37.

33. Gayatri Chakravorty Spivak, "Subaltern Studies: Deconstructing Historiography," in *Subaltern Studies IV—Writing on South Asian History and Society*, ed. Ranajit Guha (Oxford: Oxford University Press, 1985), 349.

34. The Women's Association of Salvadoran Women (AMES), for example, has had difficulties negotiating solidarity among certain U.S. feminist groups because of its ethical decision not to endorse the pro-choice stand on abortion. On the other hand, around such issues as rape and pornography there is general consensus.

35. After writing this essay, I had the opportunity to read two publications of relevance to it. "The Nature and Context of Minority Discourse," ed. Abdul R JanMohamed and David Lloyd, *Cultural Critique* 6 (Spring 1987), consists of nine of the eighteen essays presented at a conference on ethnicity held at the University of California, Berkeley, May 24-27, 1986. (Another nine essays will appear in number 7.) It is beyond the scope of this essay to review all the problems and insights contained in this issue. I shall limit myself to single out what headway is made beyond the knee-jerk third worldism or rhapsodic becoming-minor ("marginalism") that characterizes some of the contributions.

In "Genet's Genealogy: European Minorities and the Ends of the Canon," David Lloyd, following Deleuze and Guattari, differentiates between "minor" literatures, "defined in opposition to . . . canonical writing," and "minority" literatures, which involve "representations of developing autonomy and authenticity" (173). His espousal of a (modernist) rejection of narratives of identity, which are crucial to the struggles of oppressed minorities, is, however, implicitly criticized by Caren Kaplan and R. Radhakrishnan. In "Deterritorializations: The Rewriting of Home and Exile in Western Feminist Discourse," Kaplan warns that "there is no pure space of deterritorialization" and that social actors and critics should always "recognize [that] the minor cannot erase the aspects of the major" (194). She clearly recognizes the ways in which the struggles of the oppressed "enact a politics of identity that is flexible enough to encompass the ironies and contradictions of the modern world system" (197). I would add that this "politics of identity" also contests "canonical writing."

In "Ethnic Identity and Post-Structuralist Difference," Radhakrishnan exposes the postmodern paradox (i.e., that the postmodern, while privileging the marginal [which would include the ethnic, at least rhetorically], ignores the need to empower marginal groups, especially the ethnic) and proposes a theroy that "divest[s] itself from economies of mastery and yet empower[s] the 'ethnic' contingently and historically" (202).

The other contribution, Barbara Harlow's *Resistance Literature* (New York: Methuen, 1987), while not uncritical of the political and discursive practices of the third world and of the oppressed, makes the important point, against Kristeva's skepticism, that "oppressed people [have the capacity] to create cultural products of value" (193). In this book Harlow renders the important service of bringing to the North American reader a myriad of texts that contest domination but not by recourse to "economies of mastery."

The Man Who Mistook His Wife for a Hat or *A Wife Is Like an Umbrella*—Fantasies of the Modern and Postmodern
Jacqueline Rose

On the front of the paperback edition of Oliver Sacks's *The Man Who Mistook His Wife for a Hat* is a reproduction of one of René Magritte's best-known paintings—"The Betrayal of Images"—a picture of a bowler hat held in the center of the frame.[1] Across the bottom of the picture the illustrator for the book has added the caption "Ceci est ma femme" in graphics lifted from another of Magritte's paintings— "Ceci n'est pas une pipe." Without its caption, "The Betrayal of Images" comments on the tricks of the visual, which allows itself to suspend such an object in space (the "of" in the title is, however, ambiguous, not just betrayal by the image but the image as that which is betrayed). The painting of the pipe belongs to a related order of deception. It appears first as disavowal and then as a comment on the disjunction between visual image and referent, between visual icon and verbal sign.[2] The addition of the caption—"Ceci est ma femme"—to the first of these drawings, however, moves it into a completely different realm. From negative ("Ceci *n'est pas* une pipe") to positive ("Ceci *est* ma femme"), from disavowal to blind misrecognition, from betrayal to outrage, a gap opens up in which the question of sexual difference makes itself felt. Let's start by taking this as a way of thinking about the transition from the modern to the postmodern and note how it turns on the (mis)naming of the woman, at once utterly known and yet altogether in the wrong place.

By entitling his collection of case studies *The Man Who Mistook His Wife for a Hat*, Sacks turns his book into something of a joke (like the "unending joke" his patient William "substitutes for the world" [109]). The joke is clearly at the expense of the woman who finds herself caught in a perceptual crisis that flouts the limits of anything recognizable or knowable as a world, while also undermining the very site of knowledge itself. What is most disturbing about certain right-hemisphere disorders is that the patient not only loses her or his reality but *does not know it*. And, if the patient does not know it, there is a fundamental sense in which the disorder itself cannot be known, or properly told. Hence the striking dissimilarity between these sketches (Luria to Sacks, "Publish such histories, even if they are just sketches" [4]) and the classical Freudian case study, or even Luria's own history of *The Man with a Shattered World*, which consists to a large extent of the patient's own account of his disorder, the ability to tell the story of the illness being part of his attempt to recover faculties of whose loss he is only too painfully aware.[3] In Sacks's book, we are instead presented with a repeated crisis, not just of spatial and visual coordinates, but of the narrative function itself, which is either missing, frozen in time, or else acted out in a type of wild and meaningless superabundance—the "unending joke," "narrational frenzy," "confabulatory genius" of a William who, at every moment, had "literally to make himself (and his world) up" (103-10).

The grotesque substitution—"wife" for "hat"—therefore stands for a breakdown of narrative, identity, propriety (*proprio*ception is the word used in another case to describe the body's knowledge of the location of trunk and limbs, [68]), even as we can recognize only too clearly that other, banal concept of the "proper," which nonetheless permits the mistake (my wife, my hat, my property).

The title of Sacks's book is strangely reminiscent of another famous joke that exchanges the woman for the paraphernalia of everyday life. "A wife is like an umbrella. Sooner or later one takes a cab" appears in Freud's *Jokes and Their Relation to the Unconscious* as an example of the conceptual joke that works through allusion by omission: "a bewildering and apparently impossible simile, which however, as we now see, is not in itself a joke; further an allusion (a cab is a public vehicle); and, as its most powerful technical method, an omission which increases the unintelligibility."[4] As with the Sacks title, the starting point is one of bewilderment, but this time the joke merely *postpones* its intelligibility (it is this, finally, which makes it a real joke). Simile as opposed to metaphor (a wife *like* an umbrella, wife *for* hat), comparison rather than substitution, the joke is baffling but *tendentious*. It plays on that moment of seeming nonsense as part of a knowing intent. This is a cynical joke that mocks the institution of marriage. Its meaning is therefore suspended but not lost. As such, it belongs more to the language of modernism (with which Freud's book historically coincides) or at least to one of its frequent definitions—a felt alienation that can only find expression in the form of indirect speech.

Furthermore, insofar as the joke is available for interpretation, its sexual implications can be read beyond, or even against, that original intent. First, an affront to the woman (the butt of the joke), then, an attack on marriage ("not an arrangement calculated to satisfy a man's sexuality" [111]). But before we have a chance to stop at this one-sided (men only) view of sexuality, we are led, via a footnote on the same page of Freud's text, to " 'Civilized' Sexual Morality and Modern Nervous Illness," in which that same institution of marriage and its accompanying morality are presented as most likely to drive the woman mad ("unappeased desire, unfaithfulness or neurosis").[5] Although Freud's analysis in this article remains firmly within the bounds of a quantitative and reductive concept of sexual satisfaction, the laughter at the woman can be used to generate its own diagnosis and critique. The joke thereby becomes an emblem of something recognized as the condition of the "modern" itself ("Modern Nervous Illness"). If this joke targets the woman, it does so not unknowingly therefore, but in a moment of staggering self-deceit.

From Freud to Sacks, what these examples have in common is the way they turn a problem of representation and of knowledge around the woman. The woman is sited twice over, but the terms of that siting have undergone the most dramatic of shifts: in trope (simile/metaphor), in the form of knowledge (alienation/total loss of self), and in the disorders (neurosis/psychosis) with which these have come to be linked clinically. Thus, Hanna Segal, in her article "Notes on Symbol Formation," describes two patients: the neurotic whose dream of violin playing can be interpreted as a masturbation fantasy, and the psychotic who, when asked why he had given up violin playing since his illness, replied "Why? Do you expect me to masturbate in public?" The symbol first *represents* the object and then *becomes* it.[6] The recurrence of the woman across my two examples, however, suggests that if there is a difference, there is also a repetition at the level of fantasy, one that might affect the way we need to think about that modern/postmodern divide.

Recent writings on postmodernism often seem to reproduce some of the key terms of these examples, evoking—often metaphorically—their psychic economy, bypassing for the most part this question of the woman on which they could equally be said to rely. Repeatedly, the dominant concept seems to be that of psychic deficiency, that is, of a function that has been lost. At their conference on postmodern identity, the Institute for Contemporary Arts in London gave the book by Oliver Sacks a central and organizing status, thereby making the idea of deficiency the key image for the postmodern age ("The Real Me—the question of identity in the postmodern age").[7] Compare, for example, these quotations:

> if he has lost a self—himself—he cannot know it, because he is no longer there to know it.

> not merely a liberation from anxiety, but a liberation from every other kind of feeling as well, since there is no longer a self present to do the feeling.

The first is from Sacks (34), the second from Fredric Jameson's article "Postmodernism or the Cultural Logic of Late Capitalism."[8] Or place any of Sacks's sketches alongside Jameson's description of the postmodern body—"bereft of spatial coordinates," immersed "up to your eyes and your body" in a hyperspace that "has finally succeeded in transcending the capacities of the individual human body to locate itself, to organize its immediate surroundings perceptually, and cognitively to map its position in a mappable external world" (83). Like the premirror child, Jameson wanders the new city space and cannot find, or know, himself there. Which does not prevent him from knowing the woman—the extraordinary moment in his article when, talking of the 1960s' Warhol figures, he refers to "Marilyn herself," named on an earlier page as Marilyn Monroe, but offered here with all that familiarity that makes the woman so available for intimacy, so utterly *knowable*, one might say (63).

For Jameson, the psychic economy that corresponds to this vision of the postmodern is schizophrenia. He is not alone in evoking it as his model for postmodernism, but he goes further than most in the negative judgment he brings to it. "Schizophrenic fragmentation" is the psychic economy, "psychological squalor" at least one of the dominant forms of cultural production, in the postmodern world (73, 53). The argument is based quite explicitly on the idea of a historical/psychological mutation since Freud: "little enough in common anymore . . . with the hysterics and neurotics of Freud's own day" (63). The form of our contemporary cultural pathology has altered: "alienation of the subject is displaced by the fragmentation of the subject" (63). This is the opposite of Deleuze and Guattari's schizophrenic ethic (to which Jameson explicitly refers), and different again from that concept of paradoxology that Jean-François Lyotard links to schizophrenia, but which he uses above all to characterize postmodern science's relation of knowledge to itself.[9] What all these writers have in common, however, is something that could be called a psychic metaphorization of contemporary cultural and social space. In this context, *The Man Who Mistook His Wife for a Hat* becomes a kind of making strange, a bodying forth, of that metaphor, which it activates through the bodies and minds of the patients as they ceaselessly deregulate and regulate their inner and outer worlds.

We need to ask, however, what are the effects of this use of a psychic metaphor (or the psychic as metaphor) for the postmodern—whether the psychic can serve at this level of generality as the model for a whole epoch, whether finally the implication of the psychic and the social is best thought in this way. Why does the category of fantasy seem to figure so little? More specifically, what dramatization, sanitization, and desexualization follow from this general inflation of psychic economy across the whole of social space?[10] Dramatization because it becomes precisely the drama of all modern subjects; sanitization since, despite the idea of a crisis, the model seems to become strangely divested of some of the most difficult aspects of the psychic itself; desexualization perhaps most oddly of all, although this is no doubt an effect of the first two, because of the glaring omission of any question of sexual difference (the passing reference to sexuality—a "squalid" aside or the allusion to Marilyn Monroe).[11]

A few instances from different commentaries (which is not to collapse them into each other) can perhaps clarify this. For example, Jameson makes his appeal to the psychoanalytic account of psychosis in the following way:

> I must omit the familiar and more orthodox psychoanalytic
> background to this situation, which Lacan transcodes into language
> by describing the Oedipal rivalry in terms, not so much of the
> biological individual who is your rival for the mother's attention, but

rather of what he calls the Name-of-the-Father, paternal authority now considered as a linguistic function (72).

The description is taken from Lacan's account of psychosis, but by choosing to discard the reference to the paternal function, Jameson bypasses that traumatic point of sexual differentiation at which psychotic delusion seizes the subject—Schreber fantasying himself in the body of a woman and then penetrated by a God, the ultimate embodiment of a paternal function that has taken off into the real. Only if this question is overlooked can breakdown be presented exclusively in terms of the perceptual intensity of the signifier: "undescribable vividness," "a materiality of perception properly overwhelming" (73).[12] The description is, in fact, remarkably like Julia Kristeva's account of the hysterical icon in her article "The True-Real"—the point at which hysteria passes into hallucination, "a gaze that has no object," "a blinding field of colour and light."[13] Except that in Kristeva's account, this icon emerges when the question of the lack of distinction between mother and father "crops up again" and when, as a result of that lack of distinction, the third term gets grafted onto something in the order of a pre-object that appears to the subject with all the intensity of a symbolic order being denied (227-32). The perceptual dimension is therefore tied to a structure of fantasy. Interestingly, too, this example belongs to the category of the "borderline" (central to Kristeva's writing) which reveals that structure as it works back and forth across the neurotic/psychotic division.

What does it mean to separate the intensity from the structure or from the meanings to which, for all their circulation, that intensity can nonetheless be linked (cf. Hanna Segal's example given earlier)? It allows Jameson to talk of the postmodern in terms of a perverse euphoria at the *disjecta membra* of the cityscape through which multinational capitalism penetrates and breaks up the world. The omitted "Name-of-the-Father" returns in the hallucinogenic image of the most deadly phase of capitalism. The casualty is not only sexual differences but feminism itself—it appears simply as one of that "stupendous proliferation of social codes today into professional and disciplinary jargons, but also into the badges of ethnic, race, religious and class-refraction adhesion" ("stylistic and discursive heterogeneity without a norm" [65]).[14] For feminism, the political point and the symbolic point are, however, inseparable. For if one puts back the

"Name-of-the-Father" into the account of psychotic breakdown then — without celebrating the form of that disturbance — it nonetheless becomes impossible to invoke it without recognizing the far-reaching implications in the field of sexuality of this crisis of naming itself.

Faced with this, feminism might be forgiven for seeing the nostalgia for something felt as an earlier, and potentially reintegrated, form of self-alienation as a regret at the passing of a fantasy of the male self.

There is no nostalgia in Lyotard's *The Postmodern Condition*. The postmodern sees the end of those legitimizing narratives through which the social can fantasize full knowledge of itself. In Lyotard's argument, the general principle of postmodernism is a "heterogeneity" of language games, each with "pragmatic valencies specific to its kind" (xxiv). They work in common with the performativity principle of postmodern technological bureaucracy (they can be assimilated to that principle but can also disrupt it). More crucially, the fact of their heterogeneity means that there can be no general consensus through which the social can legitimize itself today. Lyotard bases this account on a pragmatics of language that takes "agonistics" as its founding principle, that is, language in its adversarial mode. The heterogeneity of language games to each other is therefore backed by a principle of instability internal to the utterance itself. Although Lyotard does not use it, the best illustration for me of this general principle of linguistic "trickery" is another joke-example from Freud: the Jew who accuses his cotraveler of lying when he says he is on his way to Cracow: "If you say you're going to Cracow, you want me to believe you're going to Lemberg. But I know that in fact you're going to Cracow. So why are you lying to me?" The Standard Edition beautifully indexes this one as "Truth a lie" (115, 247).

By backing heterogeneity with trickery, Lyotard brings his pragmatics into the realm of a psychic dynamic. (As Jameson points out in his "Foreword" to the English translation, the concept of narrative in Lyotard's argument starts to look like a fundamental instance of the human mind [xi]). It is a dimension that Lyotard himself recognizes when arguing for language games as the founding principle of the social bond:

> there is no need to resort to some fiction of social origins to establish that language games are the minimum relation required for society to exist: even before he is born, if only by virtue of the name

he is given, the human child is already positioned as the referent in the story recounted by those around him, in relation to which he will inevitably chart his course. (15)

The end of grand narrative as legitimizing principle of the social cannot dispense with the naming of the infant—and it is always a sexually differentiated naming—as the most fundamental narrative of all.

It seems as if Lyotard is separating his conception of language from the more psychoanalytic engagement with representation and the image that has been the focus of a number of his other books.[15] Pragmatics moves out the concept of enunciation in which heterogeneity would above all signify the (sexual) division of the subject to her or himself. This leaves Lyotard's own reference to schizophrenia floating (a possible link to paradoxology with aggressiveness as a "state variable of a dog" [59]). With all the difference between Jameson's and Lyotard's view of the lost moment of alienation (respectively nostalgia and relief), extraordinarily they both seem to manage the same cleanup in relation to the sexual act. In Lyotard's work it is only by separating language games from enunciation, the naming of the infant from the sexual trajectory of the child, that he can avoid any consideration of what might be the implications of paralogy, heterogeneity, and catastrophe for the postmodern ordering and disordering of the sexual realm. The loss of the psychoanalytic dimension leads once again to the foreclosure of any sexual politics from the account. One, furthermore, that would not require Jameson's distinction between the "just" and the "heterogeneity of desire," or between the "genuinely political" and the "symbolic or protopolitical" on which he ends his "Foreword" to Lyotard's book (xx). (I will come back to this.)

And what strange and innocent image of the social might finally be detected underneath both of these accounts? More than once Lyotard pushes terror off the limits of the social tie: "I am excluding the case in which force operates by terror. This lies outside the realm of language games" (46). Compare again Kristeva's reading of *Moses and Monotheism* as the key narration that reveals "*alterity, strangeness, disavowal of identity, separation and murder*" at the heart of the symbolic function—something she indeed classifies as the more "psychotic" discovery of Freud (223-24). To recognize this dimension, however, is to bring terror back into the very center of the definition of the social. It is also to rewrite that story of the child named as the referent of parental fantasy in the fully traumatic terms through which the "inevitable" charting of her or his course will take place. It might just be the sidestepping of this element that can also explain that final and lyrical definition of the postmodern by Lyotard as the putting forward of the "unpresentable in presentation itself" (81)— the point, indeed, at which the political floats off, but only because the issue of representation has detached itself so cleanly from the sexual dynamic of the sign.

For Jameson there is also an image of the extreme ("blood, torture, death and horror" [57]) which appears in his argument as the adjunct of class history—this subordination creates the space in which concepts like alienation and fragmentation can operate as the pathologies of different moments in time. Aggressivity can then also be localized as a distortion of postmodern visual space:

> the glass skin repels the city outside; a repulsion for which we have analogies in those reflector sunglasses which make it impossible for your interlocutor to see your own eyes and thereby achieve a certain aggressivity towards and power over the Other. (82)

(I am not sure how one can get power over the Other.) Or, again, "Pastiche is thus blank parody, a statue with blind eyeballs" (65). Alongside this runs the constant stress on the lack of "perceptual equipment" needed to match the postmodern hyperspace, as if vision were a question of perception and matching, and the look itself—prior to the third stage of capitalism—simply innocent. What nostalgia of the visual field is this, for there is clearly a visual nostalgia at stake? One that can still evoke that moment when cultural production looked "directly out of its eyes at the real world for the referent"[16] (I think this is what Eagleton means when he [twice] uses the expression "an eyeball to eyeball encounter with the real" [65, 69]). We might again compare Kristeva, who places scotomazation ("a fall into the blind spot of the retina") together with negation, repression, foreclosure at the heart of representation, a process that merely receives one of its available formations in the fantasies of the patient who had "rented the anus out to the eye" (224, 229).

This is simply to say that no discourse that pushes terror to the limits of its own self-recognition will be adequate to the way that violence functions as a fantasy of the social today (the appeal to a general symbolic function does not require that we discard the historic dimension). From their very different positions, both Hanna Segal and Jacques Derrida see in present-day nuclear rhetoric a discourse of maximum efficiency backed by the perverse desire of human subjects for the atrocity that they simultaneously dread and bring into play.[17] This might cast a different light on that image of postmodernism as the imminent takeover of the world (multinational capital or information banks). What happens to the account if we see it as itself implicated in a scenario that is somewhere most fervently desired?

In relation to postmodernist culture, any nostalgia for the innocence of the visual is especially likely to lead to a misreading of some of the most important cultural productions of today. Those precisely that bring into relation with each other the question of sexuality (and its horrors) and the ordering of visual space—those very aspects of the psychoanalytic that have been discarded from the account. For "Marilyn herself" is first and foremost a sexual fantasy in the form of the visual (as are indeed the title and the cover of Sacks's book). And feminist artists have set themselves systematically to interrogate the operations of that fantasy at the very point at which it turns the woman into its stake. "She" is also a commodity (the image as the ultimate commodity), which means that this type of interrogation of the image also challenges the reifications of everyday life.[18] As soon as the sexual, the visual, and the commodity are seen as part of a set of relations, some of the most cherished distinctions between the modern and postmodern, as well as the criticisms of the latter, start to break down.[19]

To name a few of the artists who could be said to operate in this field (is it necessary to point out yet again that not one woman figures in Jameson's account of postmodern, or indeed, modernist cultural production?). Take Barbara Kruger, for example, whose work can be seen in direct continuity with the found images of a Warhol, but who cuts across them with verbal slogans that blast open some of the dominant tropes of sexual division: "We won't play nature to your culture" is just one; it should be placed together with "You construct intricate rituals to enable you to touch the skin of other men" (protest at *and* pastiche of the same sexual economy).[20] To rephrase Eagleton (72), this is an artistic practice that crosses the postmodern "dissolution of art into social life" (the rejection of high culture) with a sexual politics, and crosses the modernist fragmentation of the image with a critical distance produced out of the very logic of the sign (that "You" of so many of Kruger's slogans that uses the "agonistics" of language to accuse and draw the spectator into the visual space).

What would happen to the wanderer in the city who lights on one of these images as poster?—Kruger's work is produced as art object and as fly poster, which means that it can appear in the gallery and in the street. This in itself dispenses with that reading of the postmodern as the consequence of an earlier avant-garde's own failure to successfully challenge the institution of art.[21] Or, when confronted with one of Jenny Holzer's neon signs "Protect me from what I want" splayed across Caesar's Palace in Las Vegas, or one of the *Survival* series stuck onto parking meters and public telephones on the New York City streets ("Savor kindness because cruelty is always possible later"), or more recently the announcements to be aired on network television, the first one of which is, "You are caught thinking about killing anyone you want." There is a violence in these slogans that works at the level of content, but also, and more crucially, in the disruption caused by their presence and by the very mode of address. They add to the confusion of city space and then appropriate that confusion for a blatant political intention. What would it mean to ask that we be able, in any simple sense, to *orientate* ourselves in relation to them. (Note that for Jameson the concern about postmodern disintegration is in fact backed by an insistence that all postmodern art, whatever its degree of intended protest, is in fact "received with the greatest complacency" [56]—the subject in all his complacency suddenly returns to rule out the possibility of any effective political dimension in the realm of postmodern art.)

Other artists like Cindy Sherman and Mary Kelly work more directly on the sexuality of the image. Sherman's self-portraits present themselves as the self-conscious stagings of female narcissism in its inflated and depressive modes. Kelly's most recent work, *Interim* crosses the modern and postmodern as part of its own self-understanding—it inscribes femininity in a space that stretches from the "attitudes passionelles" of Charcot's hysterics (how "far," how comfortably far, can we in fact assume ourselves to be from the "hysterics and neurotics of Freud's own day"?) into the language of consumerism and popular romance. Something that can still perhaps be recognized as the modernist formality of the image and its writing is therefore constantly linked to the consumerism of today. And central to the work's own commentary is the woman's psychic implication in and seduction by these images, which appear as both persecuting and desired. This may well constitute an important displacement of the political distinction between culture as either affirmation or critique. In the example of *Interim*, that passage and play across different cultural moments is also the narrative of the woman who ages—like the women's movement itself, which pauses, takes stock, and then redefines itself. This is no simple celebration of renewal à la Lyotard, since it contains more precisely and historically the idea of an ongoing movement that is also a self-transformation and critique; but no nostalgia either, since, for the woman, nostalgia is always an addiction to the image and fantasy of a flawless self. Kelly's latest work could be said to take the feminist slogan "The personal is political," inflect it through an interrogation of the image and its fantasies, and thereby turn it into a commentary on the movement of historical and cultural time. Seeing this question in terms of the political movement of feminism might indeed be one way of rethinking the temporal narrative (nostalgia, breakthrough) on which so much writing on postmodernism seems to be based.[22]

To sum up with a number of points: If the psychic is to be evoked as a model of the social (as diagnosis and/or metaphor),

—sexual difference must be seen as centrally part of that account, or else the fantasy of the woman will merely reduplicate itself, whether as squalor or as one of the interchangeable trappings of everyday life;

—terror cannot be pushed to the outer limits of that conception without risking its return in the form of a hallucinatory fantasy onto which nothing, and certainly not cultural production, can get any kind of grip;

—the visual field can only be understood as always already distorted and subject to the psychosexual in the full range of its effects—this if we want to avoid the worst of the eyeball-to-eyeball encounter (what kind of a fantasy is this?).

A question remains. What does it mean to compare a wife to an umbrella or to confuse her with a hat? What discourse can there be today that does not either take on and question those fantasies or else find itself condemned to repeat them across that still incomplete division between modern and postmodern time?

NOTES

1. Oliver Sacks, *The Man Who Mistook His Wife for a Hat* (London: Duckworth, 1985, Picador, 1986). Subsequent references will be cited in the text.

2. See the commentary on this painting by Michel Foucault, *This Is Not A Pipe*, trans. and ed. James Harkness (Berkeley and Los Angeles: University of California Press, 1982), especially Magritte's own quoted comments: "Sometimes the name of an object takes the place of an image. A word can take the place of an object in reality. An image can take the place of a word in a proposition" (38) and also pp. 47-49 of the text.

3. A. R. Luria, *The Man with a Shattered World, The History of a Brain Wound*, trans. Lynn Solotaroff (London: Jonathan Cape, 1973).

4. Sigmund Freud, *Jokes and Their Relation to the Unconscious*, 1905, The Standard Edition of the Complete Psychological Works, Vol. VIII (London: Hogarth, 1960), 110-11. Further references will be cited in the text.

5. Freud, " 'Civilized' Sexual Morality and Modern Nervous Illness," 1908, Standard Edition, Vol. IX, p. 198.

6. Hanna Segal, "Notes on Symbol Formation," *The International Journal of Psychoanalysis* 38 (1957), 391.

7. This paper was originally written for, and presented at, a symposium held at the Institute for Contemporary Arts, in London. See *Identity*, ed. Lisa Appignanesi, ICA Documents, 6, 1988.

Sacks in fact divides his book into two sections: Losses and Excesses. As he points out, neurology has no term for the latter.

8. Fredric Jameson, "Postmodernism or the Cultural Logic of Late Capitalism," *New Left Review* 146 (July-August 1984), 64. Further references will be cited in the text. For a much fuller critical discussion of Jameson, see Robert Young, *Political Literary Theory* (London and New York: Methuen, forthcoming).

9. Gilles Deleuze and Félix Guattari, *The Anti-Oedipus*, trans. Robert Hurley, Mark Seem, and Helen R. Lane (Minneapolis: University of Minnesota Press, 1983); Jean-François Lyotard, *The Postmodern Condition: A Report on Knowledge*, trans. Geoff Bennington and Brian Massumi, Foreword by Fredric Jameson (Minneapolis: University of Minnesota Press, 1984). See also Terry Eagleton, "Capitalism, Modernism and Postmodernism," *New Left Review* 152 (July-August 1985). Additional references will be cited in the text.

10. The exact relation being posited is very difficult to specify. Jameson states that his point is not some "culture-and-personality diagnosis" but that the account of schizophrenia serves as a "suggestive aesthetic model" (71). The distinction breaks down, however, when he writes later that "everything in our social life—from economic value and state power to practices and to the very structure of the psyche itself—can be said to have become cultural in some original and as yet untheorised sense" (87).

11. The remarks that follow do not address *The Anti-Oedipus*, which would require a separate discussion.

12. Much of the problem stems from Jameson's persistent reference to Lacan's account of schizophrenia. In fact, Jameson's description comes from Lacan's discussion of the paranoia of Schreber as part of a general treatment of the question of psychosis. It is this slippage that allows Jameson the concept of schizophrenia as the general model for psychic breakdown. Thanks to Fiona White for pointing this out in discussion.

13. Julia Kristeva, "The True-Real," trans. Sean Hand, *The Kristeva Reader*, ed. Toril Moi (Oxford: Blackwell, 1986), 232. Further references will be cited in the text.

14. There is, at moments, a striking similarity between this critique of the heterogeneity of specific interest groups and some of the discourse of the Right against the demands of feminist and ethnic groups.

15. For example, *Discours, figure* (Paris: Klincksieck, 1971). For a discussion of this book and of some of the problems in its specific use of psychoanalysis, see Geoff Bennington, "Lyotard: From Discourse and Figure to Experimentation and Event," *Paragraph* 6 (October 1985), 19-27.

16. Fredric Jameson, "Postmodernism and Consumer Society," in *The Anti-Aesthetic, Essays on Postmodern Culture*, ed. Hal Foster (Port Townsend, Wash.: Bay Press, 1983), 118.

17. Hanna Segal, "Silence is the Real Crime" (Paper presented to the first meeting of Psychoanalysts against Nuclear War, Hamburg, 1985, and to the London History Workshop, "Psychoanalysis and History" group, on 15 February 1986, to be published in the *International Journal of Psychoanalysis*, 1987); Jacques Derrida, "No Apocalypse, Not Now (Full Speed Ahead, Seven Missives, Seven Missiles)," *Diacritics* (Summer 1984), 23.

18. For the best discussion on this relationship between femininity and the emergence of consumer capitalism, see Rachel Bowlby, *Just Looking, Consumer Culture in Dreiser, Gissing and Zola* (London and New York: Methuen, 1984).

19. The relationship between feminism and aspects of postmodern culture is discussed by Andreas Huyssen, "Mapping the Postmodern," *New German Critique* 33 (Fall 1984), 5-52, and by Craig Owens, "The Discourse of Others: Feminists and Postmodernism," in *The Anti-Aesthetic: Essays on Postmodern Culture*, ed. Hal Foster (Port Townsend, Wash.: Bay Press, 1983), 57-82.

20. The link between Kruger and Warhol was pointed out to me by Peter Wollen, whose book on postmodernism is forthcoming (London: Verso; Bloomington: Indiana University Press).

21. This is the basic argument of Peter Burger, *Theory of the Avant-Garde*, trans. by Michael Shaw (Minneapolis: University of Minnesota Press, 1984). Kruger's posters have been displayed on the streets of Ireland, Las Vegas, San Francisco, and Berkeley and recently in London as publicity for the Channel 4 television series "The State of the Art."

22. For Kruger, see the Catalogue of the ICA Exhibition of her work held in London, 1984, especially the article by Jane Weinstock; for Holzer see the interview "Wordsmith: An Interview with Jenny Holzer," *Art in America* (December 1986), 108-15, 153; for Kelly, see the Catalogue of the Riverside Exhibition, London 1986, especially the essay by Laura Mulvey which gave me the idea about feminism and time.

Wild Signs:
The Breakup of the Sign in Seventies' Art
Hal Foster

In an essay a few years ago, I pointed to two basic positions within postmodernist art: one aligned with neoconservative politics, the other associated with poststructuralist theory.[1] In all apparent ways, I argued, these practices are diametrically opposed: Neoconservative postmodernism proclaims a return not only of historicist figuration (after the supposed amnesia of modernist abstraction) but also of the privileged artist (despite contemporary diagnoses of his [sic] death). Poststructuralist postmodernism, on the other hand, produces a critique of precisely those categories and configurations. Moreover, neoconservative postmodernism tends merely to counter formalist modernism with a practice of pastiche (the false populism of which covers for an elitist traditionalism). Poststructuralist postmodernism, on the other hand, works explicitly to exceed, in its various texts, images, films, and objects, both formalist aesthetic categories (the disciplinary order of painting, sculpture, etc.) and traditionalist cultural oppositions (high versus mass culture, autonomous versus utilitarian art). Yet, I argued further, what seems diametrically opposed here is in fact dialectically connected. The pastiche of neoconservative postmodernism does not redeem historical figuration or integral subjectivity any more than the textuality of poststructuralist postmodernism deconstructs them; rather, each practice marks the disintegration of both these forms. Whether in the guise of a neoexpressionist painting or a multimedia performance, each practice manifests the process of spectacular reification that is so intensive in late capitalism; in particular, each attests to a fetishistic fragmentation of the sign—which poststructuralist theory often valorizes and postmodernist practice often performs—that is fundamental to the cultural logic of capital.[2]

Yet, this short history of the sign remained very speculative and sketchy; here, then, I want to take it up again in relation to certain models of art in the 1970s. For it seems to me that the fragmentation of the sign, if not grasped as such in much art and criticism of the period, is nonetheless structural to them, so much so that for it *not* to become evident required a certain disavowal. So, too, I want to suggest that related poststructuralist theories of the time—especially ones that reject the concept of totality—also make internal this capitalist logic of reification and fragmentation, and ironically nowhere more so than when they presume to be most post-marxist. Of course, such a symptomatic reading of art and theory runs the risk, often associated with Lukács, of reducing cultural practice to a mere reflection of socioeconomic forces. Here, however, my premise is the more proper marxian recognition that theory is only as developed as its object (in this case, art) and that both are caught up in the contradictions of the moment in which they are formed—in short, that cultural categories, including concepts of the sign, possess a historicity that it is the task of criticism to apprehend.

Autonomy and Textuality

But, exactly how does one historicize the (post)modern sign? Several genealogies can be contrived, and I want to pose a few here, partly to reinscribe them later in relation to the art of the seventies. The first two, one well known, the other less so, derive from signal poststructuralist texts of Derrida ("Structure, Sign and Play in the Discourse of the Human Sciences," 1966) and Barthes (*S/Z*, 1970). I select these (rather than, say, the Foucauldian typology of the sign in *The Order of Things*) not only because they implicitly historicize the sign in relation to two specific shifts, one associated with market capitalism, the other with high modernism, but also because as they do so they reveal certain preconditions of the poststructuralist moment.

In *S/Z*, Barthes is on the lookout for slippages (linguistic, narrative, sexual, psychological, social, political) in the symbolic order of the world of the 1830 Balzac story "Sarrazine"—slippages prompted by the enigmatic (non)center of the text, the castrato Zambinella, "a figure in a complicated relation to the phallus,"[3] to say the least. Early in the story Balzac laments, vis-à-vis the mysterious keepers of the opera singer, the new social system of bourgeois money: "No one asks to see your family tree because everyone knows how much it cost." Barthes in turn theorizes this passage from the old feudal regime of hierarchical origins—of fixed wealth (land, gold)—to the new bourgeois regime of equivalent signs—of promiscuous paper money—as a shift from the order of the index to that of the sign:

> The difference between feudal society and bourgeois society, index and sign, is this: the index has an origin, the sign does not: to shift from index to sign is to abolish the last (or first) limit, the origin, the basis, the prop, to enter into the limitless process of equivalences, representations that nothing will ever stop, orient, fix, sanction. . . . [T]he signs (monetary, sexual) are wild because . . . the two elements *interchange*, signified and signifier revolving in an endless process: what is bought can be sold, the signified can become signifier, and so on.[4]

Yet, this historicization of the sign in relation to the cultural order of market capitalism—"an order of representation" that will soon prompt the first modern art—is conceived in terms far more appropriate to the cultural order of *late* capitalism—"a limitless process of equivalences." No doubt this condition of "wild signs" is emergent in the moment witnessed by Balzac, but it is not dominant until our own moment (which is, after all, often described as one of spectacular simulacra)—until, that is, the conjuncture from which Barthes writes 140 years after Balzac. Here, then, Barthes projects elements of a contemporary political and libidinal economy onto its beginnings. This suggests that the shift from the order of the index to that of the sign is completed (or rather repeated to the point where it is grasped as such) only in the present of his own text, that is, in the seventies. And such a shift does in fact govern salient aspects of the art of the period.

Derrida also projects a poststructuralist concept of the sign onto history; yet, unlike Barthes, he does so not in relation to the linguistic order of market capitalism (i.e., of early modernism) but implicitly in relation to the linguistic order of high modernism (i.e., of monopoly capitalism). In "Structure, Sign and Play in the Discourse of the Human Sciences," his famous deconstruction of Lévi-Straussian anthropology, Derrida writes of a "rupture," at which point it became necessary to think the concept of structure outside the concept of a fixed center or presence:

> This was the moment when language invaded the universal problematic, the moment when, in the absence of a center or origin, everything became discourse—... that is to say, a system in which the central signified, the original or transcendental signified, is never absolutely present outside a system of differences. The absence of the transcendental signified extends the domain and the play of signification infinitely.[5]

Pressed to specify this decentering, Derrida alludes to the Nietzschean critique of truth, the Freudian critique of self-presence, and the Heideggerian critique of metaphysics; yet, it is surely the Saussurean concept of the diacritical sign that most directly allows this new "play of signification." In any case, all these references allow us to identify the rupture remarked by Derrida—in structure, language, representation—as the rupture of modernism; and the epistemic connection between structural linguistics and modernist art is clear. ("The extraordinary contribution of [cubist] collage," Rosalind Krauss has written, "is that it is the first instance within the pictorial arts of anything like a systematic exploration of the conditions of representability entailed by the sign."[6]) Significantly, however, Derrida refuses to locate this decentering historically: "It is no doubt part of the totality of an era, our own," he states enigmatically, "but still it has always already begun to proclaim itself." Could it be that he here intimates the preconditions of his own recognition: that this decentering is only grasped as such—is only *lived* as such—in his own poststructuralist present? As with Barthes's "limitless process of equivalences," so with Derrida's infinite "play of signification": though surely related archaeologically to the ruptures of market capitalism (Barthes) and high modernism (Derrida), they are only "achieved" in our own late-capitalist, postmodernist moment, of which poststructuralism is a symptomatic discourse, one that comprehends earlier ruptures in the sign only because it reflects yet another rupture that it *cannot* comprehend for the simple reason that it participates in it.[7]

Two related genealogies of the sign may clarify this symptomatic aspect of poststructuralism. For both Jean Baudrillard and Fredric Jameson, (post)structuralism narrates a process of progressive abstraction, first of the referent (as announced by structural linguistics), and then of the signified (whereby in poststructuralism every signified becomes another signifier). It is easy enough to relate this process to the dynamic of (post)modernism: abstraction of the referent in high modernism (e.g., again, our world of simulacral images [Baudrillard] or schizophrenic signifiers [Jameson]). For both critics, the ultimate agent of this abstraction is capital: "For finally it was capital which was the first to feed throughout its history on the destruction of every referent . . . in order to establish its radical law of equivalence and exchange."[8] In this way an important historical relationship is suggested among the different stages of (post)structuralism, (post)modernism, and capital, whereby the former function as cultural codes—critical and collusive—of the latter. Indeed, not only does the diacritical logic of the structuralist sign (of signifier and signified) replicate the diacritical logic of the commodity (of use-value and exchange-value), as Baudrillard suggests, but so too may the poststructuralist critique of the sign promote the very "fetishism of the signifier" that is fundamental to the ideological code of late capitalism.[9] Jameson historicizes the same dynamic in terms of reification:

> [I]n a first moment [i.e., of structural linguistics, of modernism], reification "liberated" the sign from its referent, but this is not a force to be released with impunity. Now, in a second moment [i.e., of poststructuralism, of postmodernism], it continues its work of dissolution, penetrating the interior of the sign itself and liberating the signifier from the signified, or from meaning proper. This play, no longer of a realm of signs, but of pure or literal signifiers freed from the ballast of their signifieds, their former meanings, now generates a new kind of textuality in all the arts.[10]

Later, I want to test this model of a "new kind of textuality in all the arts" in relation to recent art theory, but first its aggressive historicism must be tempered, for the abstraction of the artistic sign does not proceed so evenly—there are repressions, repetitions, and resistances to factor in. Now, one logic of modernism is indeed to bracket the referent, first, in order to approach an autonomy of the sign (as, say, in Cézanne), then, to explore its arbitrariness (analytically in cubism, anarchically in dadaism); but this modernist "liberation" of the sign does not lead directly to a postmodernist "play" of signifiers. In the postwar reinvention of the avant-garde, modernist autonomy (or, in the language of Clement Greenberg, self-referential purity) is reestablished as the criterion of art—precisely *against* any (dadaist) arbitrariness of the sign. And, yet, after abstract expressionism, this very arbitrariness is in turn reestablished, especially with figures like Robert Rauschenberg and Jasper Johns. In fact, with Johns the arbitrariness of the sign is pushed to the point of the dissolution remarked by Jameson—to the point, that is, where signifiers (in Johns's letters, numbers, color names, etc.) do become literal, "freed from the ballast of their signifieds."

But this incipient textuality is also in turn countered with minimalism, a contemporary of structuralism that in its obsession with "objecthood" apparently achieves the autonomy of the artistic sign demanded by the dominant logic of modernism . . . only to see this autonomy dispersed across an "expanded field" of art that is again textual in nature (pop art, photorealist art, conceptual art, process art, body art, diaristic art, performance art, earth and site-specific art, video art, institution-critical art, feminist art . . .).[11] In fact, this dialectic—between a minimalist autonomy of the artistic sign and its textual dispersal across new forms and/or its pop collapse into mass-cultural ones—is operative throughout the culture of the sixties (for example, in avant-garde cinema between the structurally autonomous films of Michael Snow on the one hand and the disruptively textual films of Godard on the other).[12] However, in the late sixties and early seventies, the textual term of this dialectic comes to dominate, and the question is, how does this textual transformation occur?

Let me begin with a test case. Frank Stella is an exemplary painter of late modernism, a principal proponent of autonomy (or, again, self-referentiality). His early mature work (ca. 1959-65) is mostly based on fundamental forms such as crosses and stars whereby depicted design and actual support are (nearly) coincident. In this work, Stella is concerned to (re)ground the structure of painting as firmly as possible in the stability of simple signs.[13] That he does so, however, under the pressure of the historical *in*stability of the sign is suggested by his later work. For example, in his "Protractor" paintings, design and support are at once so coterminous and so conflictual that the pictorial sign is held together even as its fundamental *dis*unity is exposed. By the mid-seventies his work is given over more and more to this instability. Indeed, Stella exacerbates it: he first fetishizes particular signs of modernist painting (e.g., conservatism) and then simulates whole codes of historical painting—to the point in the eighties where one might find signifiers of linear perspective, of the three grounds of landscape painting, and of the modernist grid all a jumble in one construction. In short, the progression of his art from simple signs to fragmentary signifiers participates in the very negation of form, bespeaks the very dissolution of the sign, associated with the abstractive process of (post)modern capital. This negation is as transformative as it is decorative, as critical as it is replicative.

And it is hardly unique: this process is operative throughout different art forms of the late sixties and early seventies; in fact, it may be this alone that connects them. Faced with the dissolution of the artistic sign, some artists sought to reground it—first, fetishistically in various new materials, and processes (as in minimalism, process art, "postminimalism"), then, literally in the presence of the body, of the site, of actual space-time (as in body art, site-specific art, performance). Meanwhile, other artists underscored this dissolution of the sign—either demonstrated the reification of artistic language (as in much conceptual art) or enacted its material fragmentation (as in the many ephemeral installations of the period). Often presented as resistant to the commodity status of the art object, these strategies seem in retrospect to partake, indirectly at least, in the very fetishism of the signifier that, again, for Baudrillard, is part and parcel of our consumerist "passion for the code."

In any event, few artists grasped the disintegrative dynamic of the sign at this time. (There are exceptions: certainly Robert Smithson reflected, particularly in his textual site/nonsite works, on the concept of a structure outside the concept of a center.) In fact, this dynamic was not adequately critiqued until the institution-critical art and the psychoanalytical-feminist art that came to the fore in the United States only in the mid-and late-seventies. Contemporaneous with the Althusserian and Foucauldian critiques of ideological state apparatuses, institution-critical art implicitly rejected the position of an infinite "play of signification" in favor of an investigation of its institutional affiliations with power, whereas feminist art explicitly deconstructed "the tyranny of the (phallic) signifier"[14] in favor of nonsexist forms of cultural production and reception. But, again, in the early seventies, these aspects of the artistic sign were not yet foregrounded in art. Indeed, the terms necessary for such an understanding were only established in American art theory near the end of the decade—and then not entirely consciously, for the two texts that I have in mind are silent on the historical forces that determine the very fragmentation of the artistic sign that they otherwise narrate.

Indexes and Allegories

In "Notes on the Index: Seventies Art in America" (1977), Rosalind Krauss seeks a principle that might order the pluralistic art of the decade, and she finds it not in the art-historical category of style but in the semiotic order of the index. "As distinct from symbols," she writes, "indexes [e.g., footprints] establish their meaning along the axis of a physical relationship to their referents."[15] Right away this model refocuses such characteristic art of the seventies as body or installation art—as an indexical regrounding of art in presence subsequent to an erosion of representation.[16] Yet, Krauss argues, this shift to the indexical also occurred over fifty years before with Duchamp, who, after the cubist abstraction of the referent, confronted the arbitrariness of the sign: "It was as if cubism forced for Duchamp the issue of whether pictorial language could continue to signify directly, could picture anything like an accessible set of contents" (202). Indeed, not only did Duchamp *foreground* the instability of the sign (e.g., in the metonymic confusions of the homonymous phrases scribbled on his "optical machines," in the sexual confusions of his alterego Rose Selavy), but he also *regrounded* the sign in indexical marks (of which, as Krauss notes, the painting *Tu M'* [1918] is a virtual catalog, replete with shadow images of the readymades, a play of linguistic shifters in the title, and even a representation of an index finger). According to Krauss, these indexical operations govern all the work of Duchamp, whether photographic (she reads *The Large Glass* "as a kind of photograph") or readymade, since the photograph as a "sub-or pre-symbolic" trace is inherently indexical and the readymade is "a sign which is inherently 'empty,' its signification a function of only this one instance, guaranteed by the existential presence of just this object" (206).

In the second part of her essay, Krauss relates these Duchampian strategies to seventies' art, and, in fact, the "trauma of signification" that prompted the one recurs to prompt the other: on the one hand, an abstraction of the sign—first in cubism, then in minimalism—and, on the other, a predominance of the photographic—first in the mass culture faced by Duchamp, then in the consumer culture embraced by pop. (The Duchampian strategies of seventies' art also fit nearly in the Duchampian genealogy of the last twenty-five years—midway between the recovery of the readymade in minimalism and pop in the sixties and its elaboration in appropriation art in the eighties). Here, Krauss again relates the indexical to the photographic, the structure of which she defines first as a "reduction of the conventional sign to a trace" and then, after Barthes, as a "message without a code" (211). Now, one purpose of this connection between the indexical and the photographic is to order the diverse forms of seventies' art under a single principle—"the registration of sheer physical presence"—whether this be indexical, as in installation art, or photographic, as in video. But the more important purpose is to grasp the logic of this "presence" as a substitute for a "language of aesthetic conventions" (209) that breaks down in the seventies as it had at the moment of Duchamp. In short, according to Krauss, seventies' art also faces a "tremendous arbitrariness with regard to meaning," and its primary response is to resort to "the mute presence of an uncoded event" (212).

This is a brilliant account of much seventies' art, but its insight into structural logic makes for a partial blindness regarding historical process.[17] The very premises of the indexical model of seventies' art—that artistic signs can be "empty," that cultural messages can exist "without a code"—are disproved by later artists involved in a critique of (art) institutions and representations: for these artists, no body or site, representation or event, is ever simply present or uncoded. Indeed, some artists (e.g., Michael Asher, Hans Haacke) who elaborated on indexical art in the seventies came to treat site-specificity not phenomenologically in terms of mute presence but discursively in terms of institutional power. So, too, other artists (e.g., Martha Rosler, Sherrie Levine) who elaborated on photographic art of the seventies came to treat the documentary status of photography not as a message without a code to explore but as an ideological function to critique. In fact, just as the first artists would conclude that, far from uncoded, (institutional) sites actually overcode art, so too the second would conclude that, far from uncoded, (photographic) representations are actually texts that may project an effect of the real but do so only according to the logic of simulacral myth.[18] Of course, Krauss is hardly responsible for the limitations of her object; on the contrary, she outlines its logic so clearly that its historical process may now stand revealed: the shift to the indexical in seventies' art—the substitution of simple marks of presence for an eroded referent and an erratic signified—is a response to the progressive dissolution of the late-modernist sign; and this dissolution reflects the penetration of the artistic sign by the capitalist dynamic of reification and fragmentation. Such is the political unconscious of this semiotic breakdown, which, precisely because it was unconscious, could not then be grasped in its historical agency.

This rewriting must now be tested against the other major model of seventies' art—that such art refuses the late-modernist paradigm of symbolic totality in favor of a new postmodernist paradigm of allegorical textuality. Posted primarily by Craig Owens, this model can be decoded as a response to the next stage of this dissolution of the artistic sign: from its indexical regrounding in presence (body or site) to its allegorical dispersal as a play of signifiers (text). And, yet, this theory of an "allegorical impulse" in art is also blind to the capitalist dynamic that governs its object: like the indexical model, it brilliantly theorizes art in terms of internal transformations of the sign, but it too elides the historical preconditions both of these aesthetic transformations and of its own theoretical construction.

If the subject of "Notes on the Index" is the erosion of the conventional pictorial sign, the subject of "Earthwords" (1979), a review-essay of *The Writings of Robert Smithson*, is the transgression of entire aesthetic categories.[19] In this early text, Owens links postmodernism (in the figure of Smithson) with poststructuralism (in the figure of Derrida) by means of the decentering operative in both practices: it is, he argues, the eruption of language at the center of art of the sixties and seventies (e.g., conceptual art, artist writings, diaristic art, textual modes of documentation) that dislocates the visual order of modernism and prepares the textual space of postmodernism. Forget that for Foucault it is this eruption that initiates the modern, not the postmodern, episteme; the important connection here is the one implied between poststructuralist decentering in language and postmodernist fragmentation in art. In "The Allegorical Impulse" (1980), Owens thinks this relationship in terms of the Benjaminian concept of allegory: postmodernist art is allegorical not simply in its stress on the ruinous and the fragmentary, on immanent spaces (e.g., ephemeral site-specific work) and contingent forms (e.g., enigmatic images appropriated from the media), but more important in its impulse to deconstruct verbal and visual categories, to disarrange stylistic norms, to transgress modernist boundaries, to exploit the gap between signifier and signified. Owens cites practices in particular: "appropriation, site-specificity, impermanence, accumulation, discursivity, hybridization."[20]

But, as is clear today, there are problems with this model, both definitional and strategic. On the first count, one cannot strictly oppose an allegorical postmodernist paradigm to a symbolic modernist one, for each impulse—the utopian, transcendental, totalistic *and* the fallen, immanent, contingent—not only is dialectically necessary to the other but is so actively *within* modernism. In fact, as Owens works out his genealogy of the allegorical impulse, he finds it via Benjamin and Baudelaire "at the origin of *modernism*."[21] On the second count, his use of Benjaminian allegory tends to be formalist in its very antiformalism; that is, in this early essay, Owens is concerned primarily with the rhetorical ways in which the allegorical mode disrupts the formal autonomy of modernist art. At this point the stake of postmodernism is aesthetic—the replacement of one (symbolic) mode by another (allegorical) one—or, at best, avant-gardist—allegorical art is valued because it transgresses formalist categories. Analysis of the economic processes and political ramifications of postmodernism is not yet developed. Thus, for example, though Owens speaks incisively of reification of language in Smithson, of history as dissolution and decay in Benjamin, of verbal and visual forms destructured in postmodernist art, he does not reflect on the greater forces that govern these deconstructions—other than to suggest that it is the impulse of this artist or that theorist. (The word *capital* does not appear once—an extraordinary fact in an essay largely based on the Benjaminian concept of the allegorical in modern culture.)

In fairness, this apolitical reading of allegory was characteristic of the American reception of Benjamin in the seventies: his concept of allegory, received in terms of *The Origin of German Tragic Drama* more than of the Baudelaire writings and sifted through Derrida and de Man, was depoliticized; and his movement toward marxism was reversed. In his more recent work, Owens has in turn reversed this reversal; nevertheless, in "The Allegorical Impulse" he, too, rewrites Benjaminian allegory in terms of Derridean textuality and de Manian illegibility. But these characteristics of postmodernist art are complex symptoms, not transparent explanations: though they do indeed point to an "erosion of meaning" (216), this erosion must finally be referred, not to the theoretical apparatus of allegory, but again to the historical process of capitalist reification and fragmentation. At the conclusion of his essay, Owens narrates the (post)modernist abstraction of the sign outlined above:

> Modernist theory presupposes that mimesis, the adequation of an image to a referent, can be bracketed or suspended, and that the art object itself can be substituted (metaphorically) for its referent. . . . For reasons that are beyond the scope of this essay, this fiction has become increasingly difficult to maintain. Postmodernism neither brackets nor suspends the referent but works to problematize the activity of reference. (235)

Significantly, this narration of the abstractive process stops short of its historical reasons, which remain precisely beyond the scope of this particular poststructuralist model. And yet, if explored, these reasons might in turn problematize the role of postmodernist art in this problematization of reference—as symptom rather than agent—perhaps along lines suggested long ago by Benjamin: "The devaluation of the world of objects in allegory is outdone within the world of objects itself by the commodity."[22]

Allegories and Commodities

Like "Notes on the Index," "The Allegorical Impulse" is hardly responsible for the conceptual limitations of its moment. In the late seventies, the fragmentation of postmodernist art almost had to be thought in terms of an allegorical play of signifiers, in part because the discursive analysis of the artistic sign in institutional-critical art, and the psychoanalytical critique of its phallocentric subject in feminist art, had not yet taken hold in the United States. Feminist art was a particular blind spot: the conjuncture that prompted it in Britain — a nexus of feminist criticism and Althusser, film theory and Lacan — had not fully developed here. However, a reading of institutional-critical art had emerged by 1980; significantly, it too applied the Benjaminian concept of allegory but in its marxian formulation—of the allegorical as a critical mode of aesthetic practice in the culture of the commodity. Presented primarily by Benjamin Buchloh, this reading regarded the allegorical less in Derridean terms of textuality than in Barthesian terms of myth—or ideology—critique. Buchloh noted strategies similar to those of Owens—"appropriation and deletion of meaning, fragmentation and dialectical juxtaposition of fragments, and separation of signifier and signified"[23]—but he positioned them differently: not only in a genealogy of institution-critical art (from Duchamp through pop and Marcel Broodthaers to Dara Birnbaum and others) but also as dialectical responses to the montaged sensorium of (post)modern life. In this way, Buchloh returned recent allegorical art not only to its archaeological beginnings in capitalist technique but also to its historical subject: reification.

But problems have arisen with this allegorical practice too. One such problem, noted by both Buchloh and Owens, is its rapport with a melancholic posture—a posture of political passivity before a social world so reified as to appear inert, the history of which is then regarded almost posthistorically as so many ruinous tableaux vivants for aesthetic contemplation. Thus, art that was deemed allegorical (e.g., Robert Longo, Jack Goldstein, Troy Brauntuch) is in fact melancholic: its concern is the enigma of the historical or the opacity of the significant more than the critical redemption of lost moments or appropriated meanings. Such art is also spectacular: it is seduced to the point of replication by the late-capitalist transformation of events, objects, even people into so many images to consume. (Indeed, its "allegorical" aspects—an aesthetic contemplation of the historical, a rhetorical confusion of the temporal and spatial—"were discussed in 1928 by George Lukács as the essential features of the collective condition of reification" (56), a condition that late-capitalist spectacle merely elaborates upon.) With this aesthetic of spectacle, such art has inaugurated a new moment or model for art of the present: call it, after the indexical paradigm and the allegorical impulse, a conventionalist model whereby even the most materialist practices (e.g., the Duchampian readymade, analytical abstraction) become so many ahistorical conventions to be consumed, so many detached signifiers to be manipulated. Not restricted to any one style, this conventionalist art rehabilitates lost referents, only to reproduce them as simulacra; in so doing it does not contest our political economy of the sign but rather plays right to its market machinations. In fact, this art extends—to a degree that seems almost conscious—the fetishistic fragmentation of the artistic sign under discussion here.[24]

Buchloh is aware of the dangers of such a collapse; nevertheless, he insists on the potential criticality of allegorical art. Rather than rehearse the fetishism-effect of commodification (as conventionalist work does), such art can take this process apart as its own critical procedure:

> The allegorical mind sides with the object and protests against its devaluation to the status of a commodity by devaluating it a second time in allegorical practice. In the splintering of signifier and signified, the allegorist subjects the sign to the same division of functions that the object has undergone in its transformation into a commodity. The repetition of the original act of depletion and the new attribution of meaning redeems the object. (44)

Here, as he later acknowledges, Buchloh is very close to the Barthes of *Mythologies* (1957), wherein Barthes argues that the dominant culture operates by appropriation: it abstracts the specific signs of social groups into mere signifiers that are then recoded as general cultural myths (consider, for example, the trajectory of rap music or graffiti art). Against this appropriation Barthes proposed counterappropriation: "Truth to tell, the best weapon against myth is perhaps to mythify it in its turn, and to produce an *artificial myth*: and this reconstituted myth will in fact be a mythology. . . . All that is needed is to use it as a departure point for a third semiological chain, to take its signification as the first term of a second myth."[25] This myth-robbery is the allegorical procedure of much appropriation art of the late seventies and early eighties (e.g., Barbara Kruger, Sherrie Levine, Louise Lawler): to break apart the mythical sign, to reinscribe it in a countermythical system and to recirculate it in the distribution form of the commodity-image.

And, yet, there are potential problems here as well. The issue is not strictly recuperation: that appropriation is now a museum category or that montage is now an "abused gadget . . . for sale." Rather, it concerns strategy: When is appropriation a counterappropriation and not a replication? When does montage recode, rather than rehearse, the dissolution of the sign by capital? By 1970 Barthes had revised his project of myth-critique: it presumed too much—a position of scientific truth; besides, it had become part of the doxa. Today, he argued, one must do more—shake the sign, challenge the symbolic.[26] Given the phallocracy of the symbolic, this means one thing in feminist practice: a critical attention regarding positionality in representation. However, in the pervasive conventionalist practice of the present, it means quite another thing: not a critique of the mythical sign, but a fetishistic manipulation of its shattered signifiers. In conventionalist art, "the commodity has taken the place of the allegorical way of seeing"[27] once again.

If allegorical counterappropriation is to be critical and not conventionalist, it must be practiced with social groups that are appropriated and/or excluded in the first place; this includes not only the appropriated Others of present society (e.g., indigenous cultures still subject to primitivist abstractions, Afro-American cultures ever pillaged by style industries) but also the excluded Others of institutional history (e.g., popular cultures not acknowledged in art museums, proletarian cultures not transmitted in official traditions).[28] To be most effective, critical counterappropriation must take up both these contemporary and historical agendas: it must be performed collectively with appropriated social groups in the present (collectively because these groups are in no need of salvage: they have vital traditions and resistant strategies of their own) and redemptively for such excluded groups in the past (redemptively because, as Benjamin famously remarked, not even the dead—not *especially* the dead—are safe from the history written by the victors). In this way, one must not only dislocate cultural signs from myth but also reground them in the social world of everyday experience. It is true that such a practice might presuppose an idealism of the referent—as if the use-value of a sign, once abstracted, can be so restored. It is also true that it might presuppose an idealism of the social—that by sheer will artists can become collective producers rather than isolated practitioners. But this hardly makes such a practice utopian: it simply shows that it is not only in cultural production but also in its social field that artistic and critical interventions must now and ever be made.

NOTES

1. See my "(Post)Modern Polemics," *New German Critique* 33 (Fall 1984), 67-78, reprinted in *Recodings: Art, Spectacle, Cultural Politics* (Port Townsend, Wash.: Bay Press, 1985), 120-36.

2. See Fredric Jameson, "Periodizing the 60s," in *The 60s Without Apology*, ed. S. Sayres, A. Stephanson, *et al.* (Minneapolis: University of Minnesota Press, 1984), 194-201.

3. Dana Polan, "Brief Encounters: Mass Culture and the Evacuation of Sense," in *Studies in Entertainment*, ed. Tania Modleski (Bloomington: Indiana University Press, 1986), 173. I am indebted for the Barthes reference to this provocative essay.

4. Roland Barthes, *S/Z* (New York: Hill and Wang, 1974), 40.

5. Jacques Derrida, in *Writing and Difference*, trans. Alan Bass (Chicago: University of Chicago Press, 1978), 280.

6. Rosalind Krauss, *The Originality of the Avant-Garde and Other Modernist Myths* (Cambridge, Mass.: MIT Press, 1984), 34.

7. Often an argument takes on a logic that pushes certain points to the margins; so it is here. Let me simply note two lost tangents.

The shift from the order of the index to that of the sign, as outlined by Barthes, suggests another passage (outlined by Dana Polan with reference to Jean-Joseph Goux)—a partial, problematic shift in the economy of the subject from the classical capitalist regime of repression meted out by the phallic power of the father to the late-capitalist regime of investment in which the flow of desire is actively incited. Now, if we relate this putative shift to the discourse of postmodernism, we can begin to demystify its pervasive ideologeme of *loss* (loss of social narratives, political legitimation, artistic mastery, and so forth). For the postmodern sense of loss is registered as such only by various authorities of patriarchy: it is hardly felt by feminists. Nor does this shift mark a loss in any real sense: in practical terms of power it is but a slight reformation of social regime, a partial redeployment of productive bodies. Or, as Polan writes:

> Power doesn't always take shape as the power of the Symbolic Father, and the overthrow of a centered, authoritative Symbolic may simply mean that other forms of power-relations—often more subtle than the model of a feudal focused on a lordly figure—have come into dominance. Thus, for Goux, the overthrow of the Law of the Father in the overthrow of gold not only brings about the emergence of a free-floating economic sign, but also ties this emergence to the parallel emergence of a new law that finds its force in the transnational monopoly—the new corporation whose micropolitical channels of control are so widespread and dispersed that no single authoritative father-figure is necessary to put the machine into operation. (177-78)

This shift—in the order of subjectivity, in the order of power—is related to the shift remarked by Derrida: from a concept of centered structure to a concept of a "system of differences." As Derrida implies, this rupture, which finds its expression in high modernism and its precondition in monopoly capitalism, is still with us, as indeed monopoly capitalism is still with us, now lifted to a new level of totality in late capitalism. Could it be that the ultimate referent of his "system of differences" is the system of late capitalism—a centerless system that, if not global as a regime, is nonetheless total as a differential order that governs relations throughout the world market? In this system, with its multinational deployment of capital and its international division of labor, center and periphery are indeed destructured; and yet, even as difference is thereby released, it is also continually recaptured and redeployed.

Of course, developments on two such different levels—in deconstructive theory and in late capitalism—cannot be related by a mere analogy. Nonetheless, the "field" posited by poststructuralism and postmodernism in the seventies and the "field" constructed by late capitalism for the contemporary subject are somehow related, and this relationship may be mediated, in a partial way, by the reification and fragmentation of the sign. This penetration is not metaphorical; in art it becomes actual in the sixties when, with minimalism and pop, serial production is made consistently integral to the actual technical production of the work of art. But it is only in the seventies that this penetration of the artistic sign by capital begins to be thought, in however displaced a form.

8. Jean Baudrillard, "The Precession of Simulacra," *Art & Text* 11 (Spring 1983), 28.

9. Jean Baudrillard, *For a Critique of the Political Economy of the Sign*, trans. Charles Levin (St. Louis: Telos Press, 1981), 92.

10. Jameson, "Periodizing the 60s," 200.

11. For a gloss on these terms, the first associated with Michael Fried, the second with Rosalind Krauss, see my "The Crux of Minimalism," in *Individuals: A Selected History of Contemporary Art* (New York: Abbeville Press/Los Angeles: Los Angeles Museum of Contemporary Art, 1986), 162-83.

12. See Annette Michelson, "Film and the Radical Aspiration," in *Film Theory and Criticism*, ed. G. Mast and M. Cohen (New York: Oxford University Press, 1974), 469-87.

13. "[T]he logic of the deductive structure is . . . shown to be inseparable from the logic of the sign." (Rosalind Krauss, "Sense and Sensibility: Reflections on Post '60s Sculpture," *Artforum* 12, no. 3 [November 1973], 47.)

14. Craig Owens, "The Discourse of Others: Feminists and Postmodernism," in *The Anti-Aesthetic: Essays on Postmodern Culture*, ed. Hal Foster (Port Townsend, Wash.: Bay Press, 1983), 59.

15. Krauss, *Originality*, 198. Other page references for this essay are given in the text.

16. A crucial aspect of this subversion of the representational paradigm (and, for that matter, of the abstract paradigm) is the release of the simulacrum into art of the sixties (most obviously in pop). In fact, it can be argued that modernist abstraction poses no *fundamental* break with the representational paradigm, for the simple reason that it preserves this paradigm in opposition, in cancellation. Such a break must await the simulacral illogic and serial repetition of postmodernist art, which works to erode referential logic on its own terms. Clearly, any avant-gardist celebration of this "subversion" is problematic. For more on this, see my "The Crux of Minimalism," 178-80.

17. In fairness, this is her stated interest: "I am not so much concerned here with the genesis of this condition within the arts, its historical process, as I am with its internal structure as one now confronts it in a variety of work" (210).

18. For a different reading of the photographic derealization of the image, see Douglas Crimp, "The Photographic Activity of Postmodernism," *October* 15 (Winter 1980), 91-101. Although Crimp conceives the problematic of presence in seventies' art differently than I do here (see his early essay "Pictures"), his reading has been very generative.

19. Craig Owens, "Earthwords," *October* 10 (Fall 1979), 120-30.

20. Craig Owens, "The Allegorical Impulse: Toward a Theory of Postmodernism," in *Art After Modernism: Rethinking Representation*, ed. Brian Wallis (Boston: David R. Godine/New York: New Museum of Contemporary Art, 1984), 209. Other page references for this essay are given in the text.

21. Ibid., 212. A similar criticism is made (too strongly) by Thomas Crow in "Modernism and Mass Culture in the Visual Arts," in *Modernism and Modernity*, ed. B. Buchloh, S. Guilbault, and D. Solkin (Halifax: Nova Scotia Press, 1983), 257. Also, see Michael Newman, "Revising Modernism, Representing Postmodernism: Critical Discourses of the Visual Arts," in *Postmodernism* (London: ICA Documents 5, 1986), 42-45.

22. Walter Benjamin, "Central Park" (1939) in *New German Critique* 34 (Winter 1985), 34.

23. Benjamin H. D. Buchloh, "Allegorical Procedures: Appropriation and Montage in Contemporary Art," *Artforum* (September 1982), 44. Other page references for this essay are given in the text.

24. Conventionalist art assumes the avant-gardist recognition par excellence — that art is a matter of historical conventions — but it does not act on the radical possibility of this recognition; i.e., it makes no attempt to return art to social use. Quite the opposite: it surrenders art to the vicious circle of consumerist irrelevance; and it does so by default — it has no collectivity to engage. For more on these "spectacular" and "conventionalist" tendencies, see my *Recodings*, 78-97, and my "Signs Taken for Wonders," *Art in America* (June 1986).

25. Roland Barthes, *Mythologies* (New York: Hill & Wang, 1972), p. 135. Also see *Recodings*, 166-79.

26. Roland Barthes, "Change the Object Itself," in *Image-Music-Text*, trans. Stephen Heath (New York: Hill & Wang, 1977).

27. Benjamin, "Central Park," 52.

28. Jürgen Habermas gives an example of such counterappropriation: "a group of politically motivated, knowledge-hungry workers in 1937 in Berlin . . . who, through an evening high-school education, acquired the intellectual means to fathom the general and social history of European art. Out of the resilient edifice of this objective mind, embodied in works of art which they saw again and again in the museums of Berlin, they started removing their own chips of stone, which they gathered together and reassembled in the context of their own milieu. This milieu was far removed from that of traditional education as well as from the then existing regime. These young workers went back and forth between the edifice of European art and their own milieu until they were able to illuminate both." (Habermas, "Modernity — An Incomplete Project," in *The Anti-Aesthetic*, 13). The example is not only abstract but also fictional — drawn from *The Aesthetics of Resistance* by Peter Weiss. Yet this provenance says more about the isolation of the intellectual than the paucity of the practice.

Interview with Cornel West
Anders Stephanson

Anders Stephanson: Philosophically speaking, you come out of the American tradition of pragmatism. In everyday parlance, pragmatism is often understood as adjusting in an almost opportunistic manner to existing circumstances. Philosophical pragmatism is something quite different.

Cornel West: When philosophers talk about pragmatism, they are talking about Charles Peirce, William James, and John Dewey. For me, it is principally Dewey. Three theses are basic: (1) antirealism in ontology, so that the correspondence theory of truth is called into question and one no longer can appeal to Reality as a court of appeal to adjudicate between conflicting theories of the world; (2) antifoundationalism in epistemology, so that one cannot in fact invoke noninferential, intrinsically credible elements in experience to justify claims about experience; and (3) detranscendentalizing of the subject, the elimination of mind itself as a sphere of inquiry. These three theses (mainly Dewey's) are underpinned by the basic claim that social practices—contingent, power-laden, structured social practices—lie at the very center of knowledge. In other words, knowledge is produced, acquired, and achieved. Here, the link to the marxist tradition, especially that of Antonio Gramsci, looms large for me.

AS: These claims also have similarities with some poststructuralist theory.

CW: Very much so. Detranscendentalizing the subject is, in Derrida's case, of course, a matter of the decentering of the subject, and in that regard his deconstruction clearly converges with Dewey's

three basic theses of long ago. Derrida is more than a skeptical footnote to Husserl, but he can be viewed as that; and when he is, his
deconstruction is a problematization of Husserl's quest for certainty
within the interior monologue, within the self-presence of consciousness, within the mental theater.

AS: There is obviously no pragmatic agreement on what Derrida
at times is erroneously understood to be arguing, the absurd idea
that there is nothing outside the text.

CW: He can actually be understood to claim that there is nothing
outside social practices: intertextuality is a differential web of relations shot through with traces, shot through with activity. For a pragmatist, that activity is always linked to human agency and the context
in which that agency is enacted. If he is read that way, I am in agreement.

AS: Poststructuralism is a critique of marxism insofar as it under-
mines "the worldliness of the text"; but what also stands out is the
attack on totalizing and totality. In the French context, this seems in
part an effort to escape from Sartre's shadow, in part a general reaction against the postwar dominance of marxism within the intelligentsia. In the "totalizing heterogeneity" of the United States one
might well feel more inclined to retain some notion of totality.

CW: I agree. Without "totality," our politics become emaciated, our
politics become dispersed, our politics become nothing but existential rebellion. Some heuristic (rather than ontological) notion of
totality is in fact necessary if we are to talk about mediations, inter-
relations, interdependencies, about totalizing forces in the world. In
other words, a measure of synecdochical thinking must be pre-
served, thinking that would still invoke relations of parts to the
whole, as for example the Gramscian articulation of spheres and historical blocs. It is true, on the other hand, that we can no longer hang
on to crude orthodox "totalities" such as the idea of superstructure
and base.

AS: It is curious that French poststructuralism in a way shares its
fixation on language with Habermas, an antagonistic thinker thoroughly mired in "modernity." I find the idea of language as a model
for social and political theorizing quite suspect.

CW: Language cannot be a model for social systems, since it is
inseparable from other forms of power relations, other forms of
social practices. I recognize, as Gadamer does, the radical linguisti-

cality of human existence; I recognize, as Derrida does, the ways in which forms of textualization mediate all our claims about the world; but the linguistic model itself must be questioned. The multilevel operations of power within social practices—of which language is one—are more important.

AS: This is why you describe yourself as a "neo-Gramscian pragmatist."

CW: Gramsci's notion of hegemony is an attempt to keep track of these operative levels of power, so one does not fall into the trap of thinking that class relations somehow can be understood through linguistic models; so one does not fall into the trap of thinking that state repression that scars human bodies can be understood in terms of linguistic models. Power operates very differently in nondiscursive than in discursive ways.

AS: The earlier Foucauldian distinction between discursive and nondiscursive formations remains valid for you then?

CW: He should have held on to it, just as Habermas should have held on to his earlier notion of interaction—a notion rooted in the marxist talk about social relations of production—rather than thinning it out into some impoverished idea of communication. Both can be seen as a move toward linguistic models for power.

AS: Even in the case of Foucault? His pan-power theories are, after all, discursive rather than purely *linguistic*.

CW: True. The later, genealogical Foucault would not make claims on linguistic models, but he remained more interested in power as it relates to the constitution of the subject than in power as such. Now, the structure of identity and subjectivity is important and has often been overlooked by the marxist tradition; but forms of subjec*tion* and subjug*ation* are ultimately quite different from "thick" forms of oppression like economic *exploitation* or state *repression* or bureaucratic *domination*. At any rate, "the conditions for the possibility of the constitution of the subject" is a Kantian question to which there is no satisfactory answer. To answer it, as Heidegger said in his self-critique, is to extend the metaphysical impulse in the name of an attack on metaphysics. From that viewpoint, Foucault's notion of anonymous and autonomous discourses is but one in a series of attempts going back to Kant's transcendental subjects and Hegel's transindividual world spirits.

AS: What if Foucault would have said that he recognized the existence of other types of oppression but that his field of analysis was simply different?

CW: I would have replied: "Fine, but that sounds more like the language of an academic than a political intellectual." It would have been to fall into the same traps of disciplinary division of labor he was calling into question. If, in fact, one is writing texts that are strategic and tactical in relation to present struggles, then it is difficult for me to see how one can be counterhegemonic without actually including "thick" forms.

AS: At any rate, the poststructuralist problematic seems now to have been engulfed by the general debate on postmodernism. A certain confusion of terminology marks this debate. Conceptual pairs like modernity/postmodernity and modernism/postmodernism mean very different things depending on country and cultural practice.

CW: Three things are crucial in clearing that up: historical periodization, demarcation of cultural archives and practices, and politics/ideology. Take history and demarcation for example. It is clear that "modern" philosophy begins in the seventeenth century, well before the Enlightenment, with the turn toward the subject and the new authority, the institutionalization, of scientific reason. What we call postmodern philosophy today is precisely about questioning the foundational authority of science. This trajectory is very different from that of modern*ist* literary practices, which in turn is quite different from that of architecture: the former, to simplify, attacks reason in the name of myth, whereas the latter valorizes it together with technique and form. These problems of periodization and demarcation are often ignored. For instance, Portoghesi's work on postmodern architecture seems to assume that his historical framework is an uncontroversial given.

AS: In this sense, Lyotard's initial theorization of the postmodern condition is profoundly marked by its French provenance.

CW: Yes. His book, in many ways an overcelebrated one, is really a French reflection on the transgressions of *modernism* that has little to do with *postmodernism* in the American context. In France, modernism still appears to be the *centering* phenomenon. Figures like Mallarmé, Artaud, Joyce, and Bataille continue to play a fundamental role. In the United States, as Andreas Huyssen has emphasized, postmodernism is an avant-garde—like rebellion against the modernism of the museum, against the modernism of the literary and academic establishment. Note, too, the disjunction here between cultural postmodernism and postmodern politics. For Americans are politically always already in a condition of postmodern fragmentation and heterogeneity in a way that Europeans have not been; and the revolt against the center by those constituted as marginals is an *oppositional* difference in a way that poststructuralist notions of difference are not. These American attacks on universality in the name of difference, these "postmodern" issues of Otherness (Afro-Americans, Native Americans, women, gays) are in fact an implicit critique of certain French postmodern discourses about Otherness that really serve to hide and conceal the power of the voices and movements of Others.

AS: **From an American viewpont, the debate between Lyotard and Habermas is thus rather off-the-mark.**

CW: Interesting *philosophical* things are at stake there, but the politics is a family affair, a very narrow family affair at that. Habermas stands for the grand old tradition of the Enlightenment project of *Vernunft*. I have some affinities with that tradition, but there is nothing new about what he has to say. Lyotard's attack on Habermas comes out of a valorization of the transgression of modernism vis-à-vis an old highbrow, Enlightenment perspective. All this is very distant from the kind of debates about postmodernism we have in the States, though of course one has to read it, be acquainted with it.

AS: **Agreed, but the debate has not been without effect here either. For instance, it is now often felt necessary in architectural discussions to make references to Lyotard.**

CW: It has become fashionable to do so because he is now a major figure, but I am talking about *serious* readings of him. Anyone who knows anything about Kant and Wittgenstein also knows that Lyotard's readings of them are very questionable and wrenched out of context. When these readings then travel to the United States, they often assume an authority that remains *uninterrogated*.

AS: **A case in point is the concept of "life-world," now freely bandied about and most immediately originating in Husserl. In the later Habermas it fulfills an important function as the site of colonization for the "systems-world." This, roughly, seems to combine Weber** with Husserl, but the result is in fact nothing so much as classic American sociology.

CW: When Habermas juxtaposes the life-world with the colonizing systems, it strikes me as a rather clumsy Parsonian way of thinking about the incorporation of culture into advanced capitalist cycles of production and consumption. On the one hand, Habermas has in mind the fundamental role that culture has come to play, now that the commodification process has penetrated cultural practices which were previously relatively autonomous; on the other hand, he is thinking of how oppositional forces and resistance to the system (what I call the process of commodification) are on the wane. This is simply a less effective way of talking about something that marxists have been talking about for years.

AS: Yet, it is obvious that both Lyotard and Habermas must have done something to fill a kind of lack somewhere: otherwise their reception here would be inexplicable.

CW: True. These remarks do not explain why Habermas and Lyotard have gained the attention they have. Habermas, of course, speaks with the status of a second-generation Frankfurt School theorist; and he has become such a celebrity that he can drop a number of terms from a number of different traditions and they take on a salience they often do not deserve. More fundamentally, his encyclopedic knowledge and his obsession with the philosophical foundations of democratic norms also satisfy a pervasive need for left-academic intellectuals—a need for the professional respectability and rigor that displace political engagement and this-worldly involvement. At the same time, his well-known, but really tenuous, relation to marxism provides them with an innocuous badge of radicalism. All of this takes place at the expense of an encounter with the marxist tradition, especially with Gramsci and the later Lukács of the Ontology works. In this sense, Habermas unwittingly serves as a kind of opium for some of the American left-academic intelligentsia. The impact of Lyotard, on the other hand, is probably the result of the fact that he was the first serious European thinker to address the important question of postmodernism in a comprehensive way. Deleuze, to take a related philosopher, never did; though he is ultimately a more profound poststructuralist who should get more attention than he does in the United States. His early book on Nietzsche is actually an originary text.

AS: Why?

CW: Because Deleuze was the first to think through the notion of difference independent of Hegelian ideas of opposition, and that was the start of the radical anti-Hegelianism which has characterized French intellectual life in the last decades. This position—the trashing of totality, the trashing of mediation, the valorization of difference outside the subject-object opposition, the decentering of the subject—all these features we now associate with postmodernism and poststructuralism go back to Deleuze's resurrection of Nietzsche against Hegel. Foucault, already assuming this Deleuzian critique, was the first important French intellectual who could *circumvent*, rather than confront, Hegel, which is why he says that we live in a "Deleuzian age." To live in a Deleuzian age is to live in an anti-Hegelian age so that one does not have to come to terms with Lukács, Adorno or any other Hegelian marxists.

AS: Nietzsche's ascendancy was not without maleficent effects when French theory was imported into the United States.

CW: It was unfortunate for American intellectual life, because we never had the marxist culture against which the French were reacting. Nor was it a culture that took Hegel seriously: the early John Dewey was the only left Hegelian we ever had. Nietzsche was received, therefore, in the context of analytic philosophy, and you can imagine the gaps and hiatuses, the blindness that resulted when Nietzsche entered narrow Anglo-American positivism. In literary criticism, on the other hand, Nietzsche was part of the Derridean baggage that the "New Critics" were able easily (and often uncritically) to assimilate into their close readings. As a result, we now have a "Tower of Babel" in American literary criticism.

AS: The current, however, does not run in only one direction. Is the present French interest in "postanalytic" philosophy an indication that intellectual life is being reorientated toward the United States, at least in terms of objects of inquiry?

CW: No doubt. French society has clearly come under the influence of Americanization, and West Germany, always somewhat of a fifty-first state, has moved in this direction as well. More immediately, now that the university systems in Europe no longer have the status or financial support they once had, American universities are pulling in the European intellectuals, offering money and celebrity status but also a fairly high level of conversation.

AS: **Features of what we associate with the concept of postmodernism have been part of American life for a long time: fragmentation, heterogeneity, surfaces without history. Is postmodernism in some sense really the codification of life in Los Angeles?**

CW: Only in one form and specifically at the level of middlebrow culture. The other side is the potentially oppositional aspect of the notion. Postmodernism ought never to be viewed as a homogeneous phenomenon, but rather as one in which political contestation is central. Even if we look at it principally as a form of Americanization of the world, it is clear that within the US there are various forms of ideological and political conflict going on.

AS: **The black community, for example is more "contestational" than average America.**

CW: The black political constituency still has some sense of the reality of the world, some sense of what is going on in the third world. Look at the issues Jesse Jackson pressed in 1984 and now in 1988, and you find that they were issues normally reserved for the salons of leftist intellectuals. Bringing that on television had a great impact.

AS: **Yet, the black American condition, so to speak, is not an uplifting sight at the moment.**

CW: Not at all. There is increasing class division and differentiation, creating on the one hand a significant black middle class, highly anxiety-ridden, insecure, willing to be co-opted and incorporated into the powers that be, concerned with racism to the degree that it poses constraints on upward social mobility; and, on the other, a vast and growing black underclass, an underclass that embodies a kind of *walking nihilism* of pervasive drug addiction, pervasive alcoholism, pervasive homocide, and an exponential rise in suicide. Now, because of the deindustrialization, we also have a devastated black industrial working class. We are talking here about tremendous hopelessness.

AS: **Suicide has increased enormously?**

CW: It has increased six times in the last decades for black males like myself who are between eighteen and thirty-five. This is unprecedented. Afro-Americans have always killed themselves less than other Americans, but this is no longer true.

AS: **What does a black oppositional intellectual do in these generally dire circumstances?**

CW: One falls back on those black institutions that have attempted to serve as resources for sustenance and survival, the black churches being one such institution, especially their progressive and prophetic wing. One tries to root oneself organically in these institutions so that one can speak to a black constituency, while maintaining a conversation with the most engaging political and postmodernist debates on the outside so that the insights they provide can be brought in.

AS: That explains why you are, among other things, a kind of lay preacher. It does not explain why you are a Christian.

CW: My own left Christianity is not simply instrumentalist. It is in part a response to those dimensions of life that have been flattened out, to the surfacelike character of a postmodern culture that refuses to speak to issues of despair, that refuses to speak to issues of the absurd. To that extent I still find Christian narratives and stories *empowering and enabling.*

AS: What does it mean to a black American to hear that, in Baudrillard's language, we are in a simulated space of hyperreality, that we have lost the real?

CW: I read that symptomatically. Baudrillard seems to be articulating a sense of what it is to be a French, middle-class intellectual, or perhaps what it is to be middle class generally. Let me put it in terms of a formulation from Henry James that Fredric Jameson has appropriated: there is a reality *that one cannot not know.* The ragged edges of the Real, of *Necessity,* not being able to eat, not having shelter, not having health care, all this is something that one cannot not know. The black condition acknowledges that. It is so much more acutely felt because this is a society where a lot of people live a Teflon existence, where a lot of people have no sense of the ragged edges of necessity, of what it means to be impinged upon by structures of oppression. To be an an upper-middle-class American is actually to live a life of unimaginable comfort, convenience, and luxury. Half of the black population is denied this, which is why they have a strong sense of reality.

AS: Does that make notions of postmodernism meaningless from a black perspective?

CW: It must be conceived very differently at least. Take Ishmael Reed, an exemplary postmodern writer. Despite his conservative politics, he cannot deny the black acknowledgment of the reality one cannot not know. In writing about black American history, for instance, he has to come to terms with the state-sponsored terrorism of lynching blacks and so on. This is inescapable in black postmodernist practices.

AS: How is one in fact to understand black postmodernist practices?

CW: To talk about black postmodernist practices is to go back to bebop music and see how it relates to literary expressions like Reed's and Charles Wright's. It is to go back, in other words, to the genius of Charlie Parker, John Coltrane, and Miles Davis. Bebop was, after all, a revolt against the middle-class "jazz of the museum," against swing and white musicians like Benny Goodman, who had become hegemonic by colonizing a black art form. What Parker did, of course, was to Africanize jazz radically: to accent the polyrhythms, to combine these rhythms with unprecedented virtuosity on the sax. He said explicitly that his music was not produced to be accepted by white Americans. He would be suspicious if it were. This sense of revolt was to be part and parcel of the postmodern rebellion against the modernism of the museum.

AS: To me, bebop seems like a black cultural avant-garde that corresponds historically to abstract expressionism in painting—the last gasp of modernism—on which indeed it had some considerable influence.

CW: Certainly they emerge together, and people do tend to parallel them as though they were the same; but abstract expressionism was not a revolt in the way bebop was. In fact, it was an instance of modernism itself. Bebop also had much to do with fragmentation, with heterogeneity, with the articulation of difference and marginality, aspects of what we associate with postmodernism today.

AS: Aspects of the cultural dominant, yes; but these elements are also part of modernism. Surely one can still talk about Charlie Parker as a unified subject expressing inner *angst* or whatever, an archetypal characteristic of modernism.

CW: True, but think too of another basic feature of postmodernism, the breakdown of highbrow and pop culture. Parker would use whistling off the streets of common black life: "Cherokee," for instance, was actually a song that black children used to sing when jumping rope or, as I did, playing marbles. Parker took that melody of the black masses and filtered it through his polyrhythms and technical virtuosity, turning it into a highbrow jazz feature that was not quite highbrow anymore. He was already calling into question the distinction between high and low culture, pulling from a bricolage, as it were, what was seemingly popular and relating it to what was then high. Yet, I would not deny the modernist impulse, nor would I deny that they were resisting jazz as commodity, very much like Joyce and Kafka resisted literary production as commodity. In that sense bebop straddles the fence.

AS: The ultimate problem, however, is whether it is actually useful to talk about someone like Charlie Parker in these terms.

CW: It is useful to the degree that it contests the prevailing image of him as a modernist. As you imply, on the other hand, there is a much deeper as to question whether these terms *modernism/post-modernism* relate to Afro-American cultural practices in any illuminating way at all. We are only at the beginning of that inquiry.

AS: Was there ever actually a mass black audience for bebop?

CW: Yes, Parker's was the sort of music black people danced to in the 1940s. Miles's "cool" stage was also big in the 1950s with albums like "Kinda Blue," though it went hand in hand with the popularity of Nat King Cole and Dinah Washington.

AS: What happened to this avant-garde black music when Motown and Aretha Franklin came along?

CW: It was made a fetish for the educated middle class, principally, but not solely, the white middle class. In absolute terms, its domain actually expanded because the black audience of middle-class origin also expanded. But the great dilemma of black musicians who try to preserve a tradition from mainstream domestication and dilution is in fact that they lose contact with the black masses. In this case, there was eventually a move toward "fusion," jazz artists attempting to produce objects intended for broader black-and-white consumption.

AS: Miles Davis is the central figure of that avant-garde story.

CW: And he crossed over with the seminal record *Bitches Brew* in 1970, accenting his jazz origins while borrowing from James Brown's polyrhythms and Sly Stone's syncopation. *Bitches Brew* brought him a black mass audience that he had lost in the 1960s—certainly one that Coltrane had lost completely.

AS: Crossover artists, in the sense of having a racially mixed mass audience, are not very numerous today.

CW: No, but there are more than ever: Whitney Houston, Dionne Warwick, Lionel Richie, Diana Ross, and Anita Baker. Baker is a very different crossover artist because she is still deeply rooted in the black context. Michael Jackson and Prince are crossover in another sense: their music is less rooted in black musical traditions and much more open to white rock and so forth.

AS: **In Prince's case it has to do with the fact that he is not entirely from a black background.**

CW: Still, he grew up in a black foster home and a black Seventh Day Adventist church, but in Minneapolis, which is very different from growing up like Michael Jackson in a black part of Gary, Indiana. Minneapolis has always been a place of cultural cross-fertilization, of interracial marriages and relationships. The early Jackson Five, on the other hand, were thoroughly ensconsed in a black tradition, and Michael began his career dancing like James Brown. Now, he is at the center of the black-white interface.

AS: **Prince never really played "black" music as one thinks of it. His music is "fused" from the start.**

CW: To be in a black context in Minneapolis is already to be in a situation of fusion, because the blacks themselves have much broader access to mainstream white culture in general. You get the same thing with other black stars who have come out of that place.

AS: **Michael Jackson, by contrast, is now a packaged middle-American product.**

CW: A nonoppositional instance of commodification in black skin that is becoming more and more like candy, more radical than McDonald's, but not by much. It is watered-down black music, but still with a lot of the aggressiveness and power of that tradition.

AS: **Music is *the* black means of cultural expression, is it not?**

CW: Music and preaching. Here, rap is unique because it combines the black preacher and the black music tradition, replacing the liturgical-ecclesiastical setting with the African polyrhythms of the street. A tremendous *articulateness* is syncopated with the African drumbeat, the African funk, into an American postmodernist product: there is no subject expressing originary anguish here but a fragmented subject, pulling from past and present, innovatively producing a heterogeneous product. The stylistic combination of the oral, the literate, and the musical is exemplary as well. Otherwise, it is part and parcel of the subversive energies of black underclass youth, energies that are forced to take a cultural mode of articulation because of the political lethargy of American society. The music of Grandmaster Flash and the Furious Five, Kurtis Blow, and Sugar Hill Gang has to take on a deeply political character because, again, they are in the reality that the black underclass *cannot not know*: the brutal side of American capital, the brutal side of American racism, the brutal side of sexism against black women.

AS: **I always thought rap was too indigenous a black form of expression to make it in the general marketplace. Run/DMC has proven me wrong on this.**

CW: Indeed. Run/DMC is as indigenous as you can get. Upper-middle-class white students at Yale consume a lot of Run/DMC.

AS: **Yet, the constitutive elements of rap seemed to me too fixed for it to become a permanent presence on the crossover scene: more anonymous and less easily assimilated into existing white concepts of melody and structure. This, too, is probably wrong.**

CW: People said the same thing about Motown in 1961, the same thing about Aretha Franklin, who is about as organic as you can get. She is not as accepted by mainstream white society as the smoother and more diluted Warwick and Ross, but she *is* accepted. That, from the perspective of 1964-65, is unbelievable. The same thing could happen with rap music, since the boundaries are actually rather fluid. But it won't remain the same.

AS: **Where will rap end up?**

CW: Where most American postmodern products end up: highly packaged, regulated, distributed, circulated, and consumed.

AS: **Preaching, as you said, is obviously a cultural form of expression; but is it a specifically *artistic* form?**

CW: Sure. The best preachers are outstanding oral artists, performance artists. Martin Luther King, Jr. gave white America just a small taste of what it is to be an artistic rhetorician in the black churches. Tremendous gravity and weight are given to these artistic performances because people's *lives* hang on them. They provide some hope from week to week so that these folk won't fall into hopelessness and meaninglessness, so that they won't kill themselves. The responsibility of the black preacher-artist is, in that sense, deeply functional, but at the same time it entails *a refinement of a form* bequeathed to him by those who came before. Black preaching is inseparable here from black singing. Most secular black singers come out of the choir, and the lives of the congregation hang on how they sing the song, what they put into the song, how passionate, how self-invested they are. Preaching is just less visible to the outside as an art form because words uttered once don't have the same status as cultural products; but the black preachers are artists with a very long tradition.

AS: **Since it does not lend itself to mechanical reproduction, preaching is also hard to destroy by turning it into a business. How is this artistic form of expression actually evaluated?**

CW: In terms of the impact the preacher has on the congregation. This impact can take the form of cantankerous response, or the form of existential empowerment, the convincing of people to keep on keeping on, to keep on struggling, contesting, and resisting.

AS: **It is Kant's acrobat who intervenes constantly to transform an otherwise unstable equilibrium into another equilibrium.**

CW: Well put. Black sermonic practices have not received the attention they deserve. As a matter of fact, black linguistic practices as such need to be examined better because they add a lot to the American language.

AS: **Black language creates a wealth of new words, which are then quickly picked up by the mainstream.**

CW: Usually with significant semantic changes. Stevie Wonder's "Everything is alright, uptight, out of sight" is a string of synonyms. *Uptight*, when I was growing up, meant smooth, cool, everything is fine. By the time it got to middle America, *uptight* meant anxiety-ridden, the inability of everything to be fine. Similar semantic shifts, though perhaps less drastic, take place with *chilling out*, *mellowing out*, and other black expressions. *Chilling out* meant letting things be, a sort of Heideggerian notion of *aletheia*, letting the truth reveal itself, letting it shine, letting it come forth.

AS: **Given the social circumstances of which it is a product, black American language seems to me, on the outside, not to allow very easily for prevalent white orders of theoretical reflection.**

CW: It is a hustling culture, and a hustling culture tends to be *radically* "practicalist," deeply pragmatic, because the issue is always one of surviving, getting over.

AS: **This, I imagine, demands some sharp linguistic twists for you.**

CW: I am continually caught in a kind of "heteroglossia," speaking a number of English languages in radically different contexts. When it comes to abstract theoretical reflection, I employ Marx, Weber, Frankfurt theorists, Foucault, and so on. When it comes to speaking with the black masses, I use Christian narratives and stories, a language meaningful to them but filtered through and informed by intellectual developments from de Tocqueville to Derrida. When it comes to the academy itself there is yet another kind of language, abstract but often atheoretical, since social theorizing is mostly shunned. Philosophers are simply ill-equipped to to talk about social theory: they know Wittgenstein but not Weber, they know J. L. Austin but not Marx.

AS: Apart from the musician and the preacher, black culture exhibits a third artist of great importance: the athlete. There is enormous emphasis on aesthetic execution in black sports.

CW: You can see this in basketball, where the black player tries to *style* reality so that he becomes spectacle and performance, always projecting a sense of self; whereas his white counterpart tends toward the productivistic and mechanistic. A lot of time, energy, and discipline also go into it but usually with a certain *investment of self* that does not express the work ethic alone. Ali was, of course, exemplary in this respect. Not only was he a great boxer, but a stylish one as well: smooth, clever, rhythmic, syncopated.

AS: Whence comes this emphasis on spectacle?

CW: Originally, it derives from an African sense of pageantry, the tendency to project yourself *in performance* in a way so that you are at one with a certain flow of things. By "one," I do not mean any romantic kind of unity between subject and object or pantheistic unification with nature, but at one with the craft and task at hand. It is also to risk something. Baraka has spoken of the African *deification of accident*, by which he indicated the acknowledgment of risk and contingency: to be able to walk a tightrope, to be able to do the dangerous, and to do it well. But it is a form of risk-ridden execution that is *self-imposed*.

AS: Among the various black modes of cultural expression, pictorial art has not, with all due allowances for graffiti art, been much in evidence. The black middle class seems uninterested and so does the underclass: art as a practice is esoteric and largely without rewards.

CW: Access to the kinds of education and subcultural circles is much less available to potential black artists. In addition to the racism in the avant-garde world, painting and sculpture are not as widely appreciated as they ought to be in black America. Therefore, pictorial black artists are marginal. They deserve more black support—and exposure.

AS: Beyond impediments of entry, is there not also some indigenous cultural element at work here? There are, after all, many black writers and dancers.

CW: The strong, puritanical Protestantism of black religion has not been conducive to the production of pictures. For the same reason, there is a great belief in the *power of the word*, in literate acumen. In fact, writers are sometimes given too much status and become "spokespeople" for the race, which is ridiculous. Yet, there is an openness, diversity, multiplicity of artistic sensibility when developed and cultivated in the black community. Realist modes of representation are, for example, not inherently linked to Afro-American culture. The pioneering artwork of Howardina Pindell, Emma Amos, Benny Andrews, and Martin Puryear are exemplary in this regard.

AS: It is a cliché to say that we live in a society of images, but we obviously do. Blacks watch more television than the average. Do they appropriate these images differently?

CW: There is an element of scrutiny involved. The images have been so pervasively negative, so degrading, and devaluing of black people—especially of black women—that the process has always been one tied to some skepticism and suspicion.

AS: Images are seen through a skeptical racial grid?

CW: A racial grid as transmitted from one generation to the next. This does not mean it is always critical. Think, for example, of all the Italian pictures of Jesus that hang in black churches at this very moment, pictures of Michelangelo's uncles when the man was actually a dark Palestinian Jew. Such images are widely accepted. But that particular one is, of course, different because it is sacred and therefore much more difficult to question. There is a much more critical attitude towards television. With the exception of the new phenomenon of the Cosby Show and Frank's Place, black folk are still usually depicted there as buffoons, black women as silly.

AS: Images of blacks are sometimes produced by blacks, as in many music videos. Those I have watched tend to be either sentimental ones about people yearning for the "right one" or highly charged ones featuring minutely choreographed movement.

CW: You also find a lot of conspicuous consumption: a lot of *very* expensive cars, and furs, and suits, and so forth. The American dream of wealth and prosperity remains a powerful carrot, because television producers are aware of the reality that the black audience cannot not know. Another big problem is the relation between black men and women. Different kinds of women are projected as objects of desire and quest, but they are downright white women, or blacks who look entirely white, or very light-skinned black women. Rarely do you find any longing for the really *dark* woman. And when a black woman is the star, she is usually yearning for a black man who is light—never a white man, but a black man who is light.

AS: **Black culture is, of course, as sexist as the rest.**

CW: In a different way. The pressure on Afro-Americans as a people has forced the black man closer to the black woman: they are in the same boat. But they are also at each other's throat. The relation is internally hierarchical and often mediated by violence: black men over black women.

AS: **Is it not more unabashedly sexist in its macho version? For even though popular culture as such is deeply infused with macho imagery, it seems to me that the black ditto is more *overtly* so.**

CW: Black society shows the typical range from the extreme machismo of any patriarchy to a few egalitarian relations. Nonetheless, what you say is probably true, and there are simply no excuses for the vicious treatment of black women by these men. Yet, interaction between the sexes in the black community is unintelligible without highlighting the racist and poverty-ridden circumstances under which so many blacks live. Machismo is itself a bid for power by relatively powerless and degraded black men. Remember, too, that the white perception here is principally informed by interracial relations between black men and white women, relations in which black machismo is particularly pronounced. There is also an *expectation* among large numbers of white folk that black men be macho, and black men then tend to fulfill that expectation. Those who do not are perceived as abnormal. A crucial part of this phenomenon is the question of sexual prowess: if you're not a "gashman," your whole identity as a black male becomes highly problematic. So, to a degree, the process is a self-fulfilling prophecy.

AS: **There has been an extreme destruction of the family within the black underclass. Aside from the obvious causes, why is this?**

CW: Aside from the changes in society as a whole, developments like hedonistic consumerism and the constant need of stimulation of the body, which make any qualitative human relationships hard to maintain, it is a question of a breakdown in cultural resources, what Raymond Williams calls structures of meaning. Except for the church, there is no longer any potent tradition on which one can fall back in dealing with hopelessness and meaninglessness. There used to be a set of stories that could convince people that their absurd situation was one worth coping with, but the passivity is now overwhelming. Drug addiction is only one manifestation of this: to live a life of living death, of slower death, rather than killing yourself immediately. I recently spoke at a high school in one of the worst parts of Brooklyn, and the figures were staggering: almost 30 percent had attempted suicide, 70 percent were deeply linked to drugs. This is what I mean by "walking nihilism." *It is the imposing of closure on the human organism, intentionally, by that organism itself.* Such nihilism is not *cute*. We are not dancing on Nietzsche's texts here and *talking* about nihilism; we are in a nihilism that is *lived*. We are talking about real obstacles to the sustaining of a *people*.

AS: Which is not quite how Nietzschean nihilism is normally conceived.

CW: There are a variety of nihilisms in Nietzsche, and this is not so much one in which meaning is elusive, certainly not one with a surplus of meaning. What we have, on the contrary, is not at all elusive: meaningless*ness*, a meaningless so well understood that it can result in the taking of one's own life.

CONTRIBUTORS

Stanley Aronowitz is professor of sociology at CUNY Graduate Center and a coeditor of *Social Text*. He is the coauthor, with Henry Giroux, of *Education under Siege* (1985) and the author of *The Crisis in Historical Materialism* (1981) and *Science as Power* (1988).

Hal Foster is associate professor at Pratt Institute, New York. He is coeditor of *Zone* and former senior editor of *Art in America*. He is the author of *Recodings: Art, Spectacle, Cultural Politics* (1985), and the editor of *The Anti-Aesthetic: Essays on Postmodern Culture* (1983) and *Discussion of Contemporary Culture* (1987).

Nancy Fraser is professor of philosophy and comparative literature and theory, Northwestern University. She is the author of "What's Critical about Critical Theory? The Case of Habermas and Gender," which appeared in *Feminism as Critique: Essays on the Politics of Gender in Late-Capitalist Societies*, edited by S. Benhabib and D. Cornell (1987), and of a forthcoming book, *Unruly Practices: Power, Discourse and Gender in Contemporary Social Theory*.

Lawrence Grossberg is associate professor in the Department of Speech Communication, Institute of Communications Research, and Unit for Criticism and Interpretive Theory, University of Illinois at Urbana-Champaign. He is coeditor, with Cary Nelson, of *Marxism and the Interpretation of Culture* (1987) and coauthor, with Stuart Hall and Jennifer Daryl Slack, of *Cultural Studies: A Theoretical History* (forthcoming, 1989).

Fredric Jameson is professor of comparative literature, Duke University, and a coeditor of *Social Text*. He is the author of such books as

The Political Unconscious (1981), *The Ideologies of Theory: Essays 1971-1986*, two volumes (1988), and a forthcoming book on film.

Laura Kipnis is a video artist and critic whose most recent tape, *A Man's Woman* (about right-wing women), was produced in association with Channel Four Television in England. She teaches video and film at the University of Wisconsin, Madison, and writes occasionally on popular culture and postmodernism.

Ernesto Laclau is director of the Graduate Program in ideology and Discourse Analysis, Department of Government, University of Essex. He is the author of *Politics and Ideology in Marxist Theory* (1977) and coauthor, with Chantal Mouffe, of *Hegemony and Socialist Strategy: Toward a Radical Democratic Politics* (1985). His latest book is *New Reflections on the Revolution of Our Time* (forthcoming, 1989).

Meaghan Morris is a writer living in Sydney. She is the author of "Room 101 or a Few Worst Things in the World," which appeared in André Frankovits's *Seduced and Abandoned: The Baudrillard Scene* (1984), and "Postmodernity and Lyotard's Sublime," which appeared in *Art & Text* 16 (1984). She is the coeditor, with Paul Patton, of *Michel Foucault: Power, Truth, Strategy* (1979).

Chantal Mouffe is the editor of *Gramsci and Marxist Theory* (1979) and coauthor, with Ernesto Laclau, of *Hegemony and Socialist Strategy: Toward a Radical Democratic Politics* (1985).

Linda J. Nicholson is associate professor of women's studies, Department of Educational Administration and Policy Studies, SUNY Albany. She is the author of *Gender and History: The Limits of Social Theory in the Age of the Family* (1986) and "Marx and Feminism: Integrating Kinship with the Economic," in *Feminism as Critique: Essays on the Politics of Gender in Late-Capitalist Societies*, edited by S. Benhabib and D. Cornell (1987).

Jacqueline Rose is senior lecturer in English at the University of Sussex. She is the author of *Sexuality in the Field of Vision* (1986) and *The Case of Peter Pan, or the Impossibility of Children's Fiction* (1984), and the translator and coeditor, with Juliet Mitchell, of *Feminine Sexuality, Jacques Lacan and the École Freudienne* (1982).

Andrew Ross teaches English at Princeton University and is a coeditor of *Social Text*. He is the author of *The Failure of Modernism* (1986) and of a forthcoming book about intellectuals and popular culture, to be entitled *No Respect*. He is also the cotranslator of Jacques Aumont's *Montage Eisenstein* (1986).

Anders Stephanson teaches history at Rutgers University at Newark, and is a coeditor of *Social Text*. His writings include "Of Pucks and Punches and Related Matters," *Social Text* 6 (1982), and *Kennan: Art and Foreign Policy*, to be published in 1989.

Paul Smith is associate professor in the Literary and Cultural Studies program at Carnegie-Mellon University. He is the author of *Pound Revised* (1983) and *Discerning the Subject* (1988). He is coeditor, with Alice Jardine, of *Men in Feminism* (1987).

Abigail Solomon-Godeau is a photographic critic and historian. Her articles have appeared in *Afterimage, Camera Obscura, October*, and *Screen*. A book of her selected essays, *Photographs at the Dock*, will be published in 1989.

Cornel West teaches religion and political philosophy at Princeton University and is a coeditor of *Social Text*. He is the author of *Prophetic Fragments* (1988) and *The American Evasion of Philosophy: A Genealogy of Pragmatism* (1988).

George Yúdice is an associate professor of romance languages at Hunter College, CUNY, and is a coeditor of *Social Text*. He is the author of *Vicente Huidobro y la motivacíon del languaje póetico* (1978), "Cubist Aesthetics in Painting and Poetry," *Semiotica* 36 (1981), and coauthor, with Doris Sommer, of "Latin American Literature from the 'Boom' on," in *Postmodern Fiction. A Bio-Biographical Guide*, edited by Larry McCaffery (1986).

INDEX

Compiled by Hassan Meleby